A Match Made in Hell

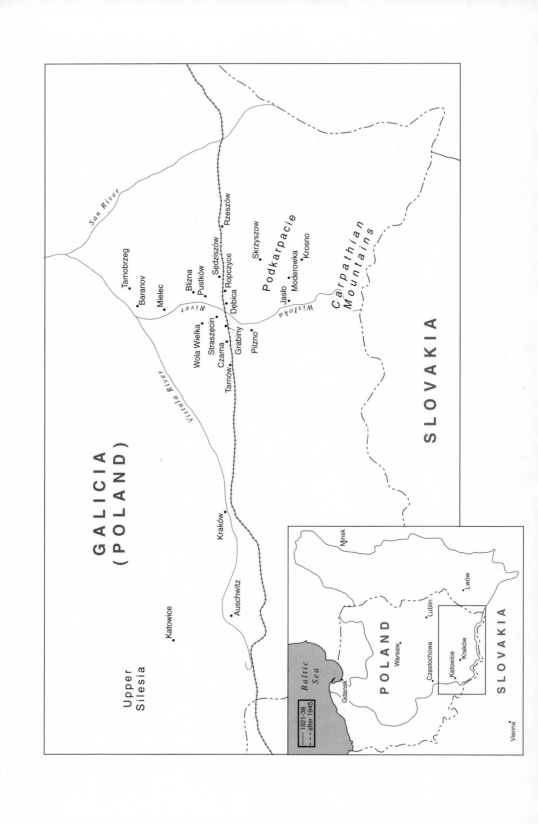

A Match Made in Hell

The Jewish Boy and the Polish Outlaw Who Defied the Nazis

Larry Stillman

From the testimony of

Morris Goldner

THE UNIVERSITY OF WISCONSIN PRESS

The University of Wisconsin Press
1930 Monroe Street
Madison, Wisconsin 53711

www.wisc.edu\wisconsinpress

3   5   7   8   6   4

Printed in the United States of America

Library of Congress Cataloging-in-Publication Data

Goldner, Morris, 1925 or 6–
A match made in hell : the Jewish boy and the Polish outlaw who defied the Nazis /
Larry Stillman from the Testimony of Morris Goldner.

p. cm.
ISBN 0-299-19390-X (cloth : alk. paper)
ISBN 0-299-19394-2 (pbk.)
1. Goldner, Morris, 1925 or 6– 2. Jews—Poland—Biography. 3. Holocaust, Jewish
(1939–1945)—Poland—Biography. 4. Kopec, Jan. 5. Guerrillas—Poland—Biography.
6. World War, 1939–1945—Underground movements—Poland. 7. Poland—Biography.
I. Stillman, Larry. II. Title.
DS135.P63 G665   2003
940.53′18′092—dc21   2003005677

To Loraine, whose "Jewish radar" set this in motion, and to my children, Jamie and Jon: read this and know how things were; and by knowing, may you and your children be blessed with a world in which such horrors are not likely to happen again.

Morris Goldner dedicates his testimony to his wonderful wife, Eda, who has given him the courage and inspiration to accomplish all that he has in his life; to his children, Renee, Linda, and Judy; and to his grandchildren, Jennifer, Bryan, Brandon, Leslie, Howard, Marci, Jessica, and Alisa.

These, in the day when heaven was falling,
The hour when earth's foundations fled,
Followed their mercenary calling
And took their wages and are dead.
                    —*Alfred Edward Housman*

Goldner was such a quiet, gentle young boy. A short little guy, soft-
spoken and submissive. I can't see him committing acts of sabotage
and resistance. Just didn't have it in him.
                    —*Home Army partisan from Goldner's hometown*

Contents

Introduction

I CAN REMEMBER CRAWLING out from beneath my father's lifeless
body. So begins the account of Morris Goldner's rescue and survival in the south of Poland.

What makes his story unlike any other is not that this frightened
teenager simply walked away from capture, or spent four years hiding
in the forests, or carried out inconceivable acts of espionage and sabotage and lived to tell about them—although these adventures alone
make his testimony a compelling one.

Clearly, what distinguishes Goldner's experiences has to do with
his symbiotic relationship—I can find no better word to describe it—
with the thirty-eight-year-old bandit Jan Kopec. This Pole, from Goldner's own tiny village, had been a wanted criminal long before the
German occupation. At the time fate brought him together with Goldner, he, too, was hiding from the Nazis in the forests, looking for ways
to profit from his criminal expertise.

Kopec came upon young Goldner quite by accident in January 1943
and, for reasons we will never know with absolute certainty, rescued
him from near death at the hands of an informer—a "friend" of Goldner's father, no less.

For eighteen months, Kopec hid the boy with him, moving constantly from one area to another, often staying in hideouts he had fashioned many years earlier. At first Kopec trained Goldner simply to
serve as his accomplice in robberies and black-market activities. But
before long he pushed the training to a whole new level, making it
possible for him to sell Goldner's services to a shadowy partisan group
that was becoming interested in the daring young saboteur.

When I first heard Goldner's abbreviated account ("the tip of the
iceberg," he told me) of these moving and harrowing experiences, I

was held spellbound. But little did I imagine that I would soon embark on a remarkable journey of learning and discovery. It unfolded during the many hundreds of hours I spent with a tape recorder, gently probing and drawing out this gentle man, gradually uncovering what turned out to be a formidable and surprisingly labyrinthine expanse of ice beneath that tantalizing tip.

There followed easily as many additional hours spent in libraries, researching historical and logistical aspects of his story. I also traveled to Poland, in search of people and places from Goldner's past. It was there I met his former neighbor, still living in the same house as he did when the Goldners lived next door. I also talked with four of Kopec's children, with several of the area's veteran partisans, and with others—some wishing to remain nameless—all of whom were happy to add recollections of their own.

Then, finally, came the writing—organizing the multifarious components of Goldner's testimony and endeavoring to put them into an accurate historical framework. Any errors that may have resulted are mine.

During this long process, Goldner and I worked closely to pool our combined insights and to excavate some of the conflicting feelings and emotions he had buried for nearly sixty years. Some of the resulting dialogue appears exactly as Goldner remembers it; other passages have been reconstructed to convey the essence of conversations Goldner can no longer replay word for word.

It's Goldner's firsthand experiences with Jan Kopec, as revealed here, that offer the world the only insight into this nefarious criminal. For Kopec's mercenary wartime activities—including his probable link to a specific, documented, Communist-backed partisan unit—don't appear in any materials I can locate from this period. This isn't surprising, given the meager records that have survived from this district. Neither are Kopec's prewar crimes—which I verified in Poland with several of his former acquaintances—archived in the prosecutor's office in that region.

Kopec's surviving children (who still live in the same area) and the grandchildren he never met do not have so much as a photograph of their late father and grandfather, much less a clear picture of who he really was. For this reason, I have substituted the name "Kopec" for his real last name, to save his gracious and upright present-day family from any possible embarrassment.

Likewise, I have changed several other names that appear here. To spare living relatives, I have used the pseudonym "Pozniak" for the heinous informer and Goldner family "friend" who captured and bayoneted the boy and his father. His sidekick in crime becomes "Grychowski." And two individuals, still living in the area where this story takes place, asked me to change their names because of sensitive information they revealed. They become "Kryzak" and "Kozera."

This said, I must point out two of the several names that have *not* been changed: Wladyslaw Reguła, Goldner's delightful former neighbor, and his daughter, Anna. When I met with them, they made it clear they were pleased to be referenced here.

Obviously, there are secrets surrounding Kopec even now, apparently built on a bulwark of mystery and intrigue forged during the rogue's lifetime. Until recently, in fact, the scope of Goldner's own understanding about Kopec's colorful background was limited as well. He knew the man's reputation, certainly, for it had been the talk of his village before the war. But the taciturn Kopec offered the boy few glimpses into his personal life. What's more, he kept Goldner in complete isolation from his contacts in the forests. Uncovering the identity and partisan affiliation of those contacts was possible only after I linked code names Goldner recalled overhearing—"Stach" and "Kruk"—to brief written and oral references by two Polish historians.

What Goldner did come to understand—and only recently, at that—was that he and Kopec not only used each other to survive, but over time, their disparate personality traits actually rubbed off on each other. As Kopec observed one day to Goldner, "Our time together has made you tough as nails. And me, I must be getting soft."

Still, for every insight about Kopec that is revealed, many more unanswered questions remain. For other than Goldner, no one alive today has any idea of Kopec's true activities during the war. The Kopec children's beliefs about their father differ from those of their father's few remaining acquaintances, all of whom spoke to me only under a promise of anonymity.

The one thing they do all agree on is that Kopec escaped in late 1942 from two years of forced labor at Auschwitz (something Kopec never revealed to Goldner). They also concur that Goldner, the Jewish boy whom they knew as Moniek, was saved by Kopec within weeks of Kopec's escape from the death camp. That Kopec hid with the boy was common knowledge among them. What the pair did together during this time was not.

Through Goldner's testimony, we learn the truth about how Kopec spent those eighteen months from the time he fled Auschwitz until the end of the war. Even so, knowing the *how* does not enable us to fully understand the *why*. Beyond the few windows Kopec opened just a crack, giving Goldner a fleeting glimpse into his psyche, we can only speculate as to what might have been in the bandit's heart and mind.

Jan Kopec, it seems, is destined to remain an enigma for all time.

But what of Morris Goldner? How did the frightened orphan adapt to being the ward of a master criminal, and how did he find the chutz-pah—the nerve—to do what was demanded of him? As Goldner reveals his expanding role in carrying out acts of sabotage and reconnaissance, it becomes apparent that many of these dangerous missions were designed specifically around him. Each new day, in fact, brought him fresh opportunities to court death.

Indeed, you may question how he escaped time and again with his life. You would not be alone; Goldner continually asks himself that very question. Part of the answer, undoubtedly, was his small stature. Then, as now, he was only five feet tall. At fifteen he appeared no older than eight or ten. Plus, he had none of the physical characteristics that were considered stereotypically Jewish. So it's possible to see why, time and time again, he was regarded by the Germans as just another impoverished, ragamuffin Polish kid, who to all outward appearances posed more nuisance to them than danger.

To his credit, Goldner was gifted with immense poise and bearing to enable this charade to work for him. Once he came under Kopec's influence, he showed no fear in risky situations because, he insists, he usually *felt* no fear. In fact, he came to fully embrace the treacherous missions Kopec devised for him.

"I had lost everything that mattered to me," he explains. "What did I have to live for?" What he wanted most was revenge against the Nazis. As he states, "If death at the hands of my enemies was ultimately my destiny, this is how I wanted to die."

Through Goldner's experiences, we're offered a first-time look at a partisan unit that paid for the services of a known criminal—a man with far greater experience in weapons, explosives, and covert operations than any of that partisan unit's own membership, many of whom were radical farmers from a small village not far from Goldner's and Kopec's own.

"Everything Kopec did, he did for money," Goldner tells us, and a confidant of Kopec confirms this assessment of what drove the man. Beyond his mercenary leanings, however, Kopec seems to have taken great satisfaction from taunting the Germans. Goldner notes that after one successful operation, "Kopec had a look of exhilaration on his face that seemed almost to say, *Hell, I'd do this again even if I wasn't getting paid.*"

When all is said and done, Goldner asks but one thing: that you think no more of him, nor less of him, from what he reveals here. "I just did what I had to do," he tells me repeatedly. He says it not with pride, but with overtones of sadness and, yes, even guilt. "Some things, I wish

I didn't remember . . . some things have been hard for me to talk about."
Then he says it again: "But I did what I had to do to stay alive."

You will read his story, and you will decide if you can understand why he acted as he did. And with each event he describes, each life-and-death resolution he makes, you may well ask yourself if, under similar circumstances, you would have done any differently.

Can any of us really say?

A Match Made in Hell

1

Rescue

I CAN REMEMBER crawling out from beneath my father's lifeless body. It was with absolute certainty that I knew he was dead, of course, in those scattered moments when I was capable of any rational thought at all. His fate was evident in the heavy weight that pressed, unmoving, upon my own injured body; in the taste and smell of blood—like rusted metal, I thought—that etched its way into my nose and mouth and throat as I lay there, too frightened and too weak to move. He was dead, my papa, and very soon I would join him. How many other sixteen-year-olds, I wondered, knew what it was like to watch death approach?

It is hard to say how long I lay there under my father's motionless form. Hours, perhaps, drifting in and out of consciousness. In random fragments the events of the past twenty-four hours came back to me, and I started a mental litany of "what ifs"—what if we hadn't gone to Pozniak's house? What if we had gone to see Reguła instead, or stolen food from a stranger, as we had often done before? Then we would not have been turned in to the ss here at the Grabiny train station. Then perhaps Papa and I might have lived. For that is exactly how I was thinking: as if I were already dead.

But I discovered that my will to live was stronger than any acceptance of death, so when I realized that the station was silent, I struggled to free myself from the prison of my father's corpse.

My first sensation was the slap of cold winds on my skin. I had nearly forgotten that it was already January. After a year and a half spent hiding in forests and fields, I had lost all track of time. The year 1943 had crept in slyly, practically unnoticed, wearing a death's head just like the year it came to replace.

3

Ignoring the chill in the air, the pain in my hip, and a searing fire across my back, I crawled on my stomach away from the tracks, toward the rear of the small station house. A few meters farther, the frozen ground sloped down for a short distance, then leveled out to where a row of red-caned berry bushes had been planted. Soaked in blood, both my father's and my own, I worked my way toward the bushes and collapsed beneath them. I was only partially hidden from the dirt road beyond but found myself too weak to move any further.

I lay there trembling, a limp rag of a boy, struggling to remain alert. It would be easy to give up now, to slip once more into unconsciousness, to join Papa in death as Pozniak had intended.

Look at yourself, I shouted in my thoughts. *Look what you faced just moments ago, yet here you are, you are alive! And your papa—your poor, suffering papa—has protected you, even in death, with his body. It is a sign— what else can it be?—that you are not meant to die here, not in this way. How dare you decide when your death should come?*

Then I thought of the shopkeeper Moishe, who for a time had been with me, with us, in the forests. How he had given up, welcomed death. Like him, I had nothing to live for anymore. Still and all, I resolved anew that I would not make it easy for those German bastards and their conspirators. I would not give them the satisfaction. *Death will come soon enough,* I said to myself, *and most certainly at the hands of the Nazis and their collaborators. But for now, if I have any choice in the matter, I will do whatever it takes to stay alive. For when I take my last breath, at least I will know I died as a direct result of my struggle to survive. I will . . .*

I thought I was dreaming when I heard a voice that was not the one in my head. "Don't be afraid, kid." From somewhere above, a whisper.

It had to be a dream, it seemed to me, for the words were in Polish, not German. Surprisingly, I found it soft and reassuring, like a Yiddish melody.

I tried to focus my eyes. I looked up to see the hazy vision of a stocky, powerfully built man. He was crouching over me. He glanced anxiously around as he removed his coat, then his shirt, seemingly oblivious to the winter cold.

I felt dizzy, still trying to focus on him. It was twilight now, making everything more difficult to see. He appeared to be in his late thirties, perhaps early forties, it was hard to tell—the war made everyone seem old before their time. His face suggested sturdy Polish peasant stock, but the skin around his eyes, his neck, hung loosely. It was as if he had lost a great deal of weight, then recently put some back on. His sandy blond hair, thinning just a little in front, lay disheveled on his head. With his shirt off, I could see the muscles of his arms. They looked like two boulders beneath tight, goose-pimpled skin. Now all he wore were his dusty trousers, tucked into the tops of his frayed leather boots, military style.

This apparition of flesh and blood knelt beside my trembling body and wrapped me in his large shirt. Then he draped his heavy coat over me, lifted me in his arms as if I weighed nothing, and carried me away from the station, away from the ashen, crumpled heap that was my father.

Again the man said, "You got nothing to fear from me. I seen what happened. I seen you crawl over to the bushes. Just do what I tell you, and I can help you. Do what I tell you, and we both might keep breathing a while longer."

I was quivering in his arms, suffering from shock, from the brittle awareness of what had happened at the station, from confusion over what might lie ahead. He carried me through the fields, heading north toward Straszęcin, the next village up the road. The village where I grew up. Where until just two years earlier, I used to live.

"Who are you?" I remember asking in a weak voice. "Where are we going?"

The man growled, a low deep sound that had no hint of its earlier gentleness. "Don't ask no more questions. Some things, you're better off if you don't know."

Had I not passed out again while in his arms, I would have probably discovered the answer sooner rather than later, for I would have recognized the house we entered that evening. It was a three-family unit just four blocks from where my own house now stood empty. The door toward the back led to a residence everyone in the village knew about, because its infamous owner, while seldom seen, had long been a topic of gossip. His exploits had begun many years before the war, and they were legendary.

His name was Jan Kopec, but for all I knew at that moment, he could have been the Messiah.

In a way he was, at least for me.

He carried me into a house—his house, I know now. But that is the last thing I can remember of that day when my father was killed, that day when I was left for dead at the train station in Grabiny. The next thing I recall is being in a field with that man Kopec, hiding in a potato dugout, but I'm told two weeks went by before he came back and took me with him into hiding.

I must confess there have been many times in my life when I've wished I could forget the terrible things I saw and experienced, just like I seem to have forgotten those two weeks while I struggled to recover from my wounds. At such times, I have to remind myself that it is good to remember, that I am here for a purpose.

I am here. I have much to say. I will be heard.

But I have not even told you my name.

Growing up, it was Moishe Goldner, Moishe being my Yiddish given name, used only within my family and by other Jews. To the Poles I was Moniek, which you would pronounce as "Moe-neck." To be honest, I felt equally comfortable with either name. Whatever they want to call me, it is still the same person they're calling, I figured. I did not distinguish between "Moishe" and "Moniek," any more than I did between "Jew" and "Pole." Could they not be one and the same?

I came into the world minutes before my twin sister, Gita. We were born on February 12 in the year 1926. Or maybe it was 1925. Few birth records survived from that time and place, mine included, and I am no longer certain which is correct.

My parents, Leap and Regina Goldner, lived in the tiny village of Mokre at that time, but we moved to Straszęcin in a neighboring district of southern Poland—the region called Galicia—when Gita and I were five or six. Mokre was my mother's home village, and her unmarried brother, Isak Flam, continued to live there after we moved. He worked as a butcher and regularly showed up at our home in Straszęcin with a juicy cut of kosher beef or mutton. Those treats, along with Uncle Isak's cheerful, outgoing personality, won me over from the time I was a toddler.

"Moishe, look how big you're getting!" Uncle Isak would say every time he saw me. But by early 1939, he was saying it with far less conviction, it seemed to me. Perhaps he only said it at all in the hope his words would make it so. For after the age of ten or eleven, when other children—including my twin sister—enjoyed growth spurts and shot up like the wildflowers that dotted the countryside every spring, I simply stopped getting any taller. Here I was, thirteen years old, yet I could not rise above five feet in height unless I stood on my tiptoes.

"Do you really think I'm bigger than the last time you saw me?" I asked one day, standing erect as if that would somehow will my body to instantly respond.

"Maybe so," Uncle Isak said thoughtfully, probably to keep my hopes alive. "Yes, I think maybe a little." And off I went, feeling taller, wondering if I would ever catch up in size to Gita. Even my parents did not know what to make of it. Papa was five-foot-eight, more or less. Mama was five-foot-four.

As it was, the sight of me standing next to Gita drew amused glances whenever we were introduced as twins, because Gita was a tall, blossoming teenager, already showing considerable emotional, as well as physical, maturity. Her dark hair fell to her shoulders in soft curls, and her coppery complexion clearly came from Mama. Our neighbor, a good-natured farmer named Wladyslaw Reguła, did not believe for a moment that we could be twins. Most everyone in the village, in fact, assumed that Gita was easily two years older than me.

Aside from being considerably shorter, I looked no different, really, than many Polish Catholic boys of my age in the village. My face was rather average, it seemed to me. I had thick, dark eyebrows, a small nose that did not fit the prevailing Jewish stereotype, full lips, and ears that stuck out just a little—like dainty handles on a teapot, I sometimes thought.

As I reflect on it, I was probably more introverted than many other youngsters in my village, sometimes prone to long periods of contemplation. Yet I was also quick to anger and, I must admit, not easily intimidated. My arms were actually rather muscular, strengthened from the pails of water I carried from the river every day. My strength was a source of pride to me. I was determined that no one would ever take advantage of me because I was small.

I was also fiercely protective of my sister. She knew that in spite of my size, I could be tough and dauntless. Once when I overheard a bully at school taunt Gita with cries of "Christ killer," I went after the boy and knocked him down. After I threw the first punch, the boy on the ground cried, "Stop! I take it back!" Reluctantly I backed off, warning him that I would meet any further comments of that nature with a far stronger response. Until he skulked away, I had not even noticed that the boy outweighed me by at least twenty pounds.

Looking back, it heartens me to think how Gita watched out for me in return. She was the one person I could tell things in confidence, without fear of betrayal. Still, when I did something foolish—and there were many such instances, I am sure—she would not hesitate to tease me mercilessly. Here is a prime example, an incident I don't recall, but which my next-door neighbor, Wladyslaw Reguła, still chuckled over sixty years later. How he remembered such a silly little thing is beyond me, but this is the story he told:

It seems Reguła was plowing the field that ran behind our house, and I was sitting in the bushes, watching him. It was a hot day, and all he wanted was to go into the shade and take a nap. So he called to me, and he said, "Moniek, how would you like to take over the plowing?" And I replied, "But I don't know what to do!" He told me just to stand behind the plow and drive around, letting the horse do all the work. "It will be fun," he added. Well, I guess it did look like fun because, according to him, I eagerly took over the plowing while he took a nap until the sun went down.

He said my sister gave me a hard time about that, and he's probably right. He heard her say something like, "I understand Mr. Reguła's got himself a new horse." Like a dummy I took the bait and assured her it was the same horse he'd always had. And she jumped in with, "No, you're wrong. He has himself a new horse, and everyone says he calls it 'Moniek.'"

My home village does not appear on many maps of prewar Poland. To get there, you might set out from Kraków, in the country's southwest, then head about forty miles due east to Tarnów. From Tarnów, if you continue a few miles east further still, almost to Dębica, you would locate the area precisely. Both Tarnów and Dębica were thriving communities, with a vigorous Jewish population. Tarnów's more than twenty-five thousand Jews, I have been told, accounted for about 45 percent of its total population—the highest percentage of Jews anywhere in Galicia. Dębica, a smaller community, added another several thousand more.

These two cities were connected to Kraków by both road and railroad, offering travelers along the way as lush a panorama, I imagine, as existed anywhere in Europe. The rolling countryside, though cold and bleak in winter, was inspiring the rest of the year. Here patchwork quilts of fields were planted with all manner of grains and vegetables. High above the ground, wheat, rye, barley, and oats bent to the whims of the breezes; on the soil itself countless cabbages sat in neat rows, forming wave after wave of white and green (and sometimes red) leafy shells tightly folded inward, each upon another just beneath; and below ground, there burrowed a profusion of root vegetables, including carrots, turnips, parsnips, beets, and potatoes—always potatoes.

Punctuating the countless acres of fields were dense stands of forests. Pines and birch, sometimes yielding to linden or poplars, were plentiful in this part of Poland, especially northeast of Kraków, where they followed northward along the Vistula River, then wandered down through the town of Mielec and south to Dębica. Continuing even further south, the terrain became noticeably more rugged, the forested green hillsides thrusting higher to meet the foothills of the majestic Tatra Range of Poland's Carpathian Mountains.

In between Tarnów and Dębica, though much closer to the latter, my childhood village of Straszęcin sat amidst great forests. Here the fertile fields were nurtured by the nearby Wisłoka River, which separated our village from Dębica. Only two Jewish families lived in this small farming community—ours and, about a block to the south, the family of a shopkeeper whose first name, like mine, was Moishe. Try as I might, I cannot recall his last name. Everyone, even the Poles, called him Moishe, because he would only answer to his Yiddish name. Unlike me he refused to accept having "Moishe" changed to the Polish "Moniek."

"I am a Jewish Pole," he often said, "not the other way around. My name is Moishe and my gentile neighbors can call me by my name, or not call me anything at all." Then he added: "I call them by *their* given names, don't I?"

He was a gentle and generous man in his sixties, educated as a pharmacist, I believe. He lived with his wife and three nearly grown daughters at the back of his little store. For many years it had been the only store in town, a true general store, selling a wide range of goods: foodstuffs, some clothing, cooking utensils, kerosene, farm implements, paint, vodka and brandy, and, of course, medicine.

But by 1937 I was old enough to understand that growing anti-Semitic factions within the Polish government argued to replace the nation's predominantly Jewish shopkeepers with stores owned by gentiles. "Patronize your own" was the catchphrase of the day, and a law was passed requiring each store owner to post his name outside his shop. So it was not surprising when a second store opened a few blocks away from Moishe, owned by an ethnic Pole. Moishe, however, was far more generous in extending credit during those devastating economic times; his business remained reasonably strong, as far as I know, if not especially profitable.

About a block north of Moishe's house and store, along the road that forked left toward Wola Wielka, where my paternal grandparents lived, stood my family's modest home. It consisted of one large room, nothing more. Needless to say, no one had much privacy. Yet once I began going to school in Dębica during the week, living there with my Aunt Enna, I actually looked forward to weekends in my own house. I had quickly discovered that living away from home did not hold the allure I once imagined. My schedule allowed little time for anything but school and study, and I found it difficult to adjust to city living.

The outside of my family's home, like most houses in the area, was built of simple pine planks. The steep roof, with its steplike surface of straw thatch, sloped down below the top of the exterior walls to create an extensive overhang. A stone chimney vented the heat from the wood-burning oven inside. There was one door and only one small window, as glass was hard to come by. A small shed on the side—it was not quite a barn—held feed and provided shelter for our animals:

one small horse, several hens, and two, sometimes three, dairy cows. An outhouse stood to one side of the cowshed. On the other side a cache was dug into the ground, a root cellar of sorts, where we stored vegetables for the winter.

Our modest living quarters had a floor of wooden planks, plain whitewashed walls, low ceiling beamed with sturdy larch. No electricity. No running water. Furnishings consisted of a wooden table with a long bench on each side and a simple cupboard for dishes. At one end of the room sat three beds, made of wooden planks set on short legs, each covered with a straw-filled mattress. The only color in the main room came from the stove, which dominated the other end. Its ceramic-tile exterior was a cheerful yellow, which I found almost as welcoming as the aroma wafting from the oven when Mama baked the Sabbath challah bread.

Beyond our home and few possessions, my father owned two small fields of less than five acres, known then as "dwarf holdings." In typical Polish fashion they were not near each other. One adjoined our property in Straszęcin. It was planted with potatoes and wheat. A second field, in Wola Wielka, had been given to Papa by his father. I had always assumed somebody was paid to tend these fields, but I was never really sure. All I knew was that with Mama peddling milk during the week and Papa on the road buying and selling cattle, they had no time left for farming.

How my grandfather and, ultimately, my father accumulated farm property, I never knew. True, many Jews tended to be merchants, craftsmen, business owners, and professionals. But Jewish farmers were really not all that unusual. I am quite sure my parents never thought of themselves as farmers, though, in the sense of growing crops. They were in the dairy and cattle business, and the fields they owned were incidental.

On the north side of our property, Wladyslaw Reguła lived with his wife and two children in an equally simple house a little further back from the main road. Reguła's son, Stanislaw, was about the age of my sister and I; his daughter, Anna, was three years younger. I often played with Stanislaw, and frequently Anna tagged along. But after a time Stanislaw and I would sneak off on our own to play cards for money. This ended one day just after I turned twelve. I gambled away all of my zlotys in just a few minutes.

"Mr. Reguła," I cried to my playmate's father after the card game, "tell Stanislaw not to take my money anymore!"

Reguła liked to recall that incident more often than I wanted to hear it. He was an energetic man of thirty-two then, with deep-set eyes and a thick shock of black hair that looked windblown even on balmy days. His gently lined face, tough as new work boots, frequently melted into an engaging smile. His hands were especially rough, callused through years of hard labor. To him working the fields was second nature, and the dirt that often wedged under his fingernails was what he called "toil soil": rich and abundant and good.

In the winter, when the fields lay fallow, Reguła sometimes got employment at the flour mill in Dębica or at the lumberyard practically adjoining the mill. Both were owned by the Grynszpan family, prominent Jews who knew my father. If I understand this correctly, it was through Papa that Reguła got part-time work at the mill, and he was not shy about expressing his gratitude.

I never heard Reguła express any ill feelings toward Jews. To the contrary, I was surprised to hear him say that he believed the Jews were a better nation than the Poles—I think that's how he put it— because they were so solid and industrious, with a much higher culture. I don't know if that's true, but I do not suppose that point of view was shared by a majority of his fellow countrymen. I imagine Reguła's experiences with our village's two Jewish families, ours and Moishe's, helped shape his atypical stance on the subject.

As for my father, he truly *was* an industrious man, with a strong body and a darkly handsome face. His outgoing personality helped him to easily make friends, whose number included several gentiles. There was Reguła, of course, and at least one other man I knew of: a longtime friend—or so my father thought at the time—named Pozniak, who lived in Grabiny, the next village to the south of Straszęcin. This man even came to my parents' wedding, I was told—one of only a few gentiles in attendance. But Papa's difficult life left him little time for shmoozing, and being a Jew in a mostly gentile village meant family was not only his main responsibility but also his primary social circle, if you could call us that.

Now and then on a Sunday, however, Papa would slip out of the house and stop by Moishe's store while most everyone else in the village was at church. It felt good to speak Yiddish outside his own family, Papa said. There was a time, he told me, when the Jews who were welcomed into Poland spoke *only* Yiddish, a thick, fourteenth-century German dialect. But as I was growing up, we—like many other Jews— found it advisable to use our country's national language outside the home.

If my parents experienced any overt anti-Jewish sentiment in these prewar years, I never heard them speak of it. I had my own share of "Christ killer" taunts when I was young, but unlike the times I felt compelled to defend my sister with my fists, I would usually fend off verbal attacks with words alone.

"I had no more to do with the killing of Christ than the man in the moon" was my usual response. In fact, it was not until I started school in Dębica at the age of twelve that I truly felt alienated, this time from Jew and gentile alike.

Little did I know that my days of innocent, carefree, and—as I looked upon it then—unremarkable childhood were drawing to a close.

2

Into the Forest

A S I SAID, I don't remember what happened over the next several days after the stranger carried me away from the Grabiny station and brought me to his home. I was pretty out of it, as you might say today, suffering from a gunshot wound in my hip and an injury to my back, which, I would later learn, was actually a bayonet wound. I imagine I had lost a lot of blood, although how much of the blood all over me was my father's, I cannot say.

Still, there are those who do know what happened in the days following my rescue, even sixty years after the fact. They are the four surviving children of my rescuer, who, incidentally, have remained their entire lives in and near my childhood village of Straszęcin. They were eager to relate the stories their late mother handed down to them, although only two of them were old enough at the time to actually remember seeing me.

"We were small children when Moniek first came to us, but over the years, our mother told us stories of that terrible period. Up until her death [in 1989], she talked about Moniek many times. It is true, Father found him at the Grabiny train station. He was badly wounded. Father carried him to our home, and Mother was not happy about it. She said to our father, 'We have so many children, so many mouths to feed, and now you bring me another? One who's almost dead, from the looks of him?' In spite of this, she helped clean his wounds. She gave him food and clothing.

"The Germans were looking for Father and probably now for Moniek, too, so it wasn't safe to keep him at our home. They decided to take him to a place just outside the village, to a house belonging to a woman named Walantina. She worked with Mother as a maid at the 'palace,' Stubenvoll's big estate on the hill. Anyway, after two weeks at Walantina's, Moniek was strong enough to hide with Father in the forests. And so he came back for Moniek. And that's all we know."

The first thing I recall is an underground storage area, called a *copiec*. It was dug into the earth to hold potatoes—up to a thousand pounds, I think—to keep them from freezing over the winter months. Was this our first day together after my rescuer collected me from that woman, from Walantina? I cannot say.

The dugout was simply covered with straw and earth. Ventilation came from a slender wooden flue. There were several such storage areas in the field; for some reason, this one was empty. Perhaps the potatoes it would have normally contained had already been conscripted by the Germans. The man who brought me there said he had discovered the empty space some time earlier and had been using it regularly for shelter.

"Are you comfortable?" he asked me once we settled into the cramped quarters.

"Perhaps if I were a potato . . ." I shot back, surprised at my own sarcasm.

He ignored this.

I leaned back, breathing in the damp, musty air. The smell of earth was a welcome respite from the smell of death. Or were they one and the same? Each time I moved, a small pile of dirt tumbled to the ground behind me.

"Actually, this is something of a luxury," I said, realizing that at least the chill wind was no longer penetrating my bones. "I have spent days in places a lot worse." I tried to push those memories out of my mind, but they were always there, lurking just below the surface, as much a part of me as a root is of a plant.

The man grunted. "You will experience worse places again. I promise you that."

I did not doubt it. Then it occurred to me; I still had no idea who he was. So I asked his name.

"Kopec," he told me, using only his last name. His eyes were fixed on mine as he said this.

My jaw must have dropped as if I had just bitten into a hot coal. The very mention of the name "Kopec" sent a wave of shock through me. I do not think I had ever seen him before, but I knew at once who he was. Ever since I could remember, people in the village had talked about him.

My mind churned, struggling to bring forward the bits of gossip and hushed conversations I had overheard years ago, before the war, from the time I was old enough to understand.

"The most feared man in eastern Galicia."

"King of the bandits."

"He's crazy—he'd just as soon kill you as look at you."

"A dangerous man. Controls the black market in this area . . ."

"He's never been caught. Everyone's too afraid to turn him in."

Could this really be the man who spoke so softly to me at the station, who carried me gently in his arms and on his back to safety? It was hard for me to believe. Why would he risk his own neck to rescue me? Him, of all people! As far as I knew, there wasn't a more notorious criminal in all of Poland. My mind continued to race with some of the things I had overheard while I was growing up. Anecdotes about the man's bank robberies, home invasions, things far worse. Daring exploits so shocking, it seemed to me they could not possibly be true.

"You know my name, I take it," Kopec growled. He studied my face.

I nodded, but I did not shy away from him.

"You heard stories about me? Things I done?"

"Yes . . . some."

"You believe them?"

"I don't know. Maybe. Yes."

"And you're not afraid of me?"

I was tempted to say, *Yes, I do fear you, knowing what they say you are capable of.* But instead I mumbled, "You rescued me. You kept me safe. You . . . saved my life."

"Fear is good. Never forget that, kid. Fear can be used to your advantage. They—" Kopec's hand swept in an outward arc, indicating everyone and no one. "They all fear me. Even the Krauts, only maybe they're too stupid to know it yet. They'll come to fear you, too—what you can do to hurt them."

I did not know what to say. A chill sliced through my body.

"It's also good to fear your enemy in return," Kopec continued. "Not no cowering kind of fear—a respectful fear, you know what I'm saying? It makes you careful, helps keep you alive. And you got to know who your enemy *is*—not just the Krauts, but also them goddamn informers. They fear the Russians more, but let me tell you, they're full of shit. The Reds may be no better in the long run, who knows? But I can't believe they'll be any worse. Besides, who the hell else is going to liberate us?"

I nodded to show that I understood, although I really did not. I had

15

no political opinions of my own, just hatred, growing and festering, for those who had taken everything from me.

I looked up at Kopec and asked, "When you found me in Grabiny . . . what did you see? How long were you there? How did you happen to be at the station in the first place?"

"Don't think about that," Kopec growled. "You're here now, that's all you need to know." I thought he was done, but then he went on, "No, you also need to know this: as long as you're with me, you will do what I say, go where I tell you, fart only when I say you can fart. You got a hell of a lot to learn, and that will take time. School starts tonight, after dark, so shut your mouth and get some sleep."

School! I never thought I would miss it, dream about it, long to have those days back again.

Before the war, my school day in Dębica began at 8 A.M. Each morning I went to a regular Polish school a short distance from where I stayed, at the home of Aunt Enna Silverman, my mother's sister.

School in general was hard for me, or more likely I did not apply myself enough. Regular classes finished at two in the afternoon, giving me a one-hour break before I walked over to the synagogue, where I attended cheder—Hebrew school—until five-thirty, Sabbath eve excepted. Before long I would be called for my bar mitzvah. That, at least, was the plan.

The synagogue itself, built in the eighteenth century, was a handsome building on Krakowska Street. Its sturdy, sloped metal roof rose gracefully to a plateau where it reflected the brilliance of the sun. Conversely, the elegant stained glass of the tall, arched windows below drew in the light, intensified it, gave it color and meaning. Over the windows, on the outside, wrought iron bars were positioned to form Stars of David, repeated in grids one after another.

Within the sanctuary itself, though, I felt ill at ease. The city boys were mainly Chassidic, their long *payes*—sidelocks—just one visible expression of their faith. I had been raised to observe the Jewish holidays, including the Sabbath as a day of rest; I kept kosher, and I was, after all, studying for my bar mitzvah—but I did not wear sidelocks like most of the other boys, did not dress in the traditional black caftan and felt hat, did not practice my religion with anything near their fervor.

"Are you a goy?" they often taunted me, using a Yiddish term for "gentile." "You dress like a goy!"

"I don't have to look different to be Jewish," I would reply, which left me open for the retort, "But you do look different. Different from us, and *we're* Jewish."

There would never be a meeting of the minds, it seemed, between us so-called assimilated Jews and the Chassidim.

By the time Friday afternoon came around, I could not wait to get back home. Straszęcin was a two-hour walk from the center of Dębica, and that was when I took short cuts, trespassing through various fields. Whenever possible I would try to hitch a ride on a horse-drawn wagon heading in that direction. This also left me with more energy to handle the one chore that waited for me when I arrived—filling buckets with water from the stream that ran under the wooden bridge just south of Moishe's store.

Friday evenings—Shabbat—were always special to me, because it meant that for the next forty-eight hours, our family would be together. Come Monday mornings, Papa would leave the house before dawn and head on foot (or hitch a ride when he could) for the *targowica*—cattle market—in Dębica. There he would spend a few hours examining the cattle that were brought in and buy as many head as he could afford. He tried to sell as much livestock as possible directly to the butchers and slaughterhouses in town.

Once, when I had a day off from school for some reason, he insisted that I accompany him to the slaughterhouse. I remember crying that I did not want to see them kill the poor cows, and he tried to assure me that the animals never felt a thing. In a kosher slaughterhouse, he said, they don't bludgeon the cattle with a heavy mallet. Was what I witnessed that much better? A heavyset man with beard and sidelocks approached the first steer, and in an instant a quick flick of his knife severed the animal's windpipe. Then another man came along, tied a rope to the steer's hind legs and used a pulley to hoist up the dead animal. Papa told me this allowed the blood to drain onto the thick carpet of sawdust below. "See?" he said. "No suffering."

Let me tell you, I suffered. I was sick to my stomach and not the least bit convinced.

Anyway, what Papa could not sell in town, he would take to the rail yard—the main east-west line went right through Dębica—and load the cattle, amidst much snorting and bellowing, onto boxcars. Then he followed in a comfortable passenger train. Most of the time he headed west, to Tarnów, where he would sell all he could. If necessary he would continue on to Kraków. This usually kept him away from home most of the week.

But every Friday Papa would be on the train headed toward Straszęcin, getting off at Grabiny, the nearest station. An hour or so later he would come up the road to our house, tired and sore, the dust of well-traveled roads on his pants and heavy leather bags over his shoulders.

17

Inside the bags were his week's earnings, but most of this money would disappear the following Monday, when he'd start the cycle over again. My father was not a wealthy man by any stretch of the imagination, but from time to time he tried to put aside a few zlotys in savings. He had opened a Swiss account some time earlier, with a little help from his father in Wola. Neither Papa nor my reasonably well-to-do grandfather trusted the Bank of Poland, what with all the runs on the bank. Surely, Papa often remarked, his small savings would be in good hands, protected for him and his heirs, in Zurich.

After washing up my father usually changed into a clean shirt and a fresh pair of pants—his Shabbat uniform, Mama always teased, because he wore the same shirt every Friday evening. He would join us as we prepared to welcome the Sabbath.

Earlier on each Friday afternoon, my twin sister, Gita, usually helped Mama knead the eggy dough, which they braided and placed in the stove. From there it tantalized us for nearly an hour with the comforting, earthy aroma of intermingling wheat and yeast. Finally the challah loaves emerged, plump and golden, as they joined the Sabbath candles to help transform our simple wooden table into a festive holiday setting.

As often as possible in those days before the war, Mama cooked a chicken for the Sabbath meal. Now and then she even put a few eggs on the table, but only if Papa had a good month. In those days it was an extravagance to eat what you could otherwise sell. As the old saying went, "You don't eat a chicken unless either you or the chicken is sick." Much of the time we settled for vegetable soups and dairy products at the Shabbat dinner, similar to most other meals. Meat was seldom on the table because it was costly and because we had no way to preserve it, except in the cold of winter.

Once in a while Papa arrived home with a chunk of beef given to him by one of the butchers he sold to. And sometimes Uncle Isak came down for the weekend with morsels from his own butcher shop. On those occasions Mama would add the meat to the evening's soup or stir small bits into the kasha—the buckwheat groats—and I would savor every mouthful, chewing slowly and carefully. It was almost as if some inner voice was telling me to make the most of every bite, for soon such moments would be nothing more than a faint and painful memory.

I awoke toward nightfall, drenched in sweat. Nightmares, again. Not fantasies this time. Real. For a moment I did not know where I was, until I saw potatoes, then Kopec. He was shaking me.

"You started to cry out," he hissed. "That can get both me and you killed. Stop with your goddamn dreams, understand?"

Easier said than done, I thought. But I knew he was right about the noise.

For the next several hours, while we waited for darkness, I tried to make conversation. Kopec did not respond. The only exception to his sullen demeanor came when I asked about his family. Kopec told me his eighth child, a boy, had been born while I was recuperating. He opened up just enough to say how he envied men who could be home with their wives and children.

"For my children's sake sometimes I wish I been in another line of work," he admitted. "It would be better for them if I was . . . someone different. But I didn't think about them things before, and now . . . hell, now it's too late." Then with a twinkle, he added, "Besides, nobody's better at the things I done."

I didn't know how to respond, so wisely, I think, I kept quiet.

"What I do now is for my family. It takes money to feed eight kids, and as long as I breathe, they'll have food on the table. Anyway, the war offers surprising *new* opportunities for a man of my background."

"What do you mean?" I asked.

"I mean there's ways to get money, just like there's ways to get food and clothing. You gonna be a big help to me in doing that, a little runt like you."

"Tell me what to do."

"Oh, I'll tell you," answered Kopec. "And you'll be safer with me than if you was on your own. But staying alive will depend on how well you do what I show you. You also got to keep your nose out of anyone else's business who may be doing things with us."

"Others will be involved?"

"I have an arrangement with . . . some other people you don't need to know nothing about. I'm going to keep you separate from them. It's better that way, you understand, kid?"

I nodded, although once again, I was not sure I understood at all.

"Now, shut up and rest until it gets darker. I don't like staying this close to Straszęcin. They could be looking for me here. We're going to be far away by daybreak."

It was a pattern of survival I had already adapted to, this constant moving from one location to another. After all, I had already been hiding in the woods for a year and a half. During that time, though, I had stayed pretty much in the same general area. Now Kopec would watch out for me, for reasons I still could not comprehend. I imagined we were like two nocturnal creatures—owls, maybe—flapping about to find a place where we might be free from harm for one more day, and then another . . .

"Along the way," Kopec was saying, "we'll get us some food, maybe some clothes, money, who knows?"

"You make it sound easy," I remarked.

Kopec snickered and grinned—in spite of himself, I imagine. "Hell yes," he said. "In this war it's always easy. Long as we don't run out of bullets."

War did not reveal itself to me through the sounds of the German Luftwaffe overhead or the incendiary horror of homes and buildings in flame. Other areas of Poland were introduced to the new reign of terror in such a devastating manner, but as I look back on that first day of September 1939, I recall hearing of the invasion through an urgent clamor that swept through my public school in Dębica. Just hours earlier German forces had crossed the border, and Hitler had addressed the Reichstag with a declaration of war.

For me the news had little immediate impact. The skies above my head were clear and would stay that way for some time. The closest the war came to me, in those very early days, was forty-eight hours later, when a lone German plane released a few bombs over nearby Tarnów, damaging the main post office and a hospital. At the time I was not even aware of the bombing.

I ran home from school that day—it was a Friday afternoon, I remember—acknowledging only that there might be a few new hardships ahead. My parents had already discussed the possibility of war, but I could not imagine my life being much different than it was, no matter how Mama and Papa tried to prepare me for the inevitable changes that even they could not fully imagine.

The moment I entered the house, my sister greeted me with, "Moishe, have you heard the news?" She chirped the line with such excitement, I thought maybe she was about to announce a windfall of some sort rather than word of the Germans sweeping across the border.

Before I could draw a breath to assure her the news was all over Dębica, she continued, "We heard it over the radio. The Germans have crossed into Poland with tanks and dive bombers and . . . and . . ." She choked back sobs. I realized that what I took for enthusiasm was really a jumble of fear and confusion. Gita, for one, had sensed that our lives were about to be immeasurably altered.

In the next moment Mama came over from the stove, where she had begun to prepare the Sabbath meal, and put an arm around my sister, while extending her other arm toward me. She held us tightly.

"Let's not talk of war now, not on Shabbat. Somehow, we'll all get through this," she said, no doubt trying to convince herself as well. "Come, give me a hand. Soon your father will be home."

But Papa did not make it home before sundown, when the candles were lit and the meal had begun. Nor did he make it home anytime that evening, or the next day. Frantic with worry, Mama reassured Gita and me that Papa was fine, that the Germans were nowhere in the area, that transportation had merely become disrupted with the news of war, so Papa was having difficulties getting home.

Actually, she had hit upon the truth, because we soon learned that the rails and roads in our area were at a standstill, for a time, while the country absorbed the news of invasion and bravely, but with complete futility, tried to resist.

And when Papa dragged his body in the door that Sunday morning, having walked nearly half the distance from Kraków, we all hugged him greedily.

Mama knew he would not be home for long, but Gita and I were stunned beyond words when, two days later, Papa appeared at breakfast and announced that he was leaving, possibly for a very long time.

"You're *leaving* us?" Gita was incredulous.

"How will Mama manage?" I asked.

Mama spoke softly, reassuringly. "Your father and I have discussed this for some time. He has to go now, before the German soldiers come this far east. There may be no other opportunity."

Papa looked at us and sighed. "To earn my living, I have to travel from town to town. You know that. Do you think that will be possible once the Germans take over? Think about it: what will I do? Become a ganef—a thief—like that man Kopec who lives just over the bridge? I've heard there's work across the Russian border. I have to find out."

I recalled shreds of conversation between my parents during the prior year. My father had a brother and two sisters, who emigrated to America in 1915, long before my twin and I were born. They wrote frequently, begging Papa to join them, to bring us with him, but he had always resisted. His life in Poland was not so bad, he said, and more important, his own parents steadfastly refused to leave. He insisted that his place was to be near them. Now he was leaving after all, leaving out of desperation, looking to salvage something, anything, to ultimately help his family.

Papa leaned forward, gave Gita a tender kiss on her forehead. Then he hugged me and called me by the Yiddish endearment of my name. "Moishele," he said, "take care of your mother and sister."

I saw tears in Mama's eyes. She was an attractively slim woman, my mother, two years younger than my father and not often given to such displays of emotion. After hugging Papa one final time, she pulled away and patted down her dress in a prim and proper gesture, perhaps to help regain her composure.

A moment later Papa walked out the door, his leather bag bulging as it lay slung over his shoulder. He was headed on foot for the eastern border, emigrating, it turned out, with hundreds of other Jewish men from the Tarnów and Dębica area.

Of the many men from this region who fled east in those early days of the occupation, a great number remained on Russian soil until the war's end. Most of them, I would come to learn, survived. But other poor souls returned to Poland disconsolate and disillusioned, where they were to face an entirely different destiny.

On the Friday after my father left, as I walked home from Dębica for the weekend, I witnessed the first German soldiers—they were Wehrmacht forces—to arrive in our area. They appeared to be hardy, spirited young men, even courteous, often smiling and waving to us. Accompanying these forces was a dusty convoy of trucks pulling tanks and artillery along the nearly deserted roadway.

I watched with a sense of curiosity rather than fear, for the troops showed no interest in harassing us. They were on the move, settling into the cities of Tarnów and Dębica, while others headed further east, pursuing the fleeing Polish army in the direction of Rzeszów, which we learned was being heavily bombed that very day.

For the next month I was able to maintain my well-established routine. I continued to spend weekdays in public and Hebrew school in Dębica while living with my aunt, hitchhiking or walking home each Friday afternoon. But I missed my father terribly. I fervently prayed for his safe and early return.

By the third Friday in October the weather had turned unseasonably mild, and while I might have considered walking all the way to Straszęcin, I came upon a ride almost immediately. It was a wagon filled with gravel, headed for a nearby cement plant just a mile or so from my home. The driver—a plump pudding of a man who wore a muffler around his neck in spite of the warm weather—did not invite me onto the seat next to him but indicated with a wave of his hand that I was welcome to jump onto the back of the cart. I was small, after all; the horse in front would scarcely feel my added weight over the load it was already pulling.

As the wagon plodded along, I faced the back with my legs dangling aimlessly off the edge. I kicked at the air, satisfied with my good fortune. I burrowed my rear end deeper into the gravel, making a small hollow in the stones in an attempt to get comfortable. I knew my dark-colored pants and jacket would be filthy from the dust of the rock but decided I would rather wash them in the stream when I got home than pass up such a convenient ride.

After several minutes I began to pick up small pieces of the crushed rock all around me and pitch them, one by one, off the back of the wagon. Without any conscious thought, I aimed at targets along the road.

Ping! A chunk of gravel hit a rusted piece of metal, the remnant of a discarded plow, lying in the dust.

Ping! The next stone found its mark as it glanced off an old wooden post.

Soon I began to daydream, and my thoughts became filled with questions and uncertainties, running through my mind in desultory fragments, as if I were spinning the tuning knob on a radio set.

I briefly wondered if my approaching bar mitzvah would ever take place. I was thirteen years old, and many boys I knew in Dębica had already undergone the solemn ceremony that welcomed a young Jewish boy into manhood.

Ping!

I questioned what the future might hold for me now that I was becoming aware of tension all around, yet not fully comprehending it. I had no interest in farming, I was certain of that. Perhaps I would learn a trade or sell cattle like my father. I naively hoped the German occupation would be nothing more than a temporary inconvenience.

Ping!

My thoughts turned briefly to my father, now undoubtedly settled somewhere in Russia, trying to eke out a living. At home, meanwhile, Mama was shouldering the day-to-day responsibility for her family. What would become of us if she could no longer freely come and go, peddling milk?

Mama. Every weekday morning before sunrise she rose by four-thirty, filling her large white porcelain pails with milk to sell to customers in Dębica. She had been doing this since Gita and I were born, and long before. It was a hard life, but not once had I ever heard her complain.

Ping! Ping! Ping!

I was not so much aiming at targets at this moment, as just throwing gravel involuntarily, with more thought to my shortwave band of daydreams than to the movement of my right arm.

A bigger chunk of rock, now. Not a "ping" this time, but the sound of glass cracking. Brakes squealing and tires skidding. Jarred out of my dream world, I gasped at what I had done.

The very moment my arm had released the chunk of gravel, a black car had been passing by the horse and wagon, heading in the opposite direction, toward Dębica. My small rock had found the car's windshield, pitting it near the driver's side and sending a series of fine cracks in all directions from the epicenter.

The car screeched to a stop. Its two passengers ran toward the wagon, screaming, *"Halt! Halt!"* to the puzzled driver. I was stunned as they headed for me. I sat frozen on the back of the wagon. Their tall, leather boots and spotless green uniforms came closer. On their uniforms was an unmistakable skull and dagger insignia. ss.

The Germans grabbed me roughly and pulled me off the cart. One man, as I recall, did all the talking.

"My partner thinks we should just shoot you here," he began, "but you'll come with us." Between the German I had learned in school and the Yiddish we spoke at home, the meaning of the Nazi's rapid-fire words was quite clear.

"First brush off the dust from your stinking clothes. You'll soil our car enough just by sitting in it. Hurry up. We're going to show you what happens to Polish swine who throw stones."

A good sign, I thought. He said, "Polish," not "Jewish." Still, I nearly wet myself.

Frightened beyond words, I was taken to an old building in Dębica just blocks from where my journey had begun a short time earlier. I was put in an almost empty room and given an uncomfortable straight-backed chair to sit in. The room smelled of sweat, of fear. *Who had been here before me*? I wondered. Two guards were stationed outside the door. I remained alone, terrified and in tears, for what seemed like hours but was probably not more than twenty minutes.

Then two Gestapo men walked in, their uniforms black as death. They each carried a chair that they set down directly in front of me. They sat backwards, their hands resting on the top edge of the chair backs, and they glared at me as if I were some kind of insect. One of the men seemed to be about thirty years old with a long jaw and sunken cheekbones; the other was a bit older, much bigger, with a misshapen, pockmarked face that made him look all the more menacing.

My interrogation went on for more than two hours. Why did you attack the ss car? they asked, speaking in Polish. Sobbing hysterically, I told them the truth, that it was an accident, I did not even see the car. What are your feelings toward Germany? came the next question. I have no idea, I answered, for indeed I did not. What were you doing in the wagon? Where were you going? Why were you throwing rocks?

It went on this way well into the evening, when to my surprise in walked Mama. She had been summoned by the Gestapo, interrogated separately, then finally allowed to take me home. Maybe the Germans had stomached enough of us country peasants.

"If you're brought in here again," said the big officer with the face like a fresh-dug potato, "the next time, you won't leave. You'll get an early look at what will happen to all you swine in time. Do you understand me?"

I did not catch every word but nodded my head anyway. It seemed like the right thing to do.

And then, in a strange twist of irony, Mama and I were returned home as if we were visiting dignitaries, riding in a finely polished ss car, which made the trip to Straszęcin in just under fifteen minutes.

It was shortly before midnight when we walked in the door. The sound of the German car speeding off gave way to blessed silence.

"What a nightmare," Mama said to Gita, who had been waiting anxiously at home. My sister was greatly relieved to see me, but I think she hoped there would be more information forthcoming about the trouble I had gotten into. At the moment, however, neither Mama nor I were in any mood to elaborate. Gita knew that in time I would tell her everything that had happened. I always did.

"It's not safe to go into town any more," Mama told me. "You're staying here from now on. You will not leave Straszęcin." Then, looking at Gita, she added, "None of us will."

"But Mama, what about my bar mitzvah?" I pleaded. Of course, I knew the answer. Deep inside, I had known for weeks.

"There will be no bar mitzvah. Not for you, not for anyone, I should think. Certainly not while the Germans occupy this country. Don't you see, Moishele? It's not safe to be a Jew anymore. It may not even be safe to be a goy much longer."

She could not have known the measure of truth to her own words. Within days the synagogues in Tarnów would be set on fire and destroyed by the Germans. As if that were not enough, a large out-of-control group of local Poles would join in the melee by pillaging Jewish houses.

Dębica's synagogue would remain standing, however, although its interior would be ransacked. Eventually I would learn the Germans used it as a warehouse. On the outside of the synagogue, the Germans had already removed strategic strips of metalwork that covered the windows so that they no longer formed Stars of David. And the prophetic words "die, Jews" appeared along with swastikas painted by an unsteady hand on the wall of the building.

It was finally getting through to me that while the war lasted, my life could no longer be the same. Although I had not been happy going back and forth to school in Dębica, now I felt like a prisoner in my own home. Yet I had no idea how much better my life was compared to what most families faced in the large cities.

25

For Straszęcin, a small village with its inconsequential Jewish population, was largely ignored by the Germans. But in the neighboring towns of Tarnów and Dębica, strict sanctions were being handed down in increasing numbers. Jews in the city were required to wear armbands with an identifying Star of David. Jewish businesses were placed under the management of Ukrainians or residents with German lineage, who kept the keys and handled all the money. Jewish males between fifteen and forty-five were required to work fourteen-hour days for their German masters. The list of hardships went on.

These measures were not enforced in my village at this time mainly because there were no German soldiers present to enforce them. As long as Mama, Gita, and I stayed close to home, we felt safe.

Of course, Mama could not continue taking her canisters of milk into Dębica. With winter nearly upon us and still no word from Papa, we struggled to get by. We had no need for all our animals any longer, so Mama sold our horse and one of our two cows to someone at the priest's farm adjoining the Straszęcin church. (It was quite common in those days for country churches to have agricultural as well as spiritual interests.)

"We'll still have milk and sour cream," she told us, "and eggs, God willing." Between our small field and the ample field owned by our neighbor Reguła—he was always willing to share—we knew there would be wheat and potatoes, at least. My grandparents in Wola offered to help us as much as they could, and so did Uncle Isak. His butcher shop was still in business, because Mokre—as small a community as Straszęcin—was also being ignored by the Germans.

Then there was the shopkeeper Moishe, a kind and generous man. He often gave us food and supplies on credit, and not just because we were fellow Jews—he extended credit at one time or another to everyone in need.

"You'll pay me back when Leap comes home, when Poland is again its own country," he told Mama, but I suspected that neither he nor my mother believed that would happen any time soon.

And so the year 1939 ended, with its bitter changes, and a new year began. Gita continued to attend the school down the street. But me, I busied myself helping my mother with basic chores and making repairs around the house.

Living in a farming village also meant there was usually something to eat, at least in those days. During that first winter of the war, food prices increased greatly, redistributing what little prosperity there was from the cities to the countryside. For farmers this meant getting top prices for crops in currency, or better still, through barter. Because much of the harvest went to feed the growing German army, farmers were indispensable to the occupation forces. It was my understanding that, as a result, we were treated far better than most Poles in the cities. Still, it saddened us to hear about additional hardships thrust upon the Jews in other places not so far away, including the proliferation of Jewish ghettos in Łódź, Częstochowa, Lublin, and Siedlce.

At this point the Jews in nearby Tarnów and Dębica had been able to remain in their own dwellings, although they were subject to frequent house searches. But there were other forms of degradation forced upon them: *Jews are not permitted to walk slowly,* read one decree. *Jews must be off the streets after 7 P.M.,* insisted another. *Jews cannot buy vegetables before 11 A.M.*

I may not have fully realized it then, but Mama most certainly did: the unimaginable was quickly becoming reality. Oppression was not the worst thing that could happen.

3

Kopec

ALL MY REFLECTIONS on the past were temporarily displaced by more immediate matters as Kopec and I followed the winding Wisłoka River to the north. After a while we reached a small village on the western edge of a vast wooded area known as the Blizna Forest. Kopec sniffed at the cold night air, as if the scent might tell him something. Then he declared the village satisfactory for what he had in mind.

Part of the way, he carried me on his back, although he pushed me to walk as much as I could. As we went, Kopec was silent, for all that needed to be said had been spoken just before we left our *copiec*.

The bandit had revealed what he would expect of me later in the evening. I tried not to act surprised, but armed robbery was not something I had ever thought about participating in before. On the other hand, I reasoned, after the many months I had spent on my own raiding stores and fields, who was I to make moral judgments?

Whatever it takes, I had to remind myself. *Whatever it takes.*

Kopec had also taken the time to familiarize me with the two weapons he was carrying. One was a *Steilhandgranate,* a German-made stick grenade with a metal cylinder at the end of a long wooden handle. The other was a Russian submachine gun that never left his side. It was a Tokarev PPSh41, crude but effective, with a distinctive drum-shaped magazine that looked like a large metallic wheel. This magazine extended down just behind the barrel. Kopec let me hold the gun and get used to its feel. It was surprisingly compact and light, but in my small hands it felt immense. I wanted to ask how he came to possess these weapons, one from each side of the war, but feeling intimidated, I kept my tongue.

We entered the village after midnight. It seemed to me that Kopec selected houses at random. He had a sense about these things, I would come to learn, honed through years of experience. The plan was to find a window that could be forced open just wide enough for me to slip through. Before the war people seldom bolted their front doors, but times had changed. There were bandits about.

Once I entered through the window, my instructions were to quickly open the door so Kopec could enter. At the first house I must have moved too slowly, for I opened the door to face my scowling master, who angrily whispered, "Faster next time, damn it."

Our hope was to get in and out without waking anyone, and at the first house we were successful. After a moment's hesitation I began taking what little food I could find—just a few paltry vegetables, no bread or meat—while Kopec searched for clothing and valuables. He found little of use except for a few coins hidden under the frayed cushion of a heavy chair. Before leaving, Kopec did a quick recheck of the kitchen I had already searched. He grabbed something from an otherwise empty cupboard. This puzzled me, but I had no time for questions as we fled outside.

"Next time, don't overlook something this important," Kopec said when we were away from the house. He held up a liter-sized bottle of homemade brandy, nearly half full.

A few blocks away, in the second house we entered, the door made a loud noise as I opened it from the inside. A woman called out, "Is somebody there?" from the sleeping quarters in back.

Gun extended at his waist, Kopec bounded into the room and ordered its occupants—the woman, her husband, and a young child, as I recall—to huddle together in a corner of the room. The couple trembled with fright, but at least they obeyed. The child began to cry, but Kopec paid no attention. He handed his weapon over to me.

"Watch them while I search the house," he said to me. "If they give you any trouble, kill them."

The woman gave a soft wail and protectively sheltered her hysterical child. Her husband looked on helplessly.

I hoped my nervousness was not showing. I was sure I could never bring myself to use the gun on these innocent people, and Kopec must have figured that as well; I am certain he was listening carefully for any signs of resistance. There were none, as it turned out. There seldom were. Many families knew the procedure well, you see, having been robbed repeatedly as banditry became almost routine. This apparently annoyed Kopec.

"I might have to get honest work when the war's over," he once told me, "and leave this life to all the goddamn amateurs coming in."

29

By the time we broke into the third house, I relaxed a bit, for I began to realize that the gun I held functioned perfectly well merely as a threat. I even rationalized that these people all had roofs over their heads, and beds to sleep on, and in most cases, a change of clothes. All of which was more than I had, more than most Jews had, and these Polish families were simply sharing their good fortune with me—albeit at the encouragement of a formidable semiautomatic submachine gun.

Deep down, however, I was not really comfortable with this justification. What's more, I was appalled at the thought that Kopec would use his weapon on innocent people without a second thought. Still, I knew I had better quickly adapt to his way of life if I wanted to survive, so I tried to push these moral quandaries out of my mind.

After the third robbery we reluctantly left the comfort of the warm homes we had invaded and fled back into the forest. There we paused a moment, sharing some of the food (bread! bacon and sausage—forbidden!) we had stolen from the second home. Kopec took a long pull on the brandy bottle, then passed it over to me. With a wave of my hand, I tried to decline.

"Go ahead, kid, drink some," he insisted. "This will keep you warm. It will also keep you healthy."

So I took a small sip, felt the fiery liquid slide down my throat, then took a more generous swallow. I coughed. My face reddened. And for the first time since I joined him, Kopec grinned broadly.

A half-hour later Kopec said in a quiet voice, "I hope you can walk a little farther."

I nodded. My hip still hurt, but the brandy had helped a little. I could not expect Kopec to carry me on his back all night. Soon it would be daylight, and I knew that with the Pustków concentration camp just several miles to the south, this was no place to wander about after dawn.

"Where are we going to spend the day? Do you have a hiding place in mind?" I asked.

"I been hiding since before you were born," he sneered. "I know the forests from here west to Rzeszów and south to the mountains. Everywhere I got places no one can find me. If you keep doing what you're told, and if we live long enough, you might see them all."

I digested this latest information, this new scrap of knowledge that I was being fed in only the smallest bits and pieces from the very private man who walked beside me. Finally I felt brave enough to ask, "Why do you pick houses to rob that are so far from Straszęcin?"

"Why do you ask so goddamn many questions?" Kopec growled, and I was afraid I had pushed too far. What might happen, I wondered, if the outlaw became truly angry with me?

"All right, I'll tell you why: you don't shit where you sleep" was Kopec's pithy reply. It was obviously an axiom he had followed carefully throughout his illustrious career. "I never robbed nobody within a two-hour walk of Straszęcin, and that's the truth."

"Not even in Dębica?"

"Especially not there. For one thing, it makes life easier for my family. People in Straszęcin can talk about me all they want—and I know they do—and I suppose they're even afraid of me. That's good. But show me anyone there who's ever been personally threatened by me."

It seemed to me that Kopec wore that fact as a point of pride.

"Another thing," Kopec went on, peering ahead in the darkness, "it's better to work where people don't know my face so much. Makes things easier, yes? But it's all right they heard all them stories about me."

"Are those stories . . . are they true?" I asked.

"Probably not." A short silence, followed by, "Then again, the truth just might be a hell of a lot worse."

I could not tell if he was being serious. I did not ask.

Kopec stopped suddenly, shot me a piercing glare. "I hope you're done with all your goddamn questions."

"Can I ask just one more for now?" I did not wait for his response. "Why is it you seldom go into Straszęcin, to your home, anymore? Why are you hiding from the Germans?"

In response I got a snarl and a string of curse words, but I never got an answer. In the year and a half we spent together, he talked freely and longingly about his wife and kids. But the rest of his personal life was clearly not open to discussion. At least, not to me.

Kopec, it turns out, was hiding from the Germans for a very good reason, having little to do with his criminal past. Just weeks before he came upon me at the train station, it seems, he had escaped from Auschwitz.

He kept this rather substantial fact from me the entire time we were together, for reasons I will never understand. I learned a few details of his internment and escape only recently, as a result of conversations with an elderly man I'll call Kryzak. He was a former Home Army partisan from Dębica and is one of the few people still alive today who knew Jan Kopec personally.

Although Kryzak did not know or remember all the details, he did verify this fact: In 1940, Kopec was picked up by the ss during a random street roundup in Dębica. Those roundups were staged to terrorize the local population, you understand, while at the same time helping the Nazis to kidnap able-bodied Poles for forced labor.

Who knows what brought Kopec into town that day. Likely as not he was just walking along, unaware that a block behind him, the street was being cordoned off by the ss. That's how they did it. Barricades would go up behind you as well as a block or two in front of you, and entrances to each cross street and alleyway would be similarly shut off by ss and Gestapo officers with fierce dogs. Then the Nazis would make their selection from among the group caught in their net.

By the time Kopec must have realized what was happening, Kryzak said, it would have been too late, even for the self-assured and powerful man he was. As far as anyone knows, Kopec was captured simply because he was in the wrong place at the wrong time. Kryzak thought Kopec was taken first to the prison in Tarnów, but by late summer he ended up at Auschwitz. It had opened for business just months earlier, also with prisoners from Tarnów. You probably know in those days Auschwitz wasn't a concentration camp for Jews; it began as a labor camp for Poles. To survive there for as long as he did, Kopec must have been a model prisoner. And I know from my own experiences he was strong as a bull.

From what Kopec himself told Kryzak after the war, he did construction work the whole time while in Auschwitz, and there was plenty for him to do, because the camp was expanding day by day. In 1942 he lucked into a real plum, as camp jobs went: driving a horse-drawn wagon carrying construction materials to the new camp that was being built. He and a fellow named Turek.

Each day they had to pass through several sentry points between the stables in Auschwitz I and the construction area outside Brzezinka. Within the main camp itself, they had a surprising amount of freedom; ss guards did not always accompany the laborers they knew well. Still, at the outer border, if no German guard was already present, one always jumped onto the back of the wagons as they passed through.

So one day in late 1942 Kopec learned that his work detail was about to be transferred to the political section. The whole lot of them. He knew this meant only one thing: extermination. He immediately put an escape plan into action, although certainly he must have been aware that the odds of success were against him. Kopec never told Kryzak all the details, but he did tell him this: the next day he and that Turek fellow drove their horse cart right out of the camp. They drove deep into the forest, then eventually made it on foot all the way back home. Kryzak guessed that Kopec was in Auschwitz under an assumed name; a lot of the prisoners were. But probably the Germans found out who he was, because they were surely looking for him.

Kopec came upon me at the Grabiny station shortly after he returned to the area, Kryzak said. Everyone who knew of Kopec's escape eventually became aware he was hiding with me. But day to day they never knew where. And thankfully neither did the Germans.

While there does not appear to be any written documentation of Kopec's escape—at least under his real name—there is a rather similar escape described in a book titled *From the History of KL-Auschwitz.* Tadeusz Iwaszko writes:

> A dray drawn by two horses passed the gate at Auschwitz in the forenoon. In one of the wardrobes, placed upon the dray, Kuczbara was hidden, dressed in the [stolen] ss uniform. The passing of the dray with the three prisoners aroused no suspicion, particularly as Otto Kusel was well-known to all Blockführers. When they were passing the checking post at the border of the big sentry chain, Kuczbara in his ss uniform was sitting in the back of the dray and he showed the necessary pass which they had cleverly forged. The dray proceeded toward the village Broszkowice. (86)

Given the execution of this documented escape, it is tempting to speculate what Kopec might have done to get away. Being a consummate thief, he could well have found a way to steal an ss uniform from the guards' living quarters. Then, when he met his partner Turek at the stables, they could have concealed the uniform under their prison clothes. Perhaps they set out to the railway siding to fill their wagon with bricks. But this time, instead of loading the bricks in a solid block, they left a hollow space in the center that could be reached from the front of the pile.

Suppose that somewhere between the railway siding and the sentry chain, Turek climbed into the cart behind the driver's seat, crawled into the hollow area of the bricks, and put on the ss uniform. Then, when Kopec gave the all clear, Turek climbed out and sat in the back of the wagon, as if he were Kopec's guard, waiting until they reached the border checking post.

No doubt Turek was ready with a forged pass (Kopec's work?) allowing them to leave the grounds, as they did most other days under proper ss guard. If asked at the border checkpoint where the second prisoner was, Turek might have answered in perfect German, "Dropped dead this morning." It was believable enough. At any rate, they were obviously waved through.

Once out of sight of the sentry chain, according to what little information Kopec shared with his friend Kryzak, they drove the horses deep into the woods. Then they continued on foot. What happened next is unknown, but it's probable that Kopec and his fellow escapee had some help from local villagers. Perhaps they were given civilian clothes to change into and places to hide along the way.

Whatever the exact details of the escape, Kopec's breakout was one of the few that succeeded. According to one source, out of 667 prisoners who escaped from Auschwitz and its numerous branch camps, 270 were caught. This number might actually be low, for other sources estimate that as many as 400 of those escaped prisoners were recaptured and put to death, often after long, painful torture.

Reflecting back on the spring and summer of 1940—almost three years before I wound up with Kopec—I remember feeling nothing but boredom and depression. There still had been no word from my father, and I feared I might never see him again.

The only bright spots were the days Gita and I spent with our grandparents. We loved to spend time with them, for the elderly couple doted on us, exuding a warm affection that my own parents held in check much of the time. Before the war we spent at least two Saturdays a month, weather permitting, at my grandparents' home in nearby Wola Wielka. Because it was the Sabbath, we could not ride on our horse cart. But the walk was a pleasant one, taking less than an hour.

My grandparents' home was much larger than ours, and it sat on a generous parcel of land. The house was surrounded by a narrow stream that reminded me of the moats around European castles that I had read about in school. The construction was much like that of my own home, but there were expensive touches. Decorative hardwood beams were used throughout the house, and there was an ornate front door, inlaid with planks of hardwood arranged in herringbone fashion. In the diamond-shaped center of this door was carved a grand rosette. And on the doorframe they had affixed a beautiful mezuzah of hand-painted ceramic.

Inside there was one very large main room, with the typical whitewashed walls and simple furniture, along with an alcove that led to a separate bedroom. Gita, more than I, envied the privacy it afforded. In the past we had often stayed over a Saturday night, which gave us our grandparents' undivided attention until we walked home Sunday afternoon. But we had not done this since Papa left for Russia. We would not leave our mother alone even for one night.

On one of our last visits Gita and I became especially fascinated with the photos our grandparents kept of their other three children, two aunts and an uncle, who had moved to America before we were born.

"This is your father's sister Anna," Grandmother said as she held out a yellowing photo of a pleasant-looking girl who must have been about twenty. I could not help but notice that my grandmother's hand had become taut and gnarled from years of arthritis.

"And this is Sophie," she added, taking another photo from a lined wooden box. Now her hands were shaking a little. "Both of your aunts live in New York. And this"—she took out a third wrinkled photograph, showing a man who looked like a younger version of my father—"this is your Uncle Louis. It's an old picture, but he's four years older than Leap. He lives in a place called Chicago, in the west of America, I believe."

"You must miss them, Bubbie," I remember saying.

"I miss them every day of my life. I wish you could have known them. Maybe you will someday. Maybe you'll go to America after the war. Now it's impossible." She sighed deeply. "From the time they settled there, they asked us and your parents to apply for visas in practically every letter."

"Why didn't you go when you had the chance?" I asked.

She wiped away a tear. "Because we were stubborn. Because we were comfortable here and didn't want to start all over again. Because we never thought things would get so bad in our own country. We were wrong; that's obvious now. It was a selfish thing to do."

"What do you mean?" asked Gita, a split second before I formed the same words.

"Because of us, your father refused to leave, to take you to what we've come to understand is a better place, especially for Jews. Now he's in Russia, doing who knows what, struggling to make a living, and you're here without a father at home, and—"

She broke down, crying, and Gita did the same. Only I remained stoic. *Things couldn't possibly stay this bad in Poland, could they?* I wondered at the time.

Just then Grandfather came into the room, followed by Mama. "What's with all the tears?" he asked. "Is this how we're to spend our precious time together? Why can't we reflect on all the good things in our lives? Maybe over a cold bowl of borscht?"

It broke the tension as together we walked into the kitchen. While Grandmother and Mama put food on the table, there was no conversation. Then, even though it was not the Sabbath, we bowed our heads and thanked God for all the blessings He had bestowed.

In the autumn of our last year as a family, German troops began passing through Straszęcin more often and in greater number. We had to wear our armbands whenever we ventured out of the house.

The first snow had fallen in early October. By November the temperatures had already plummeted to zero. I went out almost daily to gather firewood for our stove. It was also my job to carry water in buckets from the stream under the bridge, two blocks away. In this weather the stream was frozen, at least on the surface, so I would often have to cut a hole in the ice with a heavy tool to get at the chilly water beneath.

Mama heard some disturbing news at Moishe's store one day, no more than a rumor, she assured us: A forced labor camp had sprung up on the bank of the Wisłoka opposite our village, just a few miles to the northeast. It was in an area called Pustków. Some Jews from Kraków had actually volunteered to work there, she was told, for the Germans promised them a decent wage and other privileges during what they believed would be merely a three-month "assignment."

Little did we know that this would soon be just one of nine hundred German camps, that it would be the very camp where the Germans would try out their first portable gas chambers and crematoriums, where over the next four years more than sixteen thousand people would die. At the time Mama passed on to us only a few of the horrible things she probably heard, hiding her concern as best she could. As a result, the conversations at home often became forced as we all tried to sound somewhat hopeful.

We were in the midst of just such a discussion, over watery bowls of turnip soup, while the snow outside swirled in oblique angles driven by the fierce wind. Suddenly the door swung open. There, half-frozen and covered with snow, looking as if he might collapse at any moment, stood the gaunt, exhausted figure of my father.

"Papa!" Gita and I cried in unison.

With a gasp Mama ran to him, her chair overturning as she jumped up. She threw her arms around him tightly, then pulled back. Pushing him over toward the stove, she pulled off his threadbare coat, wet with melting snow. Then she helped him off with his boots, which were practically falling apart on their own.

He leaned against the warm brick, shuddering. For a moment I thought he might try to climb into the stove, as if that were the only way he could get warm. Papa was silent, rubbing his hands together, trying to ward off the aching, wet chill so he could embrace the family he had not seen in well over a year.

"You have some warm soup, and then we'll talk," Mama said to him.

But my father had little to say, at least in front of Gita and me. I never did learn what Papa did or where he went during these fifteen months he was away, or why, even more inexplicably, he decided to return.

36

"Things across the border are no better than they are here" was the only explanation I can recall hearing. "There's crime and poverty and a shortage of jobs, just like at home. And don't even get me started on the Ukrainians."

He looked at Gita and me with a love in his eyes that will always be with me. He sighed deeply and added, "Anyway, my place is here, with my family. Whatever happens will happen, and we'll face it together."

Then he gathered us in his arms—my tall, blossoming twin sister in one and me in the other—and said, "Now, let me look at you."

During the weeks that followed, my excitement over Papa's return would give way to more boredom and frustration. Throughout March and April our family left Straszęcin only three times, walking to nearby Wola to visit my grandparents. Even Uncle Isak's visits to our home stopped abruptly. We Goldners simply existed, living with uncertainty day after day, until we were awakened by a pounding on the door that came with the dawn one cool morning in late spring in the terrible year 1941.

It became clear to me almost from the beginning of my time with Kopec that he owed his survival to at least two very strong instincts: an innate ability to know when and where to move in the forests to evade discovery and a strong intuitive sense of who could be trusted.

In those first weeks I was with him, we covered many miles and changed locations according to Kopec's impulses and instincts. During daylight hours we hid, often underground, in root cellars and storage tunnels or in bunkers that he had dug out and cleverly concealed some time earlier. I often wondered how Kopec remembered them all.

Winter was almost behind us, but on extremely cold days, we still broke into barns and cowsheds. Kopec had been right: it was easy to take what we needed, and so far, at least, nobody had tried to resist.

When we were not asleep or robbing houses, Kopec insisted on putting me through a rigorous schedule of weapons training. He drilled me on the intricacies of several pistols, most notably the toggle-action German Luger. Then he moved on to guns and rifles, spending extra time going over the quirks of the Tokarev submachine gun. Kopec carried the Russian weapon at all times, and while that model saw a lot of action in the forests of eastern Poland, everyone regarded it as difficult to repair and maintain.

On another day I spent several fascinating hours—for I had never been a better student than when I learned about the weapons of war—reviewing the characteristics of various hand grenades. The German stick grenade, for example, was activated by removing the closing cap in the long handle and pulling the cord inside. But there were other types of grenades I needed to know about: from Germany, the *Panzer-wurfmine,* a strange elliptical stick grenade with four aerodynamic canvas fins that sprang out when thrown; and from Russia, the RG-42, which used a ring and handle much like the British and American grenades but looked less like a sleek pineapple and more like a squat, rectangular, metal oilcan.

Kopec used a pencil and paper to draw diagrams of the various guns, rifles, and grenades. He drilled me on ammunition, explosives handling, weapons of all types, and military tactics. He put a pinhole in a piece of paper so I could practice my marksmanship without wasting bullets. He even diagrammed his plans for upcoming robberies. Kopec believed in leaving nothing to chance.

There were occasions when he left me alone for hours on end at night, sometimes disappearing completely. Other times he met with various individuals (criminal gangs? partisans?) at such a distance that I could make out only shadowy figures. When Kopec returned from these engagements, he was tight-lipped about whom he had met and what was discussed. He made it clear he would indulge no questions on the subject.

So I was more than a little surprised when one night my master led me to a clearing in the forest. There I came face-to-face with a swarthy young man who wore ragged clothes along with what I am sure were German military boots.

"This is the Gypsy," Kopec said. "His name's not important."

The young man—he had to be in his mid-twenties, no older—had the dark, chiseled looks I had observed in the Gypsies who lived in the nearby Tarnów area before the war. I suspected that they, like the Jews, were interchangeable as targets for German bullets. This was the first time I had come across a Gypsy in the forest.

"Don't wonder none about how he got here," Kopec said, reading my mind. "Just pay attention to what he shows you."

For the next several nights the mysterious young man met me in the same place, training me in judo, hand-to-hand combat, and self-defense. I learned how applying pressure at the right points could bring a man down. I learned the art of the garrote and—should nothing be available but my bare hands—how to snap an enemy's neck before he had the chance to cry out.

To be honest, I was rather surprised by how readily I embraced this training. *Are you prepared to end another person's life with your bare hands?* I asked myself. *Better theirs than yours,* came my internal response, in spite of my ambivalence to life itself.

By our third night together the Gypsy declared me to be as proficient with my hands as I was—theoretically—with a weapon. Kopec was away that night, either meeting or robbing someone (or both, for the night was long).

I came right out and bluntly asked the Gypsy, "Are you a partisan?"

The young man seemed surprised by my direct question. He gave me a piercing look. "What do you know of the partisans?"

Stammering in response, I said something like, "Well, some time ago, I heard they were, uh, doing things against the Germans."

I had heard a little about the ragtag freedom fighters, gleaned that groups were being organized in the ghettos and in the forests. Still, I had no knowledge of the differing politics behind the major groups or of the growing animosity between them.

"Does Ko—" The Gypsy caught himself, then began again. "Does our friend ever talk about the partisans?"

"No, never. He does not like to talk about much of anything."

"Then you should follow his example."

I looked down, surprised by the reprimand. The response was, in its own way, the answer to my question.

As the next night ended, the Gypsy announced that he was finished with my tutoring. "There's only so much I can show you. The rest you'll learn by doing. From what I hear, you're about to get your chance."

"Why me?" I asked. "Why are you teaching me these things?"

I did not expect an answer, but for some reason, the Gypsy responded.

"Because you look like a child, you may succeed at some . . . operations, let's say . . . others of us can't get away with." Then his face softened, and his eyes locked with mine. "Soon we'll see your real measure as a man, and let me tell you something: it has nothing to do with how tall you stand."

I think that was a defining moment, the instant when I knew I would be ready for anything that followed. I still had no heart for endangering simple peasants whose homes and farms we continued to rob. But striking back against the Germans and their unprincipled informers—that would be another matter entirely.

I saw again the images of my own family being forced from our home. I flashed back to the horror I witnessed in Sędziszów shortly thereafter. It came to me then, an epiphany that transcended all prior insights: if death at the hands of my enemies was ultimately my destiny, *this* is how I wanted to die.

"Give me a gun," I said to the dark-complexioned young man who had drilled me mercilessly, "or the chance to use my own two hands, and I will not hesitate."

I was filled with resolve. No, it was something more: fury, an anger I had not felt before, a conviction long overdue. It fit me like a second skin.

"Everything I ever cared about—*everything*—has been taken from me," I continued, thinking back to the last day I was together with my family. "Now it is time for me to take something back."

4

Sędziszów

*A*CHTUNG, *JUDEN!* Open at once!"
As our last day together began, Gita and I were deep in sleep. I don't remember if it was the loud knocking that woke us or the piercing sound of Mama's terrified scream.

She had just come in from the storage shed. The pail of flour she carried flew out of her hand and clattered to the floor. Papa must have been out back when the German soldiers approached, for he was already in their custody. Soon it would be daylight. The brooding sky was becoming pale to the east.

Mama said, "Children, it will be all right," or words of that nature. I know she spoke without much conviction. She opened the door.

A tall German soldier glared at her and quickly surveyed the room beyond, looking at Gita and me as we stood by our beds, terrified. The soldier had Papa firmly in his grip. After a moment or two he relaxed his hold on my father and pushed him into the room, which nearly knocked Mama off her feet. Behind and to the side of this first soldier stood a second, his rifle pointed at us.

I guessed the tall German to be no more than twenty-two or twenty-three, and the circles under his eyes made it look as if he had been sleep deprived for a long time. *Doing what?* I wondered.

"You are being relocated." The soldier's voice held no trace of emotion. We strained to understand his rapid-fire German.

"You have five minutes to gather up one small bag per person, with a change of clothes, a cup, and any necessities you will need for the next two days. Hand me all money and valuables now for safekeeping. If we discover you have taken any such things with you or hidden them from us, you will be shot. Do you understand?" He did not wait

41

for an answer. "Leave all other possessions here. When you are reset-tled we will see about getting your things to you. *Mach schnell!*"

My mother and father hurried to comply under the watchful eyes of the soldiers. Gita put her hands to her face and began to sob uncon-trollably. I went over to her and held her loosely, uncomfortably, as if she might break. Then I pulled back, not quite knowing what else to do. Mama moved in, cradling Gita in her arms.

Although terribly frightened myself, I recall putting on a brave fa-cade. It felt like everything was happening in slow motion, as if I were dreaming it all. Quickly I threw on my clothes—dark cotton pants and a slightly soiled jersey—in silence.

"No, son, you'll go *clean*," Mama called out in a frantic voice, when she spotted the jersey I had on.

What does it matter? I thought, but it somehow seemed important to her. I changed my top.

I noticed that the two young soldiers were eyeing Gita, their expres-sions not hiding what I took to be lascivious thoughts. I wanted to pummel them, rip them apart, and I am not certain what held me back. Possibly it was that one of the soldiers briefly turned his attention to me, then turned to the other, and muttered something both men seemed to find quite funny. The only word I caught was "sheep," and perhaps that was enough for me to sense their thoughts, because at that moment I conjured up a strange image: the body of a sheep, all white and woolly, but with my own frightened face. Soon I was joined by another such creature, and then many more, each with a different face. Now there were hundreds, perhaps thousands of us, following submissively in a long line to some unseen destination. And we were pleading, bleating in Yiddish, our voices trembling in the panicked dis-harmony of terror and anguish.

We were crying, "Help us, help us."

But, of course, no one heard.

The wooden horse carts were lined up at the bridge, just past Moishe's house and store. There were four wagons in all, three already filled to overflowing with Jewish families from nearby areas like Czarna and Grabiny. About a dozen soldiers were overseeing the roundup in my neighborhood. Soon we would understand that German forces had been dispersed throughout the whole area, where the scene was re-peating itself in other small farm communities. The Nazis were herding the scattered Jewish families out of the rural countryside. To where? I wondered.

The wagon drivers were local Poles. Farmers, mostly. They sat im-passively, it seemed to me, clenching their reins, awaiting further instruction from their German masters. If they felt any emotion about what they were doing, they hid their feelings well. I recognized two of the men: Straszęcin residents, one a casual acquaintance of my father. Doing the bidding of the Germans, driving Straszęcin's Jews out of town—willingly? It was an uncharitable thought and I knew it, but there it was. I felt a wave of disgust along with my fear.

Flanked by two soldiers with drawn rifles, we left our little house behind as we were prodded toward the bridge. We walked together, my frightened little family, two by two, each carrying the one small parcel we were allowed.

When we got to the road, I looked over my shoulder and saw that Reguła had come out of his house next door just in time to witness our departure. I might have been mistaken, but I thought I saw tears in his eyes.

Gita, meanwhile, was still inconsolable. Mama, fighting back her own tears, hugged my sister closely as they walked.

"Mama, where are they taking us?" I heard her whimper. "What's happening?"

"I'm not sure," Mama answered. "Probably we're being resettled in Dębica. We've heard for months now that the Jews are all living in one area. It will be all right, my darling. Somehow it will be all right."

I wondered if deep down she really knew what to think. Had her brother in Mokre also been driven from his home that morning? And my grandparents, they were elderly. What about them?

Papa and I walked just ahead, saying nothing. He was drawn and stoic, looking only forward. Although I was frightened, I somehow had the presence of mind to take in everything going on around me: the determined soldiers, uprooting Jews as easily as taking canned goods off a store shelf; the frantic families on the wagons, including one with two screaming babies; the inquisitive bystanders, coming out of their own homes to see their neighbors being led away at gunpoint.

I remember thinking what a spectacle we must be, walking anxiously toward waiting wagons. Across the street and along the block, our neighbors watched with nothing more than idle curiosity. *Well, they're frightened too,* I decided magnanimously. And then, reconsidering: *But most likely they don't give a damn about us; to them, we're just Jews.*

At that moment I heard the sounds of two more horse carts and the shouts of soldiers coming into town from the north, along the road leading in from Wola Wielka. Even before they came into sight, I knew who would be on one of the wagons: Bubbie and Zayde, my beloved grandparents.

My family was ordered into a wagon that already held several people from another village. Moments later five more people would be shoved into our same wagon: the shopkeeper Moishe, his wife, and their three daughters. All dressed in their best clothes as if they were headed to synagogue on Yom Kippur.

As I watched them being led from their house, there seemed to be some sort of altercation. I was not sure what had started it—perhaps some resistance on Moishe's part—but the disturbance ended as the butt of a soldier's rifle sharply hit Moishe in the shoulder, knocking him to the ground. He picked himself up and then was roughly pushed with the rest of his family toward the cart. When they squeezed in, I could barely move, so tightly were we packed.

By now the sun, red as blood, had risen over the eastern horizon. The day already held the promise of warmth and light. The fields were carpeted in green, and wildflowers were blooming along the road, yellows and blues and purples in brilliant profusion. Why do I remember trifling details of such beauty amidst the all-consuming horror?

The wagons began to move. Mama put her arm tightly around Gita, who turned to look back at our little village for what would be the last time.

The wagon carrying my grandparents had also joined the procession as we rolled toward Dębica. I tried to call to them, as did my father, but they were three wagons behind; neither of our voices could rise above the cries of frightened prisoners and the staccato shouts of impatient German soldiers.

Entering Dębica's city center, we passed the synagogue, where new anti-Semitic insults had been painted on the walls. Mama kissed her fingertips, then let her arm drift toward the structure as we passed. I noticed her silent gesture and realized she meant the kiss for the Torahs inside. But the holy scrolls were long gone, I imagine. Ashes and dust.

The wagon train, of course, attracted the attention of the townspeople. They tried to gather on the street corners to watch the procession, as if we were a lively Gypsy caravan. Whenever more than three or four Poles grouped together to stare, they were quickly dispersed by German soldiers. There were no Jews among the onlookers, of course. Those still remaining in town were somewhere behind ghetto walls, unseen by us as we passed by.

"Mama, we're leaving Dębica," Gita cried with alarm as we continued eastward. "If we're not being resettled with the Jews here, where are we going?"

My mother tried once again to reassure her. "Perhaps Ropczyce," she said. "Or Rzeszów. Maybe the ghettos there have more room for families like ours."

But I am certain Mama was finding it difficult to come up with any logical possibilities. She looked over to me, and I could sense the hopelessness in her eyes. Then she began to stroke Gita's hair and sing softly to her, a Yiddish melody that I cannot recall. I would give anything to hear it again, sung just as Mama sang it on that last day I heard her voice.

I looked away as Gita's body shook with sobs. I looked away because I was crying too.

Throughout the day our grim caravan grew larger, as more wagons—each overfilled with Jewish families from other small villages—joined the procession.

Dębica was far behind us now and Ropczyce as well. There were at least thirty wagons, each driven by a dour-faced farmer, flanked front and back by German soldiers. We had no protection from the intense sun, which glinted down from a nearly cloudless sky. I felt ashamed that as the day wore on, I had to relieve myself right where I stood inside the wagon. I took little solace in the fact that I was not alone in this regard.

After a time Gita had stopped her wailing, but now two of the shopkeeper's daughters began to sob quietly. I could hear Moishe and his wife speaking softly to them. A few feet away Mama and Papa were also speaking in a low whisper. Words between a husband and wife: simple endearments perhaps or—who knows?—expressions of regret? Despair at their inability to protect Gita and me?

I looked over to my sister, but she was staring listlessly at some distant point. I left her alone, deciding that her mind, for the moment, was probably in some better place. Anyway, there was not much I could say. In spite of our occasional bickering and teasing, we were close, the two of us, and I regret now that I did not feel up to the task of offering her some comfort. My own heart ached with dread and uncertainty.

The day melted into early evening. Crying and conversation had been replaced by a solemn gloom of despondence and apprehension. Where would this relocation take place? What additional sacrifices would we have to make?

Hours later the tension was palpable as our wagons rolled to a stop, and dusk settled over us, dank and oppressive, in the little town of Sędziszów.

When the drivers returned to their villages with their empty wagons, did any of them cry for us? Did they feel a sense of shame or horror or pity or revulsion? Did they stop to realize that maybe after all the Jews had been taken away, they were likely to be next?

I wonder.

Wladyslaw Reguła, our next-door neighbor, at least he cried for us.

He said he did, and I believe that now. Nearly sixty years later, the images of his neighbors being forced out of their home were still fresh in his mind.

"I watched Moniek and his family being taken away," he reminisced. "I cried when I saw it happening. What did they do to deserve such a thing? They were good people. I knew they were taken to Sędziszów. Everyone in the village knew because they were taken in wagons driven by Polish farmers who were forced to transport them and they were witness. They reported back what happened in Sędziszów. We heard there was a lot of killing. At the time we believed that everyone . . . that everyone had died."

I'll tell you precisely what happened. German soldiers pushed us out of the wagons with the same disdain you might give to rotting meat. They marched us a short distance to Sędziszów's central square.

"This town is smaller than Dębica," Gita observed as we walked, all of us still together as a family. "Why would they move us here?"

"Maybe it's just for the night," I offered. "The horses can't pull us day and night without a rest." At the time it seemed to make sense.

Mama said, "We'll know soon enough." She was no longer trying to make sense of anything. Papa, meanwhile, had lagged behind, looking for his parents. He assumed they would be moving more slowly, somewhere further back in the line.

The German soldiers barked, "Faster, faster," as they herded us toward the square.

"Soon your journey will be over," added another, and he laughed, dauntingly, high and shrill.

I gasped as we turned a corner and faced the central square. Although night had begun to settle in, the square was brightly illuminated, crisscrossed by dozens of harsh floodlights. I had never seen this many German soldiers in one place. My senses were heightened, every nerve synapse wound tight. The air, it seemed, was unusually still. From somewhere behind me lingered the smell of excrement.

And then I became aware that up ahead, a few ss men were busily separating members of each family as they came to the head of the line.

"Women and small children, to the right," I could hear them hollering, over a jumble of pleas and cries. "Men, straight ahead. Quickly, or you will be shot!"

"What are they saying?" Gita cried out, although she probably understood the German only too well.

"Moniek and Papa will be in a different line," Mama answered, with tremendous apprehension in her voice. "Only for a while, I would hope." Then, to me: "Son, stay by your father. He's just behind."

"I will, Mama," I said, as we drew very near to the separation area.

46

I was filled with emotion, choking back sobs. I called out, "I'll see you soon. You too, Gita."

With the tumult all around, I could not be sure if they heard. I looked back to see if my father had located my grandparents, but I could not spot anyone I knew in the jostling crowd of desperate souls.

"Women and small children, to the right. Men, straight ahead," came the orders again, this time louder, more emphatic.

In moments we were right beside the impassive Nazi officers who were splitting apart family members. I saw them gesture angrily for me to continue directly ahead. I looked over my shoulder as Mama and Gita were pushed to the right. Mama reached out to touch me one last time, but the crush of people separated us. There was anguish in her face as she was swept, with Gita, into the group of women and babies being held to the right of the square. They were flanked by a curious lineup of large wooden barrels, empty sentinels to the horror that was about to unfold.

I found myself among a large group of men. I immediately looked toward the entrance of the square, hoping to see my father. All the time more frightened families were continuing to pour in and face separation. Papa was nowhere to be seen. The women and their screaming children were now to my left, waiting expectantly. Waiting, waiting . . .

As I looked around, I became aware of another group forming far to my right, being forced single file, more or less, into a long line at the edge of the square. In that assembly I saw only handicapped and elderly people, men and women both. That's when I realized the men in my own group were all reasonably fit and healthy, none appearing to be much older than fifty.

Looking back toward the elderly group, I began to scan the anxious faces. My heart leaped when I saw them: my Bubbie and Zayde, there, near the far end of the line. They were apprehensively touching their fingertips together and trembling, like two fragile autumn leaves. I wanted to call out to them, but with the reigning pandemonium, I was too far away.

In the next moment I heard the throaty sound of an engine. I watched as a senior SS officer arrived at the square in the sidecar of a chauffeur-driven motorcycle. From both his entrance and demeanor, the man was clearly in charge of this *Aktion,* as the Germans called their operations of terror. I would never forget the intense look that I saw in his face: fanaticism, perhaps, or just pure hatred. *Was there really any difference between the two?* I wondered. Years later someone told me that man was Adolph Eichmann. I don't know if he was or not. Does it really matter? Evil is evil.

47

A howl of anguish rose suddenly to my left—cries of such piercing pain, it struck me as being almost inhuman in origin. I turned in that direction, toward the women's group, searching for Mama and Gita. I could not spot them, because soldiers had moved in among the frenzied women. What I saw taking place there, just meters away from where I stood, paralyzed me with such horror, I cannot find proper words to describe what I witnessed and what I felt. How can words describe such inhumanity?

This can't be happening! I thought at the time, and I think it anew each of the hundreds of times the scene replays itself, even now, in my nightmares. For this is what I see:

ss men are singling out all the women with babies and small children, brutally driving them at bayonet point toward the barrels. *Give us your garbage!* they are shouting in German. *Put your babies in the barrels!* The mothers are screaming louder than the children, if that is possible. They cannot believe they understand what the soldiers want them to do. The ss monsters push them harder, force them toward the barrels. Then one after another, they pry the babies from their mothers' protective arms and stuff the beautiful, innocent children into the barrels as if they are nothing more than freshly pickled cucumbers. As each barrel becomes filled with babies, the ss man slams its cover tightly into place and moves on to the next barrel.

One of the officers seems particularly amused by this activity. A frail child of two, perhaps two-and-a-half, has squirmed out of his grasp, screaming for her mother. She flops to the ground, where she shrieks louder still. At first it seems that the soldier is going to bend down and pick up the girl, but instead he kicks her and laughs as her tiny broken body lands several meters away. Teeth clenched, he picks the broken child up by her feet, as if she were no more than a discarded doll, and jams her headfirst into an already crowded barrel.

I am still reeling from this horror when across the square, just a short distance to my right, I hear a different sound. I spin around in time to see the last rutilant flashes of heavy machine-gun fire. In agonizing disbelief I witness the river of red that begins to flow downhill between the gray cobblestones.

I scream, but my cries cannot be heard over all the other screaming, over the sobbing, the sounds of people vomiting, of people dying, of beautiful little babies in closed barrels, suffocating. All I want to do is to escape the insanity. I cannot explain why, but at this moment I do not think about finding my father or about staying in the square to be near my mother and sister. Instead, operating purely on instinct, or panic, or maybe insanity, I turn my back on the carnage taking place all around. And—choking back tears and bile and the stench of death—I simply walk away.

Trembling, I stumbled into the night, exiting the square from the side opposite of where I had entered a short while earlier. Initially I blended into a small group of villagers who were shrinking back into the shadows, watching the slaughter. From there I walked away without so much as a second glance from the preoccupied soldiers. It was almost as if I was invisible.

Soon the chaos faded into the background, the bright lights of the square no more than a weak smudge against the inky sky.

I came to a farm just outside the town and made my way toward a stack of hay piled in an old cow barn. How long was it since I had been awakened by the pounding on the door? Eighteen hours at least. I burrowed into the hay, closed my eyes, tried to get the images of death out of my mind. Over and over again I envisioned the helpless babies and saw my grandparents fall to the ground. But after a time a numbing silence washed over me like a benediction. Out of sheer exhaustion, I slept.

When I awoke hours later, the sun had already risen. Like a boy possessed, I headed back toward Sędziszów's central square. I was guided not by any rational thought, but rather by no conscious thought at all. My feet were sore from the thin-soled shoes I had been wearing, and my lightweight jacket did little to ward off the morning chill. Still, foolish as it sounds, I walked, zombielike, drawn back in search of my family.

When I got to the square, it was deserted. Even the barrels were gone, their human contents nowhere to be seen. A few blocks farther, I came within sight of barbed wire barricades, heavily patrolled by German soldiers. A makeshift ghetto, I realized. This time my common sense took hold. I stopped in my tracks before I could be spotted. Then I turned away, hurriedly leaving the wretched town for a second time, more frightened and confused than ever.

I walked for more than twelve hours, skirting the larger cities of Ropczyce and Dębica, back to my home village of Straszęcin. With every step I heard sounds in my head: voices in German (*Soon your journey will be over, ha-ha!*); voices in Yiddish (*Son, stay by your father. He's just behind.*); voices that transcended all languages, that manifested themselves only in screams and wails of mothers and babies and small children.

And while I could not get the horror out of my mind, another part of my brain spun a fantasy that it had all been just a bad dream. Back home my family would be waiting for me.

"Oh, Moishele," Mama would say, "now that we're all together again—you, Gita, Papa, and me—we'll leave Poland; we'll go to our family in America where everything is wonderful and the war won't touch us."

It was possible, was it not?

But the house stood empty. Neither my parents nor my sister were there. My grandparents did not stop by to shmooze with me; Uncle Isak did not show up, grinning, with a juicy cut of brisket. *Has he been taken away, too?* I wondered.

I considered knocking on Reguła's door, or going to the house across the street, but it was very late, and I was not sure whom I could trust. So I kept on walking, deep into a stand of birch trees, where I collapsed onto the forest floor, which welcomed me as if it were a feather bed. I slept in fits for a few hours, disoriented and alone, wondering what to do, where to go next.

I awoke drenched in sweat. Musky droplets of perspiration matted my soiled shirt to my body. In my head the cries of babies were joined by the sound of machine-gun fire. And voices, speaking German. Not a dream, it had been real. The elderly, the babies, they were gone. But where were my parents? What about Gita?

Refusing to acknowledge the dangers I would face—or more to the point, simply not caring—I once again set out on foot, heading back east to search for my family. For the third time I was drawn back into the evil that had consumed Sędziszów.

It was early morning when I got there. I had walked all night, guided only by the faint light of a quarter moon. I ignored the cold and the soreness of my feet and the emptiness in my stomach. I gave little thought to myself at all until I began zigzagging through the city, walking alongside groups of townspeople. Now was not a time to draw attention to myself. To all appearances, I hoped, I was just another ragamuffin boy, a dispirited little Polish kid looking for something to do to pass the hours in this war-torn town.

My search ended at the railroad station.

There, amidst a hive of commotion and activity, I saw a line of boxcars, like the ones that had transported my father's livestock. This time the cars were being loaded with human cargo.

Pressing forward with a small group of curious bystanders, I frantically scanned the anguished faces as women were poked, prodded, and brutally shoved into the sturdy freight cars. There must have been a hundred people in each one, confined to spaces that were built to hold—what, perhaps a dozen cows?

Then I saw them: Mama and Gita. Over the next few moments my last image of them would be engraved on my conscious mind for all time, an image too horrible to remember, too cherished to forget.

50

I can see her still, this tragic figure of my mother, standing just inside the open door of the third boxcar. Her arms are wrapped protectively around Gita—poor, terrified Gita—while her eyes dart over the crowd of indifferent soldiers and Polish onlookers.

Seconds before a soldier slides the door shut and fastens it securely with wire, Mama spots me in the crowd. Our eyes lock, I am sure of it, and her head nods almost imperceptibly. She seems to tighten her hold on Gita in that instant, stroking my sister's beautiful raven-hued hair, yet all the while her eyes are fixed on me, her expression never changing. I can only guess what words are on her unmoving lips, stifled in her throat, for fear of giving me away. I only know that in this last, selfless moment, she has, through her silence, saved my life.

Devastated, I turned away from the train station, wondering what became of the men's group. I was sure Papa had to be with them somewhere. I entertained a fleeting thought about sticking around to look for him, but wisely, I think, I did not.

Instead, for the third time in as many days, I walked away from Sędziszów unhindered. Again I headed back to Straszęcin, seeking the anonymity of the surrounding forests. I was bewildered, unsure of what to do next. It was the first time in my life that I had been totally on my own.

This time I harbored no illusions that my family might be back at the house. I also knew it would be dangerous to seek shelter there, but I did stop by briefly to look in the window. No point in going inside; the house had been looted. Cleaned out by Germans? Neighbors? Even the stove had been partially disassembled. To use for replacement parts, I suppose.

For the next several days I kept to myself, cowering in the forest, finding little in the way of food. I had never before known such hunger. My only nourishment came from a few early-growing vegetables, which I stole without hesitation from the fields at night.

Finally I summoned the courage to call on Reguła, and when the sky grew dark, I cautiously made my way through familiar fields and tapped lightly on my neighbor's side window.

At first there was no response, so I pounded harder. Someone was coming into the room. A face peered out at me. Reguła opened the window, and I saw tears—this time there could be no mistaking them—flooding down the man's cheek. Behind his moist face, flickering kerosene lamps created ghostly shadows that danced mischievously on the wall.

"Moniek, is it really you?"

I assured him it was.

51

"Thank God, you're alive! We heard from the drivers that everyone who was taken to Sędziszów must have been killed."

"Not everyone." I said evenly. "I escaped."

Reguła did not hide his feelings. "I cry for you. I cry for your mother and father and sister. I cry for us all. Where have you been hiding?"

I told him: Everywhere. Nowhere.

"Stanislaw was upset when you were . . . taken." Reguła's voice was still clearly agitated. "As for Anna, she was inconsolable."

Anna! I swallowed hard.

"For the present, I think it will be best if you and I keep your escape a secret. In time I'll let the children know you're all right."

I nodded. The thought of seeing Anna once more, sharing my grief with her, made my pulse race. But I knew her father was right. It would expose her to tremendous danger. I was an outlaw now, and my crime, as far as I could tell, was that I was born a Jew.

"You're a very brave boy," Reguła said with a gentle smile.

It occurred to me that I did not feel brave. I had, in fact, no feelings at all. Part of me had been taken away with the others.

Reguła regarded me with clear concern. "The nights can be chilly. You shouldn't be in the forest. I have no place to hide you in my house, but I have an idea. Meet me in the back."

Behind Reguła's house, on the side opposite from where our house stood, was a tiny storage shed. In it our neighbor kept dried food for his animals and a supply of hay. With his hands Reguła dug out a sort of cave, no bigger than a wash basin, behind the dried food.

"You should be safe here for a while," Reguła told me while I crawled into the tiny space. "And the rest of my family doesn't have to know. As for the Germans, they may not realize you're missing, at least not yet, but I don't put anything past them. Better that you stay out of sight."

He left me inside the meager hollow with some bread and cooked potatoes, then covered the opening with hay. I tried to push the madness of Sędziszów out of my mind, at least for a little while, but that was impossible. I dozed off and on, but my thoughts kept returning to my parents, to my sister Gita, to my grandparents, their fingers touching—or so I imagined it—even now, even in death.

And Anna. Before the horror, there was Anna.

I am back in the late spring of 1940. For the first time I am seeing the girl next door in a whole new light.

Confined to my small village since my rock-throwing incident the previous fall, I am consumed by loneliness. At the same time my hormones have stirred up uncomfortable and unfamiliar feelings. Add to this mix Anna herself, blonde and ebullient, who at age eleven has already begun to show the first signs of physical maturity. She emerges one day from her cottage as if it has been her chrysalis, or so it seems to me. Suddenly, she's no longer the little tagalong neighbor kid. It's not her brother, Stanislaw, whom I want to spend time with now; it's Anna, and I pursue her almost daily. She does not discourage me. She is flattered, I imagine, by the attention of an older boy. Plus, from what I can tell, she has always shown a liking for me.

Initially, her father's storage shed becomes our secret meeting place. But as the summer progresses and the wheat grows taller, we sneak off into the neighboring fields. There, hidden amid the tall stalks, we talk and share chaste, playful moments.

"Why do the kids at school say bad things about the Jews?" she asks me. We are lying on our backs, side by side, looking up at the fast-moving clouds through the heads of the wheat stalks that sway above us. "They barely know any Jews, but they call you all Christ killers. You didn't kill Jesus Christ, did you?"

I grin at the question, although I know it isn't funny. "Not that I can remember," I say. Then, growing more solemn, I add, "I guess they don't like that we're not Catholics like they are. They think that to be Polish, you have to be Catholic."

"I'm Catholic and I wouldn't say anything bad about you. My father even says the Jews are smarter than we are. Do you think you're smarter than the other kids? Are you smarter than me?"

"That's ridiculous, that's what I think." I roll over on my side, facing Anna, and prop myself up with one arm. My voice gives away my sudden alarm. "You haven't told your father about our spending so much time together?"

She smiles. "Of course not, silly. He likes your family, and he certainly has no bad feelings about Jews, but I don't think he'd like me sneaking off like this with one. Even if it's you."

"My mother would feel the same way," I admit. "And my father too, if he were here. Even before the Germans came, my parents said the goyim will turn against us if there's war."

"What's a goyim?" Anna asks.

"It's a word in the language we use at home. It means gentiles. Non-Jews. We use that expression so much, I never think to use the Polish word, even when I speak Polish."

"Well, your parents are wrong. The war has come, and my family hasn't turned against you. They never would. They hate the Germans." Then she asks, "Does Gita know we go off to . . . talk?"

"Gita knows everything about me."

Anna gasps.

"Don't worry, she can keep a secret. We watch out for each other."

Anna sits up, pulling up her legs and wrapping her arms around them. She rests her chin on her knee. "I wish I had a twin. Stanislaw always picks on me. He'd tell my parents in an instant if he knew we were here."

"Then we won't ever let him find out," I tell her. Impulsively, I pop up also and grin at her. "Besides, I've seen how he looks at my sister, so he shouldn't be one to talk. Gita can't stand him, by the way."

And we giggle, sharing this moment of innocence and delight, of secrets and wonder, while overhead the clouds fill and darken, moving swiftly toward the east, as if to escape the storm front that's coming in just behind.

Twice Reguła came to his storage shed to check on me and bring me fresh food. My brief reveries of Anna made me feel ashamed, after the grim reality of what I had just experienced in Sędziszów. I cursed God, or more precisely, cursed the obvious fact—obvious to me, anyway— that there clearly *was* no God. It was far easier to accept the absence of such a being than to try and understand how He could let such massacres happen.

I knew what the consequences would be, of course, if I were discovered. Harm would come not just to me. All the Regułas, Anna included, would be subject to—who knew what? Sheltering a Jew was as punishable a crime as *being* a Jew.

Not wanting to put my neighbors in jeopardy, I slipped away quietly the next day and scampered back into the forest. I was determined to make it on my own. At least it was summer, with temperate weather that might help me learn to live with only the shelter I would find in nature. Soon enough autumn would come, the temperatures would drop, and hiding in the forests would require far greater survival skills. I shuddered at the thought.

Before long it became evident to me that I was not the only one in hiding. As I went foraging for food at night, I occasionally saw places where carrots had been uprooted and cucumber vines had already been picked clean, suggesting that others were stealing food as well.

Once, as I was approaching an enticing garden just north of Straszęcin, I caught a fleeting glimpse of a frightened figure—an older man, from the way his form moved rather stiffly—shuffling off into the shadows.

But for the time being I stayed to myself, trusting no one, quite unaware that to the east the Germans had just marched across the Russian border. The war was expanding. The invasion of eastern Galicia and Russia had begun.

54

5

Saboteur

E VERYONE IS LOW ON ammunition," Kopec informed me a few days after my last meeting with the Gypsy. He did not clarify his choice of the word "everyone." "Besides, you need a weapon for yourself."

I had been thinking the same thing. The weapon of my rage was no longer enough. "The time has come to see how good a student you been. What you're going to do for me could cost you your life, but without bullets we're good as dead, anyway."

I felt a surge of adrenaline. I was a new Moishe/Moniek Goldner, no longer a shy boy but a man, eager to prove myself.

"Tell me."

Kopec explained the plan. There would be others nearby, out of sight, but the success of the operation—and whether or not I lived through it—would rely solely on me. The details were simple, yet my mentor forced me to rehearse my actions over and over.

"No," Kopec said more than once, like an acting coach shaping the movements of an eager young thespian. "It's got to look like you don't see them coming. Work on your goddamn timing, kid."

Then he added a piece of motivation no acting student ever heard from his teacher: "The slightest screw up and *we* might get away. But you, kid, will most certainly end up dead."

"Let's go through this one more time," I said.

Two hours later Kopec was satisfied.

It was to be a daylight operation, so we set out the following morning before sunrise. It had rained during the night. The ground was damp as Kopec and I trudged for nearly two hours through forests and fields. Already the sky was beginning to take on the color of cream as we arrived at a carefully chosen point just outside a small village. Podgrodzie, perhaps. There we crouched in a narrow ravine along the main road that connected Tarnów to Dębica. If others were present, as I had been led to believe, I did not see them.

We waited in silence. From time to time, Kopec checked the watch he had stolen from a wealthy landowner months before. Somewhere nearby a raven gave a shrill ca-caw, ca-caw, as if sounding a warning. I felt both fear and excitement intertwined. My senses were charged with anticipation.

At last Kopec said, "It's time. The Krauts may be crazy bastards, but they are punctual." He looked at me sternly. "You know what to do, kid. Get the hell out there and do it."

I nodded and said good-bye, not knowing if it was a temporary or a final farewell and equally uncertain whether I much cared one way or another.

From a small cache of weapons Kopec carried inside the lining of his coat, he took out a grenade and handed it to me. Russian, this one. The "oil can." I gripped it firmly, depressing the handle. Then I pulled the pin, letting it fall to the damp ground. Once I released the handle, there would be just five seconds until the grenade exploded. A lot of terrible things could happen in that short time. I pushed the thought out of my mind.

The jacket I wore—not my child's jacket but another, one that was far too big for my five-foot frame—was perfect for the plan. The long sleeves hid the grenade, which lay cradled in my right hand. In my left hand I carried a narrow branch, pulled from a dead tree an hour earlier.

I climbed out of the ditch, where Kopec remained crouched, and headed for the road. With a quick glance back at Kopec's expressionless face, I turned toward the southwest and began walking. Not along the side of the road, but right down the center.

To unknowing eyes I was a small boy wandering aimlessly, a frail gamin with no sense of purpose, no place to go, and all the time in the world to get there. From time to time I poked my stick into the surface of the road, scattering little clumps of stones that were still damp from the rain.

Then I saw it, far ahead, at a point just before the road disappeared over a hill: an approaching vehicle, just visible over the crest, coming toward me. Right on schedule, I thought. Kopec or someone else had done his homework.

I looked down, staring only at the road directly in front of my feet. I kept on walking. My pulse raced. Fear rose in me like boiling water. Not fear of dying, as I think back on it; fear of not succeeding. I needed to do this one thing well, to take something back from *them*. It would make my own inevitable death—if not today, then tomorrow—more justified.

"It's got to look like you don't see them coming." Kopec's words echoed in my head. I continued the charade, poking my stick offhandedly in the dirt, more meandering than walking.

The oncoming vehicle rattled as it bounced along the road, approaching rapidly. It was almost on top of me. Still I pretended not to see it.

I heard the blaring of a horn. The open-topped transport, filled with perhaps a dozen shouting German soldiers, had spotted me.

"What the hell's that kid doing in the road?" was the gist of what I overheard. The German word *Kind* was a good sign; they did indeed take me to be a child.

"Move! Get out of the way!" they shouted.

I looked up suddenly, a startled rabbit seemingly frozen by unexpected movement. I wondered for a moment if they would simply run me down. Then came a sound that helped me breathe easier: the loud squeal of brakes.

As the truck screeched to a stop just a few meters in front of me, I jumped to my left as if to get out of the way. In the same smooth movement, I swung my right arm in a practiced underhanded arc, pitching the grenade with just enough impetus to roll it halfway underneath the transport. Or so I hoped.

Five seconds. Four seconds.

I turned to run. I heard soldiers start to jump off the truck.

Three seconds.

The sound of rifle shots. Aimed at me?

Two seconds.

More shouting. Then an explosion of tremendous force, louder than any sound I had ever heard. The ground, shaking. Pieces of truck and flesh and bone, flying everywhere. My small body, running, exhilarated, miraculously unscathed by the raining fire and debris—my doing, my devastation.

From somewhere beside the road Kopec came bounding out. Three men were with him, two of whom I had not seen before. The third was the Gypsy, who ran past, grinning as if this were some sort of game.

"Well done, little one," said one of the strangers, a seedy fellow who, Kopec later told me, had killed the one officer with the presence of mind to jump off the truck just before the grenade exploded. The officer apparently had been in the process of pointing his rifle. At me.

"Wait here," Kopec shouted to me. I did as I was told.

Feeling triumphant, I watched as the four men quickly scoured the area for weapons and ammunition that had survived the blast. Like scavengers they combed through both body and truck parts alike, taking whatever had not been blown to bits. There was a sense of jubilation among the men as they amassed pistols, rifles, and—most valuable of all—rounds of ammunition.

The three men, their arms loaded with weapons and bullets, ran off as Kopec came back to where I was standing. He was carrying a pistol, ammunition, and two pairs of boots he'd pulled off the feet of dead German soldiers.

"Let's get the hell out of here," he said.

We ran until we were well away from the road, back in the protective shroud of trees. Only then did we pause for a moment to rest. For the first time since the operation had begun, Kopec turned to look at me.

"How you feeling?" he asked me. He was breathing heavily.

"Like I could do it all over again," I said, and meant it.

"Trust me, you will." Then he reached over and handed me a pair of the boots he'd taken. "These are for you, kid. I'm sure they're too big, but they got to be better than those pieces of shit you're wearing now."

I put them on. They were rather large for me, but they felt wonderful. *So this is what it feels like to walk in the footsteps of a Nazi*, I thought.

But Kopec was not finished. "I think you earned this too," he said without emotion. He handed me the captured Luger. Its textured steel was still warm from the tight grip of the young Wehrmacht soldier who had been holding it, until the blast had ripped his arm off at the elbow.

I examined the pistol closely, turning it in my hands, reverently, as if I had just been introduced to a new best friend.

I had.

During this period—March and April 1943—we continued to move from place to place, first staying in the familiar areas around Tarnów, Dębica, and Sędziszów, but then heading north toward Tarnobrzeg. Kopec had mumbled something about a scheduled airdrop up there. In those days, before the Germans caught on a few months later, we often hopped onto freight trains heading in whichever direction Kopec decided to go. I think a great deal of our movement was directly related to the whereabouts of Kopec's contacts. One name I overheard was Kruk—a partisan code name, I assumed, because it meant "raven"—but I was always kept apart from these people.

Still, in spite of my earlier success that led to our new cache of weapons and ammunition, Kopec had not yet asked me to participate again in further acts of sabotage against the Germans, even though he seemed to be getting more involved himself. While I watched (sometimes) or was ordered to lay low nearby (more often), Kopec involved himself in such activities as unscrewing the rails, cutting telephone lines, or wreaking havoc on German-managed farms and businesses.

One day I watched as Kopec and others slipped into an estate somewhere north of Tarnobrzeg. The owner had been brewing beer for the Germans. Kopec and his cohorts destroyed all the brewing equipment along with whatever stockpile of beer they could find. I wanted to join in the melee, but Kopec said I was not needed. "I'm saving you for more important things," he told me at the time.

Kopec and I left the others right after that raid, and the two of us headed south again, back toward Dębica. But a short time later Kopec learned that the group he had joined in destroying the brewery got into a skirmish with a German patrol, and several of the men had been killed. When given this news, from what I can recall, Kopec merely shrugged his shoulders.

Later he said to me, "Kid, one reason other people die in the forests is because they move around in groups and hide together. Now you understand why I operate alone, why I go under cover alone. Except for you nobody knows where I go to sleep."

"Then how do you make contact with the people I've seen you with?" I asked.

"I know how to find them" was all he said. "But never do I let them find me."

Days later, in yet another hiding place in another nameless forest, Kopec handed me a package. It was about three feet square, weighing maybe ten or twelve pounds, securely tied with twine. I wondered how the packaging materials had come to their hiding place deep in the forest. I knew enough not to ask what was inside the package; as it was, I had a pretty good idea.

"Take this into Dębica," Kopec said, as if walking into the large city was of no consequence at all.

I knew Dębica was teeming with Germans, and I had heard (from a Pole who was babbling nervously as Kopec and I robbed him at gunpoint) that the Jews had all been taken from the ghetto several months earlier. I was given an address near my Aunt Enna's apartment—former apartment. I committed the number to memory.

"They'll give you an envelope in return," Kopec continued, gruffly. "Don't come back without it." Then came a change in tone. "Be careful, Moniek," he added.

It was the first time he had called me by name.

After dark I set out on the three-hour walk into the city. I knew that if I was caught, I would be killed—particularly in light of the weapons or ammunition I was undoubtedly carrying in the package—but I felt less fear than when I faced the German transport. My Luger was tucked securely into my waistband, and I would have no qualms about using it. After all, I had been trained well. The way I figured it, I had nothing left to lose. I would do whatever Kopec told me to do. It seemed like the best chance I had to get through the war, slim as those odds might be, and the most meaningful way to die if I did not.

At the late hour when I arrived in the city, the streets were quiet. I stayed in the shadows, alert for any German soldiers who might be patrolling. From an alleyway directly in front of me, a noise made me jump and pull out my pistol. A scrawny cat, not much bigger than the rats it had been chasing, jumped out and skittered away.

Breathing only a little easier, I eventually made my way to the assigned address. It was on a narrow side street, a small apartment above what was once an apothecary shop. The shop's windows had been broken and the interior stripped clean, by Germans, or Poles, or both. Not recently either, but months earlier. Maybe longer, from the way things looked.

I rang the bell.

"Who?" came the single word, which floated down like a feather from a window above.

"I have something from a friend," I answered, following Kopec's instructions.

Moments later I heard footsteps coming down the stairs. The door opened.

"Quickly, get off the street," said the man who stood there, a tall, thin fellow of about thirty-five. He was missing two of his bottom teeth, and even in the shadows I could see the teeth that remained were yellowed and crooked. The man wore dirty pants and an undershirt, nothing else. Perhaps he owned nothing else.

Standing behind the door at the bottom of the stairs, the man snatched away the package I was carrying. He eyed me suspiciously.

"Now he sends a boy to do a man's work?"

I was in no mood to explain. "I got it here, didn't I?"

The man flashed a brief smile. "Wait here."

He took the package, then climbed up the stairs, and disappeared into his apartment. I heard the package being ripped open, and a moment later there came a faint intake of breath as the man evaluated what was inside.

After a time he came back downstairs and handed me a thick envelope in return. To the touch the envelope felt like it was stuffed with paper. No, not paper. Money. I wondered where it might have come from.

"Tell our friend he's outdone himself this time." The man grinned. Then, as an afterthought: "Can I trust you with this?"

I tucked the envelope into my trousers. "Do you have a choice?"

The man chuckled. "Hell, the man seems to always know what he's doing, crazy as he gets sometimes."

Cautiously he opened the door a tiny bit and looked out. All remained quiet. "Go," he said. "And remember, you were never here."

That rankled me. "Mister, you're in the same danger as the rest of us. Only difference is, you got a roof over your head."

Then I slipped out into the treacherous night, dissolving once again into the shadows. Soon I put the city behind me and covered my head with a canopy of stars.

Spring. Another forest near Dębica. And standing directly in front of me, a glowering man who, Kopec told me, had been a German officer.

"Call him Walkyrie," Kopec said, using his code name.

"I've heard a lot about you, young man," said the German in his own language.

I eyed the man warily. He was in his thirties, from the look of him, certainly no more than forty. He was taller than Kopec, pleasant looking, with hair as dark as Hitler's, from the photos I had once seen of the monster. It seemed to me he did not fit the Aryan stereotype any more than Hitler did. He was dressed like everyone else in hiding: peasant clothes, probably stolen, seldom washed.

I looked past the German and addressed Kopec icily. "What are you doing with the enemy?" My hatred was rising like reflux, burning in my throat.

"It's all right, kid," Kopec said in a calm voice. "He don't care for Nazi politics. He defected some time ago to join . . . others in the forest."

Why did Kopec avoid using the word "partisan"? I wondered, calming down just a little.

Severity crept back into Kopec's voice. "Remember, I tell you who you trust and who you don't. This man's not like them other Krauts. If I can accept that, so can you. You're going to spend a lot of time with him. He's going to teach you German like you was born there."

At that I raised my eyebrows, not hiding my skepticism. For the first time I looked directly at the former Nazi officer, who returned my stare with no change in expression.

Kopec went on, "You already know some Kraut words, yes? Your people speak some form of it, I been told. But that's not enough. You got to speak it good and understand it when it's spoken back."

"Why?"

"Why? When you took that package into Dębica—that was nothing. There could be times when you're surrounded by the German sons-of-whores, by the ss, the Gestapo, maybe, and you'll be pretending to be an orphaned Polish kid with no money, no nothing. If they buy your act—and you better hope they do—the stupid bastards won't expect you to understand them, so you can maybe learn things that I can use. Who knows, what you overhear might even save your own miserable neck."

He had been looking at me, but at that moment he glanced away and added, "I can tell you that from experience."

I looked up at the German, who seemed to be growing impatient with the long explanation in Polish.

"When do we begin?" I asked in German, which clearly surprised both Kopec and the man standing before me.

The man's face softened slightly. "Now," he said. "We begin tonight. I have better things to do than spend my summer being a schoolteacher."

Learning fluent German came easily to me, not only because my family spoke Yiddish at home but also because I had learned some German in school. Now I was being tutored several nights a week by a man who met me in varying locations that Kopec had prearranged. On many of the other nights Kopec and I continued to rob homes and churches in surrounding villages, stockpiling as much food as we could.

I came to respect my German teacher and often wondered what had prompted the soldier to leave the Nazi party, to take up with people who I assumed were partisans. I developed various scenarios: The man was half Jewish and was about to be found out. Someone in his family had been victimized or killed by the ss. Or maybe the man simply had a foreboding that the Nazis would not win the war. He might have changed sides for reasons of conscience, or fear, or some personal vendetta—the forests of Poland were alive with the fantastic and the impossible, as I well knew. My own situation was just as unlikely, yet here I was, alive (so far) because the area's most wanted criminal decided to rescue me and train me as his—what would you call it?—apprentice?

Go figure.

"Kid, we're going after more weapons. I need you this time."

I jumped at the chance. Although just over a month had gone by since I lobbed the grenade under the German transport, Kopec and his "associates" were always looking to expand their cache of arms and ammunition.

"Do I do it the same way as before?" I asked.

"Not if you don't want to die. The Krauts, they only *look* stupid. They usually learn from their mistakes. Could be this time, they see a kid in the road, they only slow down to shoot. Or run you down without slowing at all."

It made sense, and I was grateful he had reasoned it through. It seemed to me that although he was exposing me to considerable danger, he really was trying to keep me alive as long as possible. Whether his motive was strictly self-serving or whether he really cared about me, I was not sure. Did it matter?

"So how do we stop the Germans long enough to take care of them and get their weapons?" I asked.

"Cows," came the terse reply.

I imagine my jaw dropped, but once he explained the plan, I had to admire his ingenuity. Or had I been giving Kopec credit for the schemes of others?

What we did was this: First, we "borrowed" three cows. That was the easy part, cutting some wire and walking the cows away from their pasture. Kopec and I did that ourselves, just before dawn on a mild spring morning. Hours later we were joined by a third man, who carried animal collars and some long, narrow metal bars. I had never seen this person before, and no name was given. He and Kopec put the collars around the cows' necks. Then we maneuvered the cows in a horizontal line, spacing them apart so we could fasten one bar from the first collar to the second, and another bar of equal length from the second to the third.

Kopec and his mysterious friend had already selected a nearby road where German trucks had been seen with some frequency on previous days. Of course, we had to hope for a single truck, not a convoy. In case of the latter, we would have had to abort the plan and run like hell. One had always to try and prepare for the unexpected.

We positioned the three animals so the middle cow was in the center of the empty road, which meant the other bovines were in the scrub and brush alongside the road, one on each side. Kopec and I walked beside the cow on one side of the road, the third man doing the same on the other side. By guiding these cows on each end, we were able to keep the middle cow pretty much in the center of the road. In theory we humans were blocked from view by the cow beside us; any approaching car or truck would not immediately sense a trap, we hoped.

Moments later we walked and waited.

We did not wait long. Coming up the road was a truckload of German soldiers. The driver leaned on the horn as the truck approached. Kopec and I strained beside our "guide" cow to keep the middle animal in the road. Sure enough, the truck slowed down, and we heard one German shout, "Move, you fucking cow. Get off the road," as if the beast could be intimidated like the local population. Several soldiers jumped off the truck, their eyes only on the obstacle in their way. Seconds later, at about the time they should have become suspicious of the metal bars joining the cows, grenades landed at their feet, tossed by the three of us on opposite sides of the road.

I heard shouting in German. A burst of rifle fire was aimed in our direction, cut short by one explosion, then a second.

This was my cue to flee back to our hideout. I had been ordered not to stick around—another sign, I guessed, that perhaps Kopec wanted to minimize my risks. It was not more than an hour or so later that Kopec himself returned, declaring that the ploy had been a success.

"Dead Germans and live ammunition," he gloated. "What could be better than that!"

On the final nights of my lessons, Kopec often disappeared until daybreak. Several times he stayed away for more than twenty-four hours, doing who knows what; I knew enough not to ask. During one of his lengthy absences, I grew tired of sitting alone. So even though there was still afternoon daylight, making it risky to move about, I decided to walk into Straszęcin. Kopec had left me with enough food—vegetables mostly—from an earlier raid, but I got it in my head that in the village I might be able to steal some fresh bread or even a chicken. It was not the smartest decision I could have made, but I was buoyed from my previous adventures. Mostly I just needed a change.

I was crossing a field near the road that passed between Dębica and Straszęcin. My Luger was concealed within the waistband of my trousers. I guess I must have been a little too complacent, because I never saw or heard the German soldier until it was too late. He spotted me from the road and shouted at me to halt. As he approached, his rifle was trained on me, of course, and my mind raced with how I might handle the situation. I hoped I did not look my age and that he would not discover my weapon. And that I would have no need to use it, for I might not emerge the winner of such a confrontation.

"Do you speak German?" he asked.

"Yes, I can speak German," I answered. Never did I dream that my lessons would pay off so quickly.

"What are you doing here?"

"I'm walking into Straszęcin, to visit a friend," I lied.

I could see he was becoming suspicious. Not because of *what* I said, it turned out, but because of how well I said it. "How is it you speak German so perfectly? Perhaps you are a Jew?"

"No, of course not." I was not sure what more to offer.

"But you speak German far too easily for a kid from around here," he said.

"That's because my father is a Pole and my mother is German." I do not know where I came up with that bullshit, but it slid out as smoothly as if it were the truth.

He considered my response for a moment, then said, "Well, be on your way."

With nothing more than that, he let me go. It hit me then how lucky I had been. The fear I had not felt moments before suddenly rose within me. Needless to say, I did not push my luck by continuing into the village. As twilight gathered, I made my way back to the forest, where I was happy to wait in solitude until Kopec came back.

He returned to our lair just before dawn of the next day, carrying four pairs of supple German boots, two uniforms—one of them stained with blood—two rifles, several rounds of ammunition, and a handful of German marks.

"I was worried about you." The first words out of my mouth.

I tried to understand my conflicting emotions. I still feared Kopec a little, wondered what he might do to me should I no longer prove useful to him; yet I also needed him, depended on his survival instincts, had even grown to like him. Or had I confused fondness with gratefulness?

"I can handle myself" was Kopec's characteristically surly response.

I had decided not to tell him about my encounter with the German soldier, since I was not supposed to have left our hiding place. Besides, I could see he had been through an encounter of his own.

Holding up his treasure, he said, "While I was out, a couple friends dropped in on me. The pleasure was all mine. The surprise was theirs."

I asked him what happened, hoping to hear the details. It was a balmy night. We were aboveground, sitting on the mossy forest floor. To my surprise, Kopec actually started talking.

"I meet some . . . friends . . . earlier in a wheat field near Lubzina. We lose track of time. Before we know it, the sky is already starting to get light. The others go their way; I go mine. I got a hiding place not too far from there, but to get there, I got to cross the main goddamn road. You know, the road that connects Dębica and Sędziszów."

I knew it well. I had been on that road in a long procession of wagons, was on it still, in my nightmares. *Mama, we're leaving Dębica,* my sister Gita cried night after night. *Where are they taking us?*

I tried to focus on Kopec's story.

". . . not a good situation after dawn. There I am, crouched down in an ash grove that goes right up to the road."

I waited breathlessly while Kopec took a hearty gulp of vodka. He wiped his mouth with his sleeve, took another pull from the bottle, let out a loud belch.

"I don't see no vehicles, so I go to run across. Then from the woods on the other side, just up the road, two Krauts come out. On foot, heading toward Dębica. My guess is they been marching prisoners into the woods at dawn to shoot them, but who knows. Who the hell cares? I look on it as a gift from God. When they get within range, I aim at their heads, to spare the uniforms. Nail the first one in the temple, have to put two bullet holes in the second one."

He appeared lost in thought for a moment; then he continued, "Lucky for me, no one comes along while I pull the bodies into the woods and grab me their uniforms. I cover the bodies up best I can, with dirt and branches, but they'll be found before long. Then who knows how many innocent sons-of-bitches will have to pay?"

He shrugged, put the bottle to his lips once again. "Well, what can you do? Meanwhile, there's two less Krauts than there was yesterday, and the uniforms will fetch a good price."

"From the partisans?" I asked, feigning innocence.

"Your goddamn questions again," Kopec snarled. Then he began to brood. I was sorry I had pushed him just when he was actually talking to me with more than grunts and short phrases.

Apparently the mood had not been totally broken. Maybe he had second thoughts about the tone he took with me, because after a while he turned and said, "Kid, you been doing real good getting used to life on the run. Like living in the forest is not so hard for you."

"I had more experience than I ever wanted," I said. "I was hiding in the forests for a year and a half before you found me at the Grabiny station."

I could see furrows start to form across his forehead. I am sure he had no idea what I had been through or how many times I had already come close to death before the day he came along and saved me. I waited to see if he would ask me for any details of this painful period, but he did not.

I shared some of them with him anyway. And for a while he listened.

6

After Sędziszów

T HOSE SUMMER MONTHS that I was on my own, having walked away from the massacre at Sędziszów, were pure hell. Not a moment went by that I did not think about my family.

Physically I was doing all right, I suppose. I knew the fields well and helped myself to vegetables throughout the summer. There were carrots, cucumbers, cabbages, and by August, ripe, juicy tomatoes, all of which I greedily devoured. I also located fruit trees that had been planted in the area. I picked apples and plums, not much caring if they were ripe or not. Under a luminous moon I even found chunks of bread and other goodies curiously placed between the leafy tops of carrots in the field Reguła had been working. I suspected he knew I was nearby, that my raids were no secret to him. Turns out, I was correct. His daughter, Anna, recalls how she brought dinner for her father, back in those days, when he was working the field. He admitted to her that he often left part of his meal for me, knowing I would find it during my nightly forages. To me, coming across the food was like finding the afikomen—the hidden matzoh—during Passover, an observation that brought on another flood of memories.

Fortunately I did not encounter any Germans searching for escaped Jews. During daylight hours, however, while I remained hidden in the forests or in deep ditches or in fields of tall wheat, I observed more soldiers on the roads than ever before.

Still, I had many moments of panic, like one time when I decided to leave the cover of the forest well before nightfall. My clothes had become so soiled and gamy, I could not wait another day to rinse them out in the river. The moon was just a meager slip, making it too precarious to walk along the river after dark.

I had located a flat rock in the shallows near the riverbank. I began kneading my wet shirt and pants against it, much like my mother kneaded the challah dough. Suddenly I became aware of footsteps coming through the forest toward the river. They were muffled, tentative—someone approaching cautiously, trying to be silent but not quite succeeding.

I quickly submerged my naked body in the cold river, lying flat and motionless against the shallow bottom near the bank. The water covered all but my head. I waited to see who would emerge from the woods, but I did not have the slightest idea what I would do if they were Germans or even local Poles. I blinked several times in the diminishing light, trying to focus, as one solitary figure hesitantly emerged from the cover of trees.

The intruder came into the open and continued toward the river, clearly unaware of my presence. Once I got a good look at him, my tension melted away like butter on a warm stove. I recognized the familiar face of Moishe, the shopkeeper from my village. Like me, he came to wash his clothes, including the fine white cotton shirt he wore the day his family, like ours, was taken from Straszęcin. He, too, had somehow escaped!

Moishe looked older and more gaunt than I remembered. He was in his early sixties, it was true, but his thinning hair seemed whiter, and his unshaven face reminded me of the beggars who used to wander through town, looking for food or other handouts. We're all beggars now, I realized. I wondered how bad I must look myself, then dismissed the thought because I really did not care.

Holding my wet clothes in front of me, I climbed up from the river. "Moishe!" I called in a loud whisper. "It's me, Moniek—uh, Moishe—Goldner." I remembered the man's dislike for the Polish adaptation of our identical first name.

"Little Goldner, it's really you?" the shopkeeper cried ecstatically, clutching one hand to his chest. "Thanks to God someone else from our group got away!"

Ten minutes later, our clothes still damp, we scurried into the woods, talking softly but urgently. We marveled at the ease of both our escapes. Like me, he had simply walked away. We shared our mutual guilt and sorrow that the rest of our families, as far as we knew, were still in German hands.

I told the shopkeeper about what I had seen at the railroad station—the women shoved into cattle cars—and together we cried for our loved ones, for our own loss of freedom and dignity.

"I did not see your wife or daughters," I told him when we were settled in the forest. "But I'm sure they were on the train. There were many cars. Maybe we can figure out where they were taken, where they have been relocated."

Moishe grew angry. He peeled a loose piece of bark from the birch tree behind his back, crumbling it between his fingers. " 'Relocation' is the German term. It suggests a new home in a new place. I don't think where they are going will be much of a home."

"What are you saying?" I asked, not wanting to admit the truth of his statement. "That they will be—"

"I'm saying that where the Germans are taking them—" He stopped abruptly, looked at me, then apparently decided to choose his words more carefully. I think he said not what he undoubtedly suspected in his troubled heart, but what he felt I needed to hear.

"I'm saying it may be a long war. We'll try to survive and pray they will do the same so we can all be together again. But you have to understand nothing is certain. Nothing ever was."

The shopkeeper turned away, put his head in his hands, and sobbed quietly. As I would come to realize, he had become increasingly aware of his own frailties. He was not a young man. He did not have the strength—or drawing from a deeper well, the desire—to continue hiding and foraging for food like an animal. But coming upon the frightened son of his friend and neighbor—I was just six years younger than his own precious youngest daughter—well, that changed everything, at least for a while. It was *beshert*, he told me. Predestined. He was certain I would need him. And for the time being that was enough to supplant the guilt that haunted him every moment: the fact that he was alive and unfettered, while his wife and daughters were . . . God only knew.

"We have got to figure a way to get some warmer clothes," Moishe said late the next afternoon, after we had slept away hours of daylight curled up on our mossy bed deep within the birch forest. The weather was already turning chilly, and neither of us had so much as a jacket. I had been thinking the same thing. I wished Mama were there with us. She would know what to do.

Moishe wrung his hands. It was a habit he had, I noticed, whenever he looked back on things he could not change.

"To think that just a few months ago, I owned a store filled with most everything we need. But the shelves are empty now. They must have been cleaned out within hours of our leaving. All I know is, when I crept back into town after escaping from Sędziszów, everything was gone. Everything. Even the mezuzah on my door, can you imagine?"

I thought about how I found my own home in shambles and nodded. Then something occurred to me, triggered by Moishe's words.

"There's another store in the village. I went in there once." I actually smiled a little at the fond memory it brought back, but I pushed it away. Another time.

"Yes, K——'s place." (Here I do not wish to use the real name, although I strongly suspect I remember it incorrectly anyway.) Moishe snickered. "Our good neighbors will miss their Jew when they beg to buy on credit from *that* son-of-a-bitch."

"Does he sell clothes? Food?"

"Yes, but—"

"Then tonight, let's show him what it's like to offer credit to the needy. Of course, we won't exactly *ask* him . . ."

Moishe raised his eyebrows so high, they almost touched where his hairline used to be. "You're proposing to break into the store like bandits, like . . . like that ganef Kopec would do?" (Do not worry; I did not include this reference to Kopec as I told him the story, although I think he might have taken some pride in it.)

I was on my feet now, agitated and alive. For the first time since being on my own, I knew what needed to be done. Now I had to convince Moishe. Who would know better how to break into a store, I reasoned, than another store owner?

"With all due respect," I calmly insisted, "we need warm clothes. And in that store is where we'll find warm clothes. You said so yourself. Is it any different than stealing food from the fields?"

Moishe began to argue that breaking and entering was somehow different than digging up a few vegetables, yet he surely knew we needed clothes just as much as nourishment to survive. If our meeting was fate, I argued back, was it not his moral responsibility to help me make it through the coming winter?

"I suppose you're right," he finally said with reluctance in his voice. He looked down at his flimsy shirt and fingered the thin material. "And it's true we'll freeze to death before long if we wear only these shmattes, these rags. Still, breaking into a business, with the owner living right next door, is a lot riskier than plucking tomatoes off a vine." He paused a moment. "Let's plan this carefully. We need to think it through."

I thought, *Maybe Mama is looking over my shoulder after all.*

Then the two of us crouched down as Moishe shrugged off one moral concern for a bigger issue: figuring out how we might steal the things we would need to stay alive a while longer.

It was well after midnight on the following day when we headed for Straszęcin's last remaining store. Moishe carried a short branch and a large sheet of burlap, neatly folded, which had been used at a nearby farm to hold potatoes. I carried a thin, rigid wire, about three feet long, that I had found near the river several weeks earlier. It was one of those finds you can't imagine a use for at the time, but you hang on to it, because something in the back of your mind says, well, you never know. Moishe was delighted when I showed it to him; with any luck at all it would be a perfect tool for the job we had to do.

The night was mostly cloudy, and the relative darkness worked to our advantage as we slipped among the shadows, snaking through fields, keeping as far back as possible from houses in the village. In farm communities like Straszęcin, it was not likely anyone would be up this time of night. Still, all it would take is one barking dog to alert a homeowner that something was amiss. Then there was always the possibility of an encounter with German soldiers. Not probable at night in a rural village such as ours, but . . .

We arrived at the little store without incident. Darkness continued to close in all around, except for a faint luster above, where moonlight tried to penetrate a thin layer of clouds. The store, although badly in need of repair on the outside, was much like Moishe's place had been in both size and layout. In fact, years ago, K—— himself made no secret of the fact that he had modeled his place after Moishe's store, with the exception of pharmacy items.

"We've got everything he's got except the Jew," K—— was fond of saying, although Moishe's business, if I am not mistaken, had clearly been the more successful of the two.

As Moishe expected, the door was securely bolted. But the window was another matter. The bottom sill was about six feet off the ground, and the frame was hinged on the top so it could swing out from the bottom. Only two hooks and eyelets on the inside held it shut, and if there were enough give . . .

My partner in crime hoisted me up on his shoulders. It took all his strength, but by this time I weighed next to nothing. Besides, what choice was there? For the next few moments I worked my wire in between the sash and the casement, grateful that the eyelet must have loosened a bit over time, bending enough so that the hook was not holding the window frame tightly against the casement. Finally the wire slipped all the way through.

Working quickly, I maneuvered the wire upward and at a slight angle until it touched against the straight piece of the hook. With a series of short jerky motions, I tapped the wire up and against the hook until, finally, I knocked it out of the eyelet. With the first hook unlatched, the window gave even more, making removal of the other hook much easier. My hands were shaking as I slipped through the open window and into the store.

71

For a moment I panicked. It was so dark inside, I was afraid I might not find my way to the door without sending who-knew-what clattering to the floor. Gradually my eyes began to adjust. Moving tentatively, I found the door and slid back the bolt for Moishe to enter.

"It's too dark to find what we need," I whispered with alarm.

"Well, we're not going to compare sizes and colors, that's for certain, but I can pretty much figure out where everything is. But just to be sure, let's see if I can find . . ."

He mumbled something else, then groped his way to the main counter, walked behind it, and ran his fingers over the shelves beneath.

"There," he said, under his breath. "Same place I keep them."

I had no idea what he was talking about until I heard a scratch and a whoosh, immediately followed by the distinct smell of sulfur. The match in Moishe's hand flared and illuminated part of the room. With his free hand he grabbed several more packages of matches and stuffed them in his pocket. Then he quickly headed down the aisle toward the shelves of clothing, what little there was. I followed closely behind as the match burned down to Moishe's fingertips. Suddenly the room was in darkness again.

"We take no more chances," he said in a hushed voice as he unfolded the burlap. "The rest we do in the dark."

Relying on touch, guesswork, and visual memory from that last instant before the match burned out, we stacked warm shirts, pairs of pants, and blankets—two of each—on the burlap, which we then folded over and hastily knotted around the branch Moishe had carried in. *Like a couple of Gypsies,* I thought. Then we each grabbed a heavy, lined jacket from a rack just to our left and put them on over our own reeking clothes. The jacket I took was too big, but there was no time to look for something else.

As we groped our way toward the entrance, I thought I saw food of some kind—sausages, perhaps, or smoked hams—stacked on a table as I passed. I reached over to take one, but my arm accidentally bumped against a display of kerosene lamps, which fell clattering to the ground, their glass chimneys shattering as soundly as if I had set off an alarm.

I cursed under my breath.

We ran, Moishe and I, lunging toward the open door and out into the still-empty street. Looking over my shoulder, I saw the flickering of a lamp that had just been lit in K——'s room behind the store.

Moishe couldn't run as fast as I could, so he handed over the bundle of clothes to lighten his load. We heard shouting behind us. K——, most likely, screaming like a madman. Moishe was breathing hard as we reached the first of two fields we would have to cross before entering the protective forest, but he kept going, on adrenaline or fear or maybe even a wicked sense of exhilaration at having succeeded at something that, until now, had been against his very nature.

No one followed us as we ran. After ten minutes Moishe panted, "You go on. I need to rest a moment. I'm no youngster like you." He collapsed to the ground, gasping for air.

"We stick together," I said, sitting down next to him.

We sat in silence for a moment. Then I asked, "Do you think K——came out in time to recognize us?"

"If he did, he'll go to the Germans, that one, and they'll come searching. But it was dark. My guess is he figured we were just two more bandits. Either way, we don't go near that store again."

"You're the boss," I said.

Moishe sighed. "No, I'm just a miserable ex-shopkeeper. And you, you're a confused, innocent boy. We're both without homes and families, both without much idea of how to survive the winter. Two tragic equals, wouldn't you say?"

Neither of us looked at the other. We both lay on the cold ground, the bundle of stolen clothes beside us. For a brief second the only sound was our breathing, rapid and labored, like machinery.

Then Moishe said, "I'll tell you something else, young Mr. Goldner. Two days ago I thought our chance meeting was a sign from above that I was destined to help you, keep you going. I'm not so sure anymore."

I gave him a puzzled look.

"I think maybe it was meant to be the other way around," said the shopkeeper.

"So, you was a thief even before you met me!" Kopec chortled.

I had just finished telling him how Moishe and I had robbed the store, and he was grinning ear to ear.

"Serves the old bastard right," he went on. "My wife, she always bought from the Jew. We figured he was less likely to cheat us."

I had to smile at the idea of a lifelong bandit who worried about being cheated, but I kept that observation to myself.

"It is hard for me to believe that happened only a year ago," I told him. "We broke into that store just before the last winter hit. It came early, if you remember, just like the winter before it. Getting through this present winter with you has been easy, so far, compared to what life was like when Moishe and I were on our own."

Kopec merely grunted, then took another pull from his vodka bottle. My thoughts again went back to that previous year, and I wondered how I ever made it this far.

Back in that early winter of 1941–42, farmers scrambled to harvest whatever they could, storing away what little the Germans let them keep for the bleak months to come. To get at some of this food, Moishe and I had to break into root cellars and other storage areas, which we became increasingly adept at doing. But this was far more dangerous than raiding fields, and it required us to expand our area of operation.

As the days grew colder, we often slept in depressions or among tree roots. Sometimes we had to create our own nest, digging with our bare hands. First we covered the cold earth with straw or moss or bark, then lay on it, and covered ourselves with the blankets from K——'s store. At night, before prowling for food, we buried the blankets and covered up our hiding place. Often we changed locations, moving to another area of the forest or to other forests altogether, to throw off any trackers. We came to know intimately the woods around Straszęcin and along the banks of the Wisłoka.

By early December the temperatures plummeted so low that even our new jackets and blankets were not warm enough. Like field mice, we scurried toward the nearest dairy barn, where we moved in with the cows. We found them to be fine company and quite accepting.

Actually, there were two dairy farms in the immediate area. The church farm, where Mama bought milk to sell in Dębica, was just south of Straszęcin, over the bridge, along the road to Grabiny. But a bigger farm, with perhaps a hundred head of cattle, was quite near where my family and Moishe's family once lived. Along with expansive fields that stretched east nearly all the way to the Wisłoka River, it was part of the vast holdings of the area's largest landowner, an Austrian noble-man named Stubenvoll.

The farm was next to a fenced-off area where Stubenvoll lived in a grand house with his wife and two daughters. The "palace," we all called it.

Poland had long been a feudal society, and while everyone in Straszęcin envied Stubenvoll, with his conspicuous procession of mo-tor cars that paraded in and out of his gated compound, I don't think my neighbors disliked him. The man seldom mixed with peasants like us—he was clearly a man of position and breeding, with fine, expen-sive clothes and (we assumed) refined tastes—but if memory serves, he was always courteous to us villagers.

It was in this barn, to begin with, where Moishe and I often escaped from the cold. We crept in while everyone was asleep. We found the stalls comfortably warm as we pressed in close to our undiscriminating bovine companions. Plus there was welcome nourishment under our feet. We groveled for it beside the cows, becoming animals ourselves.

We were reduced to this: crawling on our hands and knees, sifting through clumps of manure to devour whatever feed lay on the ground. We found primarily wheat mill feeds, dried beet pulp, and fermented silage of indeterminate origins—an acquired taste, I must say.

"A year ago, who'd have guessed we'd be stealing food away from a bunch of cows?" Moishe observed.

I screened through the slop on the floor, looking for anything remotely edible. "At least we're not grazing on their hay."

"It may come to that yet, my young friend. The winter has just begun."

About an hour before dawn, before the farmers arrived like clockwork to milk the cows, we took the first sample of the morning milk supply for ourselves. At first we lay beneath the cows and squeezed the milk directly into our mouths. But after a time we supped like gentlemen, drinking from a small metal container someone had discarded.

Before fleeing out into the early morning frost, we would try to conceal all evidence of our presence. But we always worried that we might have overlooked some telltale sign that would give us away.

One December morning, with the temperature hovering near zero, we opted not to leave the barn at all. After gorging ourselves on fresh milk, we climbed the ladder to the hayloft that overlooked the stalls. There we burrowed deep into the dried stalks, where we dozed lightly throughout the day, undisturbed.

The barn brought back warm memories to me: images of my mother, whom I missed so much, and of the times I accompanied her each morning to buy milk from the priest. That was, I had to admit, the happiest period of my entire childhood, the experience I treasured above all others. I thought about those days often, reliving each halcyon moment as if I were back at Mama's side.

The reverie is always the same: I am eleven years old, sitting next to my mother on the narrow bench at the front of our small cart. I hold the reins, grinning proudly, feeling very grown up and in full command of the horse that's steadily pulling us forward.

On the cart behind us are two large canisters made of white porcelain. One has just been filled with milk, while the other remains empty for the time being. It jostles noisily as the cart bounces over the dirt road. The sky had begun to lighten just before we left home; now the sun is a sliver of melon above the horizon. My favorite time of day.

"Are you cold?" Mama asks.

"No, I'm fine, really," I reply.

I am wearing a light jacket, but the morning air is brisk. I hardly notice the chill though, because I hold the reins, and the thrill of driving the wagon has not worn off, even though I have been helping my mother for more than two months.

"I'm lucky to have a strong son who doesn't mind getting up so early," Mama is saying.

She has been awake since 4:30 A.M., guided by some internal clock that is always more reliable than the crows of Straszęcin's roosters that follow, depending on the sunrise, some time later. She wakes me at 5:00—there are still several hours until I have to be at school—but she lets my sister sleep. Gita does not share my interest in driving the cart, and besides, with me out of the house, she has a few moments of privacy to get ready for school.

My grin widens at Mama's compliment. She and I have grown close, for these mornings have given us more time together. I know she has a tough life, peddling milk each weekday morning, returning home in the afternoon to care for the household while Papa is on the road. I am happy to help, especially when it includes driving the horse cart.

"Can I drive the cart all the way into Dębica with you today?" I ask.

"You don't have school?"

"Yes, but—"

"Next time there's a school break. Then you can go with me and watch the horse while I make my deliveries in the city. You'll be a big help. But I won't have you missing classes."

I sigh deeply. It's the answer I expected.

Mama has standing orders in Dębica, regular customers who buy from her every day. The filled pail on the cart holds the milk she has just taken from our own cows. It will be sold to her Jewish customers, for the milk is considered kosher, coming from a Jewish-owned farm.

At this moment we are on our way to the priest's farm, which adjoins the Straszęcin church. Here Mama will buy milk to sell to her gentile customers. I cannot imagine what makes our cows Jewish—they look just like our neighbors' cows, and the priest's cows, for that matter. Friesians, they are. Part black, part white. But then I have always been told that I do not look Jewish either, which suggests to me that you cannot often see any difference among people any more than you can among cows.

It is a ten-minute ride from our house to the church farm. When we arrive, I help fill the empty canister with the pails of fresh milk that have been set aside for Mama. Then, heading back toward home, I again take the reins. The horse snorts, as if to complain about the heavier load, and I imagine myself as a heroic officer in the brave Polish cavalry, heading off to fight the Russians or the Germans or the Austrians or whoever Poland's enemy happens to be at the moment.

And I am still smiling as I hand Mama the reins and jump down off the seat, a block from our house where the road forks to the right. With a wave of her hand and a warm smile, Mama wishes me a good day at school.

"Tell Gita that I haven't forgotten she wants me to lengthen her blue dress. I'll do it when I get back," Mama calls as an afterthought.

And I think, *She never has a moment for herself, my poor Mama.* I stand there and watch for a few moments as she guides the horse cart down the road toward Dębica, until she becomes a speck in the distance and I lose her in the intensity of the blinding sun.

For days Moishe and I repeated our routine: down with the cows at night, up in the hayloft during the day. Several times that week workers climbed up to pitch down new hay, but the loft was big; when Moishe and I heard the heavy footsteps on the ladder, we lay still, hidden well to the back, against the wall.

But not all footsteps were so clearly announced. On our fifth or sixth consecutive day in the barn, we were sleeping deep within the insulating blanket of hay. All I knew was that one second I was back with my family in our little house a few blocks away (a dream? had to be), and in the next instant I was aware of a flash of steel—a bayonet, it came to me—piercing through the hay just inches away from my left foot. Resisting an almost reflexive urge to scream and roll out of the way, I froze with fright, my heart pounding so loudly I was sure it could be heard echoing throughout the barn. Moishe lay a few feet over—he liked to hide next to the outside opening, so he could look out onto the street below—and thankfully he also remained still.

Suddenly there came a second thrust of the bayonet, then a third, haphazardly slicing through the deep pile of hay, each narrowly missing the two human forms that lay hidden beneath. It was as if we were protected by an invisible shield.

"Nothing here," came two words in German. They were shouted by a soldier just inches away as he called out to his Wehrmacht companions below.

Holding my breath, I took in the sounds that followed: sturdy boots, heading back down the wooden ladder. A moment later, laughter, drifting up from the ground. Voices, receding into the distance. In German something to the effect of "at least there's no Jew blood to clean off our fine German steel."

I thought I was going to vomit.

"The bastards must have been tipped off we were hiding here," whispered Moishe once the Germans swaggered off.

"Who would have done that?" I asked, my heart still racing and my body trembling as if it would never stop.

While most anyone could have alerted the Germans, Moishe insisted he knew. With a dismissive wave of his hand, he spat out, "Stubenvoll, who do you think? He's one of *them*, wouldn't you guess?"

"Not necessarily."

Moishe looked outside once more; then he popped up from beneath the bed of hay, sitting upright. Several pieces of the dried grass remained in his hair, giving him the look of a scarecrow. He continued talking, his contempt evident.

"Before we were taken, Stubenvoll was cozying up to the Germans like crazy. Everyone noticed the soldiers, the ss in particular, coming and going from the 'palace.' Beer parties, orgies, who knows what the hell they were doing. Just good old Germans being Germans."

"Austrian," I corrected.

"What?"

"Stubenvoll is Austrian. That's what I was told."

"Austrian, German, what's the difference? You mark my words; they're all Nazis, every one of those bastards."

"If they knew we were here, they didn't try very hard to find us." I was not convinced that the nobleman even knew about us, let alone gave us up. Call it a hunch. "A little more effort, a couple more stabs with those bayonets, and we'd both be dead now."

"Enough talk," said the shopkeeper. "We're not going to spend another day here. Not for a long while."

We moved to the church farm, assuming it would be safer for the time being. We found silage and shelter there just as we had in Stubenvoll's barn.

And when I realized my birthday was less than a month away, it occurred to me that turning sixteen would not be the milestone that I once had envisioned. There would be no birthday hugs, no birthday surprises. Little did I know.

Kopec was growing restless and beginning to yawn, either from my stories or from the vodka. Probably both.

"You think you had it so tough, kid? While you was picking cow shit off that animal feed, I was in a place where . . ." He stopped abruptly.

"Where?" I asked, waiting for him to continue.

He fixed me with as firm a gaze as his vodka intake would allow. "You don't need to know nothing more about me. Just forget it."

I know now, of course, that his oblique reference was to Auschwitz. But while I was with him, as I have mentioned, he kept that from me.

Eventually he did brighten a little and seemed to take a renewed interest in what I was telling him. "What I don't understand is, when does your father come into the picture? That was your father who was . . . lying there . . . when I found you at the Grabiny station, yes?"

Papa. Tears began to form, but I fought them back. "I was just getting to that part," I said.

It was one of those rare winter days when the temperature had moderated and the skies had turned partly cloudy. If you listened carefully, you could hear the call of the hardy winter buntings as they hopped from branch to branch. For a Polish winter during wartime, this was as good as it got.

Moishe and I had taken advantage of the break in the weather to stay away from the nearby barns and keep to the forest. We had even stockpiled enough food to last a couple days. And we found a great place to settle in for a while, behind the protective trunks of two venerable old pines, which had nearly grown together, allowing just a fine streak of daylight to penetrate between them.

I might have been daydreaming, perhaps reliving some painful moment, but the sudden snap of a nearby twig catapulted my senses to full alert. Someone was approaching with slow, stealthy movements. Moishe heard it too.

From where we sat, we saw nothing. It was late in the day. Twilight.

For a moment, silence. Then again: the crackle of brittle brush underfoot.

Like a mole emerging from his burrow, Moishe warily peered out from behind the tree while I waited, partially hidden behind him, as if that would make a difference. After several moments a solitary man appeared. He was dressed in torn, deteriorated clothing. The man was obviously chilled and weary, quite unaware, it seemed, of anyone's presence. Moishe emerged slowly. The stranger froze in his tracks, possibly not yet comprehending the vision before him.

At that moment the shopkeeper turned toward me, and a broad smile spread across his face. It was the first time since we were together, I think, that I had seen him smile.

"It's all right, little Goldner," Moishe said, clasping his hands joyfully. "It's more than all right. It's wonderful!"

I came out from behind the tree. At first I did not recognize the bearded stranger before me. Then my heart began to leap in my chest.

For the stranger who stood there, rigid as a statue, was my father.

"Papa, Papa, Papa!" I cried as I ran to him.

"Moishele?" he gasped. "Moishele, it's you?"

We embraced, and as we hugged, tears of joy mixed with tears of anguish. The shopkeeper looked on compassionately, his own eyes filling up. He knew, I can say with certainty, that he would never be reunited with any members of his own family. Not in this life.

Through his tears Papa whispered, "Shush, shush, Moishele. The forests have many ears, and sometimes as many guns. I know, I've been in hiding a long time." He hugged me again, not wanting to let go. Then, familiar words: "Let me look at you."

I remembered him saying the same thing when he returned home from the Russian territories, just a few months before the Germans came for us. *What did you come home to?* I wanted to ask as we hugged, reunited. *Why didn't you stay where you might have been safe?*

Papa held me at arm's length, drinking me in, a wisp of a boy who still had grown no taller than five feet. I am sure I looked thinner than ever to him, but at least he could see I was alive and doing reasonably well, all things considered. Eventually Papa's gaze fell again upon the shopkeeper, and with my father's recognition of this second familiar face, we hugged, the three of us.

"They killed them, Papa: Bubbie and Zayde, I saw the soldiers kill them, and I saw them put Mama and Gita in a boxcar and they took babies and . . ." I was nearly hysterical. The words came pouring out like raw sewage, bitter and rank.

"About my parents, I know," Papa said. He choked back a sob. "I saw what happened also. And moments later, I watched you walk away. I could not get to you in the crowd, but when I saw you turn your back on the soldiers, it gave me the courage to take a chance myself a little later."

"I should not have left you there, Papa. I should have stayed for you and Mama and Gita." My body shook as I wept.

"Son, look at me." My father put a finger under my chin, forcing my face upward. "You were right to escape. There was nothing you could do for Mama and your sister—may God have mercy—and nothing you could do for me. Had you not walked away when you did . . ." Papa's voice cracked with emotion. "What matters now is the fact we're alive. And together. Such a miracle it is."

We huddled closely for a long while, bound in fear and despair, fragments of what had been two happy, loving families: a father and a son, along with an aging neighbor.

Straszęcin's last surviving Jews.

Throughout the rest of the winter, the three of us moved through the forests, staying within familiar areas. During daylight we varied our hiding places, constantly on the lookout for German patrols.

"Don't think for a minute we're safe just because we're out of the village," Papa said. "If there are three of us, there must be others, and if there are others, you can be sure someone will try to kill—" He caught himself. "Capture us."

"Why, Papa?" I asked, although I knew the answer. "What did we do?"

"You know why. They're after us because we're Jews."

It was a truth, I truly believe, my father could not have imagined a few years earlier. Papa dropped his voice and said it again, as if it explained everything.

"Because we're Jews."

"Why did we have to be Jews, anyway? Why couldn't we be Catholics like everyone else in Straszęcin?" I was crying angrily, no longer the tough young man I had grown to become with just Moishe at my side. Papa was here now; Papa was supposed to make everything right.

Papa hugged me close to him, rocking back and forth. "We are what we are, Moishele. We can't change it, anymore than we can change what's happening all around us. The best we can do is endure it, one day at a time. What will be, will be."

It was a fatalistic answer that I found unsettling, but at that moment I was not sure why.

Meanwhile, we three fugitives were each learning something new about survival from the other, and our pooled experiences made us collectively stronger. Papa might have frozen to death if not for the clothes Moishe and I had stolen from K——'s store. We had no extra jacket for him, so he used a blanket as a wrap, and it made all the difference. Papa, in return, introduced us to a few of his hiding places—an unlocked potato cellar, for one, and a barn much farther away than Moishe and I had ventured—giving us more places to hide.

For the time being we continued to avoid the nobleman's dairy barn. But when Papa heard the story of Moishe's and my close call there by Wehrmacht soldiers, he, like me, was not convinced that Stubenvoll either knew or cared about our visits.

What none of us knew—and Moishe would never have believed it anyway—was something I learned many years later: Stubenvoll, it seems, had suspected early on that Jews were hiding on his grounds, and he did nothing to discourage it. In fact, some local people report he knowingly hid a Jewish family at one time. It turns out that, although an Austrian national, he had no love for the Nazi party. He used his camaraderie with German officers (developed during frequent drinking encounters at his estate) to glean intelligence information. All the time the Germans thought he was one of them, but he was using the bastards, passing on information to partisan groups that were beginning to form. This is what I was told, at any rate, and who am I to challenge it?

At the time, however, Moishe remained steadfast in his conviction. No Austrian could be trusted. And Papa and I were not inclined to argue.

By the end of that March the shopkeeper had slipped even deeper into depression. He ran a constant fever. Fluid began collecting in his lungs, from what he told us, making breathing difficult for him. He was also having trouble walking. Each day the pain—both physical and mental—seemed to worsen.

"I've made a decision," he announced early one morning to Papa and me. We were in the church barn, crawling around like pigs, grabbing whatever stinking animal feed we could locate. Moishe pulled off pieces of cow dung that were clinging to his pants and stood up.

"I'm through running, living like an animal—worse than an animal. I can't keep hiding this way anymore. And you don't need a pathetic old man to slow you down or share your food."

"That's nonsense," Papa said. "More than that, it's suicide."

Moishe merely sighed. "What's the point of staying alive when I have nothing to live for?"

Papa tried to reason with him. He argued that the war might end soon, that maybe their wives and daughters were still alive, just as we were. That maybe they were fighting to survive at that very moment, in order to be reunited with *us*. He said at the very least it was our duty to fight for life, to make it difficult for those Nazi bastards.

Moishe, suddenly seized with another violent fit of coughing, was not moved. "Time has ended for me. I've lost all hope."

Papa shook his head sadly. "Perhaps you'll feel differently in the light of day" was all he could say.

But that night, while Papa and I slept uneasily in a freshly dug *ziemlanki*—a camouflaged underground bunker we had hollowed out in the forest soil—Moishe must have quietly risen, left his jacket for us to find, and without looking back, stoically headed in the direction of the small village where he had lived, like us Goldners, for so many years.

And over the months ahead I would come to visualize the mournful resignation of Moishe, my elderly friend, almost as if I myself had walked away with him: He is moving slowly, painfully, with his head high, feeling not fear but a calm sense of renewed determination. The shopkeeper is no longer taking care to move silently, not this time, not anymore, because he is finally able to say to hell with the Germans, to hell with the madness all around. He is simply going back to where he had made his living, in the little store by the wooden bridge; back to the living quarters where he had raised his three daughters, where his wife was always fussing to keep the modest place neat and attractive. It is not the Stubenvoll "palace" that stands behind the fence across the road, but it is *his* palace. He had lost sight of that fact over the past six months, but clearly he knows it now.

As Moishe walks, the sky is brightening toward the east, but he pays it no attention, any more than he notices the acrid burning smell in the air, blowing in his direction from somewhere up ahead. All his senses are focused on a single goal, his meager strength marshaled for one desperate purpose—to be free and safe, back in Straszęcin where he belongs, where his destiny lies.

Oh, the shopkeeper sees it all so clearly now: This is actually not an act of resignation or of suicide; rather, it is a beginning, the embracing of all life's blessings. Soon he will not need memories to fall back on or fear to propel him forward. Soon, he'll be home. And surely, if there is still a God in heaven, everyone will welcome him back, with tears of joy and with open arms.

Surely.

How do you judge another man's actions? How do you understand what motivates someone to do what you never could?

I struggled with these questions throughout that second spring of my vagabond existence. I was deeply troubled by Moishe's loss. For a few arduous months he had been the most important person in my life.

"Don't be angry with him, son," Papa said to me. "For him the pain of living had become intolerable."

I listened but did not respond. My father continued, "Look, I meant it when I said we must trust in fate. Fate led me to you, after all. And— who knows?—it could lead us both to Mama and Gita; there's always a chance. Moishe didn't see things that way. He—" His voice faltered, then it seemed like he changed what he was going to say. "I only hope that however the end came, it was fast, and may he rest in peace."

I was still not comfortable with my father's philosophy, and I continued to despair over Moishe's resignation. But after further thought I vowed I would not judge him. I had no right.

With the thaw Papa and I stayed in the forests, for the weather was tolerable and Papa felt it was too risky to stay in the barns at night. Already a heavy lock had tightly secured the church barn, a clear indication that our raids had been discovered. But our stomachs growled with hunger, and Papa thought about our former next-door neighbor. I had told Papa how Reguła helped me months before. It was time to beg favors once more.

After nightfall we skulked past our former home. It remained dark and empty. We tapped lightly on Reguła's window.

It was heartening to see our former neighbor cry with joy to see us. He also grieved with what appeared to be genuine despair as to the uncertain fate of Mama and Gita.

But he did not invite us to come in.

I wondered briefly about Anna, then realized my adolescent memories were firmly fixed in another time and place. Now, it seemed to me, I had no feelings for anyone. Except Papa, of course, to whom I felt closer than at any previous time in my life.

"Can you give us some bread?" my father finally stammered. "Something to take with us into the forests? We wouldn't have come here if we weren't desperate."

Reguła looked out at our two expectant faces. He wiped his eyes with the back of his hand, then wiped his hand on his pants. "Yes, of course. I'll give you what I can," he said in a whisper. "But then you must go quickly and not come back here. It's too dangerous for you."

Reguła gave us bread, a couple of cooked potatoes, as I recall, and a chunk of sausage. "I know you don't eat pork," he said considerately, "but it's all I have to give you."

Papa stared at the *traif*—the Yiddish word for any food, like pork, that is not kosher—and sighed. "When one is hungry enough . . . well, God will understand."

"He will," Reguła whispered. "And He will protect you. Be safe, my friends."

In tears he closed the window on Papa and me. I wondered if Reguła still looked upon me as the same boy who once laughed and loved to spend time with his son and daughter. Now my eyes had grown cold. And my disbelief in Reguła's words must have been evident to him.

Those tears in his eyes? I did not believe, at the time, in the obvious explanation—that having to send Papa and me away simply broke his heart. But I am much older now, more accepting, and I have Reguła's own recent words to fall back on:

"The night Moniek and Leap knocked on my window asking for food, it was terrible that I had to send them away. You see, other people were living with us in our house. People from the east who were deported were living here. I was afraid they might turn Moniek and his father in to the Nazis. So I told my good neighbors not to come back. I had to tell them that. I had to trust in God to save them."

Back in the forest we ate some of the food Reguła had given us, determined to save the rest for the next day. The baked potato was a special treat—for the past year, we had eaten mostly raw potatoes. It fired Papa with a new resolve.

"We're not going to sit here and starve while we wait for the crops to grow in the fields," he told me, as I licked the last bit of tender potato off my fingers. "There are hares in the forests and fields, and there are chickens in nearly every home and barnyard. There's food all around if we're willing to risk cooking it."

I popped a piece of the once-forbidden pork sausage into my mouth, forcing myself to savor it as if it were a prime cut of Uncle Isak's kosher beef.

"What about all the smoke?" I asked

Papa had given this some thought. "We'll have to experiment with different types of fuel. Maybe dried peat or bark or moss, whatever we can find that will burn. But it's still risky, because smoke or no smoke, even darkness won't cover up the scent of cooking meat."

Two nights later our food ran out. I picked a yard at random on the edge of the village and grabbed a hen, wringing its neck almost immediately to end the squawking. I was surprised by how easy it was, even though I had never before killed anything with my bare hands. Soon a great commotion arose from the other residents of the coop. I ran as fast as I could with my hand still tightly wrapped around our dinner's contorted neck.

Papa gutted the hen using a sharp piece of metal we had scavenged in another yard. Then I plucked the animal while my father dug a deep pit with a stolen shovel. He filled the pit with branches, starting a fire using far too many of our remaining dry matches. The damp winter wood did indeed produce smoke. It spiraled up with the breeze and drifted steadily toward the east. We rigged a kind of spit with other pieces of metal we had gathered, then put the hen over the fire. Quickly we scurried away, heading a considerable distance to the southwest. There we hid while our food cooked, alert to the possibility that the smoke and aroma wafting from the forest might bring unwanted company.

After an hour we crept back to the pit and dined on fresh-cooked chicken. We almost cried with joy as the warm shmaltz—chicken fat— ran down our chins, the crisp skin and tender meat reminding us of days long gone. With great difficulty we put half the chicken in our pockets, to be enjoyed another day. Then we covered over the pit so it would not be discovered.

In this same way we cooked not only chicken, but wild hares (which I learned to catch and skin with some aplomb), potatoes, beets, whatever we could find or steal. We did this once or even twice a week throughout the summer of 1942. When the matches ran out, we started fires by rubbing rocks together. Always we left the immediate vicinity while our food cooked. At least twice, when we came back and peered through the trees, we found that our fire had been discovered by a patrol of German soldiers, probably alerted by the smell. In those instances we ran off undetected, forgoing the day's meal.

With the warm weather and frequent rains, which always left Papa and me muddy and miserable, the fields again became green and the grain grew tall, providing us with alternative hiding places. But because the farmers now had an immense quota to fill for the Germans, with harsh penalties if they fell short, they did not react kindly to having their fields raided. As a result, we found it much more difficult to pilfer fruit and vegetables than we had the summer before.

In our nocturnal raids Papa and I had taken to carrying a heavy iron bar in case we needed to defend ourselves, for on several occasions we had spotted Poles patrolling their fields at night. The bars were thick and rounded, about four feet long, dismantled from a piece of harvesting equipment we found in an unlocked shed. The metal gave us a small, added sense of security, although they would have been no match, of course, for a bullet.

It was on an uncomfortable August night, I recall, that we decided to raid a field near Czarna. This particular field was one of our favorites because it backed onto a forest and the Pole who owned it lived far to the other side. Also it was large enough to provide a full buffet of choices, including the plumpest, juiciest tomatoes Papa and I had ever tasted.

We found such good pickings that night, we made a point to come back again the next evening. Creeping out of the dense forest, we crouched among the junipers that filled in the short distance between woods and field. The moon was waning, but there were few clouds to block the faint light that splashed softly over the ground in front of us. The air was stagnant and the humidity uncomfortably high. At first cautiously, then more brazenly, Papa and I headed for the tomato vines.

We were nearly there, ready to claim our prizes, when a loud rustling came from the wheat field to our right. Emerging from the willowy stalks were two tall figures. They came toward us at a dead run, screaming and cursing in Polish.

Farmers, not Germans, I realized with some relief. The figures were approaching quickly, brandishing their weapons high in the air. Not guns, luckily. Scythes.

"Should we run, Papa?" I asked. I had the foresight to speak in Polish rather than Yiddish. No need to advertise that we were Jews.

"No time," my father responded, also in Polish, and he was right. The Poles, simply trying to protect what was theirs, were upon us.

The combat was one on one: man against man, man against boy. While Papa and his attacker went at each other, iron bar to scythe, my assailant wildly swung his scythe at me in a wide arc. I easily dodged the sharp blade and darted left, behind the big man. The Pole turned to his left, preparing to sweep his blade into me as he came around, but I pivoted, changed direction, and now came back around the man's right side. Summoning all my strength, I swung my metal bar and slammed it into the man's right kneecap. The grisly crunch of shattered bone was almost as loud as the piercing scream that followed. The Pole crumbled to the ground.

I ran to help my father, but the second Pole, hearing the shrieks of his fallen partner and seeing himself outnumbered two to one, dropped his scythe, turned, and with a scream of his own, ran off back into the wheat field. Meanwhile, the injured farmer continued to writhe and scream in agony.

There was urgency in Papa's voice. "Let's get out of here. Others will be coming soon."

I walked over to the injured man, who was now retching uncontrollably. "I am not the enemy," I said in what I thought was a calm, even voice.

He looked up at me, his eyes intense with pain, loathing, probably disbelief as well.

Then Papa and I vanished into the night.

Kopec was falling asleep before I got to the events leading up to my father's death (and my own, nearly) at the Grabiny station. But I resolved that one day soon he would know. I did not think for a minute that I would live through the war to tell the story. But *someone* had to know the deceit and treachery that befell my poor Papa and me on that day, even if that someone was a hard man like Jan Kopec.

In the meantime there followed more nightly drills in the German language. But a short time later my teacher indicated he was anxious to move on, to do more with his life than wait out the war by tutoring a teenaged Jewish kid. And by this time I had mastered the language rather well.

So I was not surprised when late in June the lessons abruptly stopped. When I asked Kopec where the former Nazi had gone, he told me only that the man had been "reassigned."

I couldn't help myself. "By whom? To do what?"

"Damn it, kid, never mind."

Besides, Kopec had more to think about than dealing with my persistent questions. His wife, Stefania, had missed their last rendezvous. He had a suspicion that something must be terribly wrong.

7

Close Calls

ASIDE FROM KOPEC'S Auschwitz escape, it was enough that his increased actions against the Germans—not to mention his sheltering of me, a Jew—made it far too dangerous for him to sneak back into Straszęcin. The last time he had been home, as far as I knew, had been in January. That was when he had carried my wounded body in his arms. But at regular intervals, his wife, Stefania, met him at prearranged places in the nearby forests or, now that the wheat crop had matured to the stage where it was thick and tall, in one of several fields.

She always faced the danger of being followed, so usually she came alone. But now and then one or two of their children accompanied her, bringing food that Stefania prepared before the clandestine meetings.

I imagine the Kopec children knew what I did not: that their father had been captured in a roundup and had recently escaped. But Stefania apparently had aggrandized their father, telling her children he was a dedicated partisan, fighting to free Poland. About his criminal background, I am guessing the children knew nothing. Their mother apparently kept that detail from them, and who could blame her? From what I recall, the villagers themselves spoke of it only in hushed voices. They all feared Kopec; there was no question about that.

Kopec's children did know that I was hiding with their father, of course, and the older ones could undoubtedly remember my being in their house briefly, laid up like a wounded bird. I vaguely recall a few occasions when Kopec's eight-year-old daughter came into the forest with her mother, but we had little in common to talk about, even when her parents left us alone for an hour or so while they went off to . . . well, you can imagine.

After a time I became aware that during these trysts Kopec was giving his wife money and other goods he received from his robberies—*our* robberies. But often he seemed to hand over far more plunder than I ever saw come out of our holdups. I wondered where it all came from, for I still had not grasped the idea that Kopec was, in fact, using the war to his advantage. The envelopes I brought back to him after delivering packages were part of it, no doubt, but his real complicity in what was happening all around had yet to dawn on me.

His wife, meanwhile, was bringing not only home-cooked food but also the latest war news and local gossip. She often had intelligence information for her husband, including up-to-the-minute news about German activity in the area. I suspected this might have come from her well-connected employer, Stubenvoll, and now that I know he actually despised the Nazis, this scenario is even more credible.

Assuming Stubenvoll did pass on information to Kopec through Stefania, it was likely for one reason only: he wanted to stay in Kopec's good graces. A confidential source in Dębica recalls that Stubenvoll feared Kopec just like everyone else. The nobleman knew that "Kopec was crazy and dangerous, capable of burning down his estate or doing who knows what if he did not comply."

I wonder what terrible things specifically—beyond stealing and black marketeering, that is—Kopec did before the war to earn this widespread reputation. Maybe I am better off not knowing.

The exchange of information between Kopec and his wife, I must point out, was not a one-way street. My new mentor was also getting intelligence reports of his own and discussing them with Stefania. The Kopecs' previous meeting together, sometime late in June, was a good case in point. At that time I had overheard part of their conversation as Kopec briefed his wife on recent setbacks for Kruk, the code name I had heard before, and Stach, apparently another partisan leader in our area. I surmised these were the men he met with while leaving me alone for hours on end. According to Kopec, their group had once again encountered Germans and the "blue police," this time in a forest near Grojnica, just east of Dębica. ("Blue police," incidentally, referred to the blue-uniformed Polish auxiliary police. They were called the blue police, as I understand it, to avoid any reference to their nationality. These sons-of-bitches were intensely loyal to the Nazis, especially in the killing of Jews.) Anyway, Kopec told his wife that Stach had been wounded in the clash, while some others of the group had been killed.

"Lucky for me," he said to her, "Kruk wasn't among the dead or wounded."

"I'd be careful with that lot," Stefania warned him. "I don't trust any of them."

Kopec grew angry. "Don't you forget, you got eight children to feed. What little I can steal is nothing compared to what may come my way from 'that lot,' as you put it. Think of it, Stefania: they took thirty thousand zlotys last month from just one Kraut-run business alone! Plus there are Russian airdrops, where cash and weapons come pissing down from the goddamn sky. There's money in them forests, by Christ, and I'll get my hands on some of it."

"And what about the Jewish boy?" she asked, not hiding her disdain for me. "Here you are spending every moment with him, you who never spent any time with your own children."

"The boy will be important to help me get what I want," he said. "Even more than I thought at first. Already Kruk and the others are aware of him, of his courage. He's my ticket to bigger things. Besides, do you think I would put my own children in such danger?"

A chill ran through me as I strained to hear more. I wondered how, exactly, I could be his "ticket to bigger things."

Then his wife said, "But your children are in danger; we all are. That's what I wanted to tell you. The Germans have been coming to the house more often now, sometimes every day, searching for you. They know you're hiding, and they want you. You and the boy as well, I should think."

I wondered if Kopec had been tied to the murder of the two soldiers he told me about. Or had everything else—his long-standing legend not the least of it—simply caught up with him? *Well, since I'm going to die anyway, this is how I want to do it,* I reminded myself at the time.

But that meeting between Kopec and his wife had happened weeks earlier. It was well into July now, and Kopec was growing anxious. Stefania had failed to show up at their appointed time and place.

"She never missed coming to me before," he worried, looking in my direction but addressing no one in particular. "Either she figured she was being followed and turned back, or . . ."

He did not finish the sentence. I had never before seen him so agitated.

"I got to make sure everything's all right at home. You might as well come with me, kid. Straszęcin's your home, too," he added—thoughtlessly, it seemed to me.

"Not any more."

"Yeah." Kopec paused. "You're right, not no more. Well, you coming anyway?"

Of course, I was. "Mister, I'm safer with you than on my own."

"Who knows if you are or not?" Kopec countered. "Who the hell knows anything anymore?"

It was uncomfortably warm for so late in the day, but a light breeze picked up as we made our way to Straszęcin, just under an hour's walk from where we had been hiding. Since I first began living in the woods, I had been exposed to sub-zero temperatures and sweltering heat, and I would take the heat any day. It would have been safer to wait until nightfall before setting out, but Kopec was anxious. Besides, he figured the tall wheat would hide us much of the way.

Between us we carried a Russian submachine gun and two Lugers. We also had several grenades, safely hidden inside the lining of our filthy jackets, toward the bottom. We had torn the lining away on the top and sides, then repinned the sides back in place to create a pouch. It was the only reason we wore jackets at all on such warm days.

Coming from the south, we crossed the narrow Czarna River, which emptied into the Wisłoka a short distance further east. We heard German troops in the distance—laughter, dogs barking—so we moved carefully as we approached Kopec's home. By the time we got there, dusk had settled over the village.

Kopec showed visible relief when he found his wife and eight children safe and sound. As he hugged them all, I observed once again how this notorious thief—who plundered and robbed and perhaps even killed before the occupation made such actions more commonplace—had such a soft spot where his family was concerned.

"You should not have come here," Stefania admonished. "The village is crawling with Krauts."

"I got anxious when you didn't show up," he said truthfully. I tried to make myself invisible against a wall of the room. This was not easy. Children were everywhere.

Stefania told him she had not come to the forest because she was sure she'd be followed. "They're actively looking for you now; they know you've been hiding in the area."

"I been hunted before," he said as if it were nothing.

Stefania gave him a severe look, then glanced over at me. "I'm sure they also know you're hiding a Jew. And they know what you two been up to."

Then her voice dropped, so her children wouldn't overhear. But I caught bits and pieces.

"More than that, they know your background. I don't know if they connected you to the escape, but Stubenvoll knows, and he talks to them all the time. *Drinks* with them."

Kopec let out a snort. "He won't be no trouble. He knows me, and he's not stupid."

"Just the same, you have to get away from here," Stefania urged. "The Germans come by almost every day, and they haven't been here today."

As if on cue, there was a pounding on the door moments later. Voices shouted in German for Stefania to open it at once.

The only way out was through that door or the window next to it. Kopec and I were trapped. We could open fire, but that would just attract more Germans and mean certain death for Kopec's entire family. What happened next is pretty much a blur to me, but according to Stefania, who retold this story to her children over the years, it was she who abruptly put a plan in motion.

"Quick," she said in a hushed voice, "under the bed!"

"What?" her husband asked, as if he did not hear her correctly. Neither of us moved.

Stefania pushed him with everything she had. I followed. "Unless you have a better idea," she whispered urgently, "get under the goddamn bed!"

There was one bed in the cramped Kopec home. It was in a small separate room that formed the base of their L-shaped living space. This, of course, was used by Stefania and Jan on those rare occasions before the war when he was home. The children all slept on mats, which they rolled out into the main room each evening.

In an instant Kopec and I dove under the bed. I slid beneath it easily, but Kopec had a harder time squeezing his body under the framework. The pounding on the door grew more insistent. Soon they would break it down.

"I'm coming," Stefania yelled. She hurriedly passed on instructions to her three oldest children. They quickly responded, for the older ones rounded up all but their two youngest siblings, then raced for the bedroom where we were hiding.

The mattress sagged above us as the six kids plopped down on the bed.

Kopec and I waited breathlessly as Stefania opened the door.

This is how one of Kopec's daughters tells the story of what happened that day: "It was a scary time, that day the Germans came looking for Father and Moniek. They hid under the bed, and six of us children—all but the two babies—jumped on the bed in a line. When the two Nazis came into the bedroom, Mother sat next to us on the bed as well. Before they left, the soldiers even stabbed their bayonets through the mattress, just missing Moniek. Over the years, mother reminded us of that day many times."

The Nazi bastards must have been startled to see six children sitting in a row on the bed, their legs dangling off the side. Did they look like sweet, innocent waifs to the German officers?

After what must have seemed an eternity, but in reality lasted less than a minute, the Germans turned to leave the room. Suddenly one of the officers stopped, turned back toward the bed, and motioned to Stefania and her children.

"Off!" he said. Then again, louder. "Off! Now!"

What choice did they have? One after another, the children jumped off the bed and backed away.

As Stefania and her children looked on in terror, one officer unshouldered his rifle. His boots had to be just inches from my face as he thrust his bayonet through the straw-filled mattress with a sharp jab. One, then another. Kopec and I held our breath. As luck would have it, the bayonet's cold steel never sliced into either Kopec or me.

Why didn't the officers bother to look under the bed? I wonder. It's another stroke of good fortune I can't explain.

All I know is the two Germans left with a stern warning that they would return. And as the door closed behind them, Stefania—tough, callous Stefania—broke down in tears.

Before Kopec and I left to slink back into the forest, Stefania said to her husband, "Jan, it's bad enough you're being hunted for all the things you done. But do you have to make matters worse by hiding the Jew besides?"

I guess he was in no mood to argue. "Like I told you, he'll earn his keep" was all he said, skirting the complex motives he undoubtedly held for rescuing me in the first place—many of which, I suspect, he was just beginning to understand himself. For I choose to believe that his move toward me at the train station that first day was an emotional one, that it began before his mind started to rationalize more practical reasons for saving me and keeping me with him.

Then he added, as his wife merely shook her head, "Besides, with my plans for him in the days to come, you won't have to worry none. Odds are the kid won't survive near as long as me."

The following day Kopec and I were long gone, but the Germans paid a return visit to Stefania. This time the two ss men from the previous intrusion were accompanied by a third man, older and more severe in appearance. We found this out weeks later, when Stefania was next able to meet with her husband. She said the Germans were angry to learn we had come and gone right under their noses. She told the soldiers, as she had many times before, that she didn't know where we were hiding (which was true, at least much of the time). The older officer slapped her across her face. He called her vile names. He turned to his two henchmen. He gave them orders to take her and all of her children out back.

"And then?" asked one of the two soldiers, if Stefania understood him correctly.

"Shoot them, of course," came the reply. He said it in German but followed it with a hand gesture to be sure Stefania got the message.

At gunpoint Stefania and her eight children were marched outside. She held the infant in her arms. An older child carried the next youngest, who was just learning to walk. The littlest ones weren't sure what was happening, but they cried upon seeing the fear in their other siblings.

As for Stefania, she told her husband that she prayed silently, hoping it would be over quickly. I wondered if she wished she could tell them exactly where her husband was, in order to save her children. Perhaps she realized the information would offer no protection anyway.

She recalled that a dog barked incessantly from somewhere in back. Her children wailed. Legions of small gnats flew around her eyes, her nose.

She waited to die with her children.

Both young officers raised their rifles, each taking sight on an opposite end of this human line, ready to work their way down the row of children and meet in the middle. They awaited the order to fire.

The order never came. Eventually the Germans left them alone.

Kopec's two oldest children claim they still remember that terrifying day: lining up against the wooden fence that separated their small patch of yard from the creek behind it. They were sure they would die. But they believe they were saved because "one of the Nazis could not justify killing so many innocent children, so he talked the others out of it."

I have to say, I do not for one minute believe their explanation as to why the Germans had a change of heart and allowed them to go free. Not that such occurrences—soldiers resisting the killing of innocent children—did not happen during the war; I may well be alive because of just one such German soldier in Grabiny. I simply do not think it was the scenario in this instance.

Rather, Kopec's family was spared because of the reputation of Kopec himself. After all, a dead or captured Jan Kopec would be one thing. But to kill his family while he was still on the run would bring the Germans no closer to finding him. More than that, it would surely invite his retribution. The fellow named Kryzak who knew Kopec, he confirmed that the Germans were wary of the man. Yes, even the Nazis could be cautious about someone like him. Given his long-standing repute for being volatile and cunning, his connections to the underground, and his presumed link to others in the criminal underworld, the Germans must have known he would be a problem if anything happened to his family. Better to find and kill Kopec first, *then* dispose of his family, make an example of them, perhaps, for refusing to reveal his whereabouts. *That* was the overriding judgment that saved those children, ensuring future generations of decent, hard-working, law-abiding Kopecs.

There is another individual who also reflected on Kopec's sphere of influence. He is a former Home Army partisan commander from the Dębica area and a published historian who spoke off the record. I am not sure that he knew Kopec personally, but he knew *of* him, for this is what he said: "I can tell you why everyone was afraid of Kopec, and it was not just the man himself. It was also who he knew, his connections deep within the criminal structure, reportedly as far away as Lublin. He had very strong ties with any number of people like himself. Everyone feared what he could do, for if it came to retribution, he could call on the whole criminal underworld."

As I said, Kopec and I were far away when all this happened, unaware of the terror Stefania was facing. We were on foot, heading deep into Podkarpacie, several days' journey south of Dębica. We took our time getting there, following a circuitous route mapped primarily by Kopec's instincts, stopping to rob farms and homes in small villages along the way.

And during one of those robberies we had a rather close call of our own.

As was our usual practice, Kopec approached a house while I waited just out of sight, behind a tree. With no light other than that of a nearly full moon, I watched as he tried the door. It was bolted. He walked over to a window to see if he could pry it open enough for me to enter. I expected that any moment he would give me the okay to join him and enter the house.

Next thing I knew, he was surrounded by two men and a woman. All three carried rifles. And they were cautiously approaching Kopec as if they had cornered a dangerous animal, which in a manner of speaking, they had. *Had they been lying in wait for bandits like us?* I wondered. (*Bandits like us!* How strange to think of myself as Kopec's partner in crime.)

Kopec also was armed, naturally, but with three against one, he would expect me to start shooting first. That was why we never approached a house together and why I carried the submachine gun. Even though this was the first time I had to use it, I hesitated for only the briefest moment. From my vantage point I was able to surprise the family just as they had surprised Kopec. I took them out without getting Kopec in my line of fire.

At the time I convinced myself it didn't matter that I took the lives of three Poles, including a woman—even though these might have been innocent people just trying to defend their home. Killing them—perhaps orphaning children, who knows?—haunts me now, I admit it, and from the safety of my old age, I would gratefully undo it if I could. But back then I did not see a choice. Circumstances being what they were, it was them or us, and I did not hesitate to protect the man who protected me. It was as simple as that.

Of course, we helped ourselves to whatever we could find in the house, then continued southward. Kopec knew where we were heading, but me, I just followed. Each step of the way, we continued to evade the Germans, even as other groups and individuals also in hiding were captured and killed all around us.

This entire area was part of the larger Kraków district—Kraków being the headquarters for Nazi-occupied Poland—so it was not surprising that here would be the largest presence of military and police forces of any district in the country.

Yet Kopec and I continued to move about almost as if we were transparent, like a pane of freshly washed glass.

Luck? I wondered. *Kopec's sixth sense? Something else? How is it possible to move from place to place—stealing food and other necessities, sustaining a lucrative trade in the black market, carrying out acts of sabotage against the enemy—yet evading capture every time? How is it possible?*

Questions without answers.

8

Podkarpacie

T HE WISŁOKA RIVER, which separates Straszęcin from Dębica, me-
anders for a few miles southwest of those towns, then takes a
gentle curve near Pilzno, where it changes course, heading
south by—ever so slightly—southeast, eventually passing through the
town of Jasło on its way to the Slovakian border.

Stretching in a fairly narrow band both east and west of Jasło lies
the rugged, heavily forested region known as Podkarpacie. At least
that is what the area was called when I lived in Poland. I can still visualize the hills and ridges, the caves and hollows, the valleys and canyons,
all sweeping in a gradual arc to meet the Tatra Mountains along Poland's southernmost border. The region offered ideal hiding and meeting places for underground groups familiar with the terrain.

I had never before been that far south, but Kopec clearly knew the
area well. "It's where I head when things get hot," he said to me many
times.

On our three-day trek from Straszęcin, we moved by night, as always, helping ourselves to food from the fields and sleeping away the
daylight hours concealed deep within the forests. Toward dawn following the third night, we reached our destination. It was a stretch of
high riverbank along the Wisłoka, just north of Jasło.

"Here we are, kid. Our home for a while."

We stood on a grassy, wind-swept bluff overlooking the river. In
the surreal predawn murkiness, Kopec gestured grandly with his right
hand, indicating the nothingness that surrounded us.

I squinted, looking right and left. I saw only grass and scrub, which
rose gracefully to form a gentle knoll, then sloped gradually down-

ward. The forest began about thirty yards behind us. Ahead of us, or more exactly, ten yards below, was the river itself, flowing toward the border.

"Aren't we going into the forest?" I asked. "I don't see any place to hide around here."

Kopec flashed one of his rare smiles, although in the dim light I was not sure if it was a smile or a sneer.

"That's good," the master escape artist said, "because if you don't see it, nobody else will neither. It's hidden me good over the years."

As I watched in astonishment, my guide and protector crouched down beside the edge of the mound and carefully peeled back a layer of grass, moss, and other scrub—it looked about four feet square—as if he were removing an area rug. It exposed planks of barn siding, tightly aligned together over a square framework of two-by-fours. One by one, Kopec removed the planks of siding and dropped them into the pit below.

"What are you staring at?" Kopec spoke to me gruffly, but he was grinning. "You never walked into a room from up on top? Follow me, kid."

Kopec descended into the hole, carrying with him the mat of vegetal covering that had rested on the very top. A crude ladder had been built, also with two-by-fours, to provide access in and out of the clever hideout, whose floor rested about ten feet beneath the surface.

As my feet touched the bottom, the cavernous space was suddenly flooded with light. Kopec had fumbled around in the dark, finding a match and a kerosene lamp that had been lying nearby. It now burned brightly.

"We're going to be in the dark the rest of the day," he said, "but first, I thought you'd like to look around."

I could not believe my eyes. It was like being in a cave, only this cavern was man-made, hollowed inside the bluff and roughly framed with lumber. It was surprisingly roomy, enabling the stocky Kopec to stand and move about comfortably. The dirt floor was dry, suggesting to me that the river was still far below. A metal tube vented to the outside for air, but it would only be seen by someone down at the level of the river, looking up.

Surveying the room, I saw a large fiber mat that covered part of the floor. A blanket lay heaped in one corner. In addition to the lamp, there were assorted items that Kopec had stored away during previous visits: odd pieces of clothing, potatoes and beets, a jar of what appeared to be vodka or homemade brandy, and weapons, including Russian grenades and a rifle.

Seeing me stare at his firepower, Kopec shrugged. "There's only so much I can carry around with me. But I think between you and me, we'll put everything here to good use."

Before we settled in for the long day ahead, Kopec carried the strips of siding up the ladder and, working from below, put all but the last one in place. He used the open space to maneuver the grassy covering into place on top, then put back the last strip of wood.

Satisfied with his own prudence, he said to me, "Now if anyone walks above, they won't fall into our little rabbit hole."

With that, he extinguished the lantern, and we settled down in the cool subterranean lair to sleep away the daylight hours. We had covered a great distance, after all; both of us were thoroughly exhausted. But just before sleep came to me, some of Kopec's words ran through my head, fitting together like pieces of a jigsaw puzzle: *It's where I head when things get hot . . . hidden me well over the years . . .*

I realized he had built this hideout before the war, when he was lying low from the Polish police.

I marveled at Kopec's ingenuity—his genius, perhaps—at having the cunning and wherewithal to remain a long-time fugitive who had never been caught for his crimes. Then I drifted off, slipping reluctantly into a deep, uneasy sleep.

"Tonight, you stay here," Kopec instructed me when darkness fell. "I got to meet some people."

"Why don't they meet you here?" I asked, though I knew the rules, that I was to be kept apart. It was a lonely existence.

"You think I let anyone else know about this place? You're the first to ever set foot in it, kid." Kopec was sorting through his arms cache. "Remember what I told you? I go to them; they don't find me. I don't share my hiding places with nobody. At least not until you came along."

"What will I do down here until you return?"

Kopec selected a couple of grenades and took some fresh ammunition. "Same thing you always do: Wait. Breathe. Stay alive." Next thing I knew, he was climbing up the ladder.

For me the toughest part of my time with Kopec was these long, sequestered periods of inactivity. I yearned for more action, longed to meet Stach or Kruk or whoever it was Kopec had joined forces with. *Surely they're partisans,* I thought. *Or maybe they're criminals whom Kopec knew before the war. Come to think of it, is there really any longer a difference between the two?*

To my mind, all partisans were freedom fighters. I was not aware of the strong distinctions between the two primary groups that had formed around that time. But even if Kopec had given me direct exposure to the partisans he knew, I still would not have understood what made one group different from the other. Only recently have I learned there was the Soviet-backed People's Guard, and there was the Home Army—a larger, more organized force whose members were supported by the Polish government-in-exile, temporarily headquartered in London.

Political backing aside, the composition of the two groups differed greatly. From its formation that summer in 1942, the People's Guard (which originally came into being in 1931 as the Polish Workers Party) accepted anyone willing to fight: Jews, Gypsies, escaped POWs, and especially lawless individuals like Kopec.

Many of the antisocials who were attracted to the People's Guard joined not necessarily because they had pro-Communist leanings, but—according to much that has been written on the subject—often because they were simply looking for action. The People's Guard promised this from the very start, encouraging Jews and Poles alike to rise up against the Germans. In reality, however, this may have been nothing more than rhetoric and propaganda; Moscow's real goal, many believe, was to stir up a revolution in Poland to ensure Communist domination after the German occupation. Either way, the People's Guard gained a large following, particularly in the forests and rural villages. It supplied numerous arms to individuals willing to fight.

The Home Army, on the other hand, was far more discriminating in whom it would accept. According to a Home Army veteran from Grabiny named Tadeusz Kozera, Home Army members all took a blood oath of loyalty. "They certainly would not have done business with a man like Jan Kopec," he said. If anything, they would likely have killed him, given the opportunity, because of his growing involvement in hostile actions against the Germans. The Home Army, you see, initially considered acts of military sabotage to be ineffective and, even worse, dangerous, because it guaranteed reprisals against the Polish people. (Indeed, this might well have been Moscow's ulterior motive in encouraging the People's Guard to strike.) For this reason, the Home Army engaged largely in espionage and economic sabotage. They also actively sought out traitors and informers. But in general they did not, until much later in the war, place emphasis on purely military actions against the Germans.

In these and many other ways, the Home Army and the People's Guard clashed with each other philosophically, politically, and militarily from the very beginning. And the situation steadily deteriorated throughout the war.

But while I struggled to stay alive, I was unaware of these politics.

I must admit I do not particularly care about them now, except that they have shed some light on several of the adventures Kopec planned for me. Specifically, I've learned that Stach and Kruk were indeed leaders of the People's Guard squadron in my area. I became aware of this after coming across a book entitled *Oddzialy Gwardii Ludowej i Armii Ludowej* by historian Jozef Garas. Here is Dorothy Kultys's translation of what Garas says about these resistance fighters:

> With an initiative of the command of the Dębica area, a People's Guard attack squad was formed in the middle of 1942. Its commander, radical farmer activist Stanislaw Jaskier ("Stach"), came from the village of Skrzyszow. The squad consisted of nine people from the Skrzyszow area. . . . In March 1943, this unit joined with the partisans squad under commander Piotr Chłendowski ("Kruk"), also from Skrzyszow. The squad was always on the move—they performed operations not only in the Dębica region but also in the Tarnobrzeg, Rzeszów, Jasło, and Gorlice (Podkarpacie) regions. (363)

A veteran commander of the opposing Home Army partisans from this same region added more information in a present-day phone interview: "It's true the leaders of the People's Guard in this area were Jaskier and Chłendowski. It's interesting about Chłendowski: He was a double agent. In 1936, when there was a revolution of farmers, he was actually a police sergeant. Anyway, under the leadership of these men, the People's Guard engaged in some sabotage, certainly, but if you ask me, they mostly robbed people to survive. And they fought as much against us in the Home Army as they did against the Germans."

Clearly each partisan group had a jaundiced view of the other, which still exists to this day. But at the time I was more concerned about the hollow emptiness in my stomach and the almost constant disorientation from not knowing whether it was day or night. So I was greatly relieved when Kopec finally returned that day, carrying carrots, cucumbers, and tomatoes. And something else: a hindquarter of crisp rabbit, still warm from a fire.

"Where—" I started to ask, but Kopec raised his hand to stop me before any more words poured out.

"Never mind," he said. "Just eat. I already had my share."

As I devoured the sumptuous feast, Kopec took a drink from a nearly full brandy jar and passed it over.

"For your health," he offered. "It will also help you sleep, since you been just lying around. That will change tomorrow night, by the way, when you're going with me. There's someone wants to meet you." Before I could ask who would even know about me, he raised his hand again to silence me, repeating only, "Tomorrow night."

I shrugged and helped myself to several long swallows of the fiery brandy. The alcohol, along with the filling meal, made me drowsy. Soon, I knew, I would nod off, perhaps to dream about Stach and Kruk and all the other vague, heroic figures who were just beyond my reach in that netherworld behind the barrier Kopec had put up all around me. There they would always remain, elusive as smoke, revealing themselves only to Kopec as he pulled the strings and I responded, his willing marionette.

The next day at dusk we cautiously emerged from our hole beneath the hillock. The last rays of light shimmered on the river like mischievous sprites, bobbing along the surface of the water. While Kopec concealed the entrance behind me, I breathed deeply, taking in the fresh evening air.

I was burning with curiosity as I followed my guardian through the woods. After a vigorous walk of more than an hour, we emerged from a stand of pines to face a wheat field that grew practically to the edge of the forest. Even in the pallid moonlight it was evident that the tall grain was yellowing with the hot, dry weather. In a week or two it would be ready to harvest, after which the fields would not hide men in their midst for another year. Not that I expected to continue living that long.

In the center of the field a group of five men stood talking quietly. Four of them, from what I could see, were armed to the hilt with an assortment of Russian weapons. The fifth man stood out, not just because he lacked any visible firearms, but because he appeared older than the others—he had to be forty, maybe more. Also, while he wore the ragtag clothes of a forest dweller, he appeared—I don't know, a little tidier, maybe. A little less disheveled.

The man was tall, easily six feet, with neat brown hair that had begun to gray at the temples. His face was broad and friendly. Approachable, you might say. While the others in the assembly seemed to be somewhat on edge, their eyes darting back and forth, this man looked directly at me as we came closer.

Kopec nodded to the group but addressed the unarmed man. "This is the kid I was telling you about."

The man nodded, then smiled faintly at me.

Kopec said to me, "This man is from Kraków. He's a Catholic priest."

A priest! The man's smile broadened at my surprised response, but then it was gone.

"He been risking his life coming here," Kopec continued, "but he . . . I guess you could say he been helping these people. When he heard about you, he wanted to meet you."

"You're a very courageous young man," the priest said.

"I do what I have to do, sir," I responded. I did not know how to address a priest, having never been introduced to one before, let alone one who was not even dressed like a priest.

"Can we take a short walk together so that I may talk with you?" the priest asked.

I nodded tentatively, not sure what he could want with me. We walked out of earshot of the others, navigating between the densely planted stalks of wheat.

For the next ten minutes the priest spoke gently, softly, and I found myself captivated by him and his words. He never asked the details of what I had endured, but it was as if he *knew,* he could *feel* my suffering.

"There are some of my countrymen who see the horror of what is happening to the Jews, to others of their own background as well," said the priest, "and they're risking their lives to save and shelter those they can."

I wondered if he included Kopec in that righteous group. Was he aware that I had been saved by Kopec, as far as I could tell, for other than noble reasons?

The priest continued, "But the others—a far, far greater number— they turn a blind eye on what is happening to your people. Many even claim to welcome it. For this apathy, this ignorance, I place some of the blame on the Catholic Church itself."

He paused, took in my surprised reaction to his words, then explained.

"You wouldn't know this, but as long ago as 1936, Cardinal Hlond—he was head of the national church—Cardinal Hlond wrote and distributed messages of hate and distrust toward the Jews. *There will be a Jewish problem as long as the Jews remain . . .* that was one. Here's another: *It is a fact that the Jews deceive, levy interest, and are pimps. . . .* There's more, you can be sure, and it disgusts me, as I know it does you."

"Is that bast—is the cardinal still head of the church?" I asked.

"Not here in Poland, thankfully. True to his cowardice, Hlond fled the country with the Polish government-in-exile."

The three-quarter moon had risen high in the sky, and even here in the wheat field, between the stalks, milky light was seeping through. It highlighted the face of the priest as he talked, revealing moisture that had pooled around his eyes.

His next words were measured and bitter. It was clear to me that he felt them deeply. They have stayed with me to this day.

"I am ashamed of my own people"—his precise words—"both within the church and outside it. When the war ends and we have to answer to the rest of the world, what will we say? How will the Polish people face them?"

He turned his head away and was silent for several moments. Then, with a sigh, he looked back at me. His expression had turned cold.

"I have this feeling—this terrible fear—that when the war ends, it won't be the end of persecution, or bloodshed, or Jew-baiting. There are those of . . . my people . . . who will still need someone to fear, someone to blame."

I found myself captivated by the priest, and now my own eyes began to tear. It had been a while since my tears came this easily, and they would not come often again, not for a great many years. But there was something I needed to confess to this man, this priest, who had just made a candid confession of his own.

"I've done some bad things myself, Father." I was finding it less difficult to use the proper form of address. "I've robbed, I've . . . done things I'm not proud of, but what else could I do? How else would I have stayed alive?"

The priest put his arm around me. "These are grievous times." He said it again: "Grievous times. And what we do in war will be forgiven."

Gradually, tentatively, some of my guilt and shame began to dissipate. In its place an icy lack of emotion seeped in, like a low-pressure area displacing warmth and sunshine to herald in a less-settled climate.

"But there are those whom *I* can never forgive," I said defiantly. *"Never."*

The priest squeezed my shoulder and looked down at the ground. Then together we walked in silence back to the rest of the group, for there was nothing more to say.

On our last night before we headed back north, we enjoyed a grand repast. Kopec had stolen a plump young pig from a nearby farm. It was cooked by the men (Stach? Kruk?) who had been with the priest two days earlier. They dug an underground pit and covered it with leaves so the smoke would not give them away. I was invited to eat with the group—a rare occurrence—but there was little conversation and no talk, in my presence, of any resistance plans or other activities.

I noticed there was a bond between the men that did not seem to be shared with Kopec. He had provided the main course but was clearly an outsider in this group. Kopec himself had said as much. *I operate alone. I go under cover alone. And I don't share my hiding places with nobody.* Yet Kopec had known them before, had been here before, I was certain of it. Surely they must know about his past. Yet it appeared they trusted him.

Throughout the quiet meal the priest's words played over and over in my mind. Abruptly I turned to Kopec and cried, "Why was I so damn unlucky to be born a Jew?"

He seemed taken aback for a moment, but then he replied with one of his typically surly responses.

"That's life, kid."

He said it just like that: "That's life, kid." Then he added, "Look at me. I been running all my life."

It was a decision you made, I thought. *But me, I didn't ask to be a Jew. I didn't ask to be hated because of what I was born into.* I looked glumly down at my feet and did not say another word for the rest of the meal.

In the years that have followed, I must tell you, I have continued to wonder about the priest, who moved me to tears for one brief moment, with words and with empathy and with compassion I had seldom before experienced.

Perhaps he was one of the thousands of priests who had been captured and imprisoned—Auschwitz, I understand, was the destination preferred by the Nazis for men of the cloth—then was released (it did happen now and then!) or, like Kopec, found a way to escape.

Perhaps.

But more probably, I think, he was one of the several nameless priests of courage and conviction who belonged to a secret society led by Adam Sapieha, the archbishop of Kraków. From what I heard after the war, Sapieha and his followers were closely connected with partisan groups, performing such selfless acts as distributing baptismal certificates to Jews.

I never knew the name of the priest who talked with me, but I will always remember that I was in the company of a very special person.

And some weeks after I returned with Kopec to the fields and forests not far from my home district near Dębica, something happened that triggered the memory of that day anew.

It was late July—or had August already come?—and I was making a routine raid on a farmer's field I had visited many times before. Digging deep into the soft soil, pulling up turnips to help quiet my growling stomach, I was caught by surprise as someone came up behind me. I had been spotted by the farmer whose field I was invading.

As I remained crouched on the ground, a voice behind me said, "Put your hands in the air and get up slowly."

106

I could actually feel the rifle that was aimed at me. An audible click told me a bullet had dropped into position, ready to be fired.

Without moving I said quietly, "Mister, does one of us have to die over a couple of goddamn turnips?"

"Your hands. In the air. *Now*, you miserable thief."

As you wish, I said to myself.

I slowly began to straighten up, plucking the Luger from my waistband as I started to raise my hands. Then, spinning around, I fired into the chest of the man who stood before me. He did not have breath enough to fire back.

Forgetting the turnips, but with the presence of mind to grab the Pole's rifle, I ran back into the woods as fast as I could. And as I ran, the words I heard in the forest of Podkarpacie played over and over again in my mind.

What we do in war will be forgiven.

And I thought, *But I'm not willing to forgive. Not now, not ever. So why the hell should I expect anyone to forgive me?*

9

Grabiny

SHORTLY AFTER KOPEC and I returned from Podkarpacie, he found
a way to see his wife. The meeting took place well away from
our hiding place, and this time I was not invited to come along.
When he returned—sharing a small portion of Stefania's home
cooking that was not, it is safe to say, prepared for *my* enjoyment—he
was unusually agitated. During his rendezvous with Stefania he had
learned how close his family had come to being mowed down by German bullets.

You do not know what it's like to have no one, I thought then. *The
thought occurs to you, the possibilities are real, but still you do not know . . .*

We were changing locations nearly every day or two, basing our
strategy of movement on Kopec's intuition and now on mine as well,
for there were times when I sensed danger, too—how, I could not
say—and we fled, only to learn that a hunt for fugitives had indeed
taken place in the area we had left behind.

Kopec was leaving me by myself for up to two days at a time now,
revealing nothing about what he did or who he saw when he was away.
But when we were together, we continued our regular late-night robberies and, as a result, seldom wanted for food or clothing.

On one mild September evening Kopec handed me a package, with
a name and location in Grabiny. Grabiny—the village where Papa and
I had gone before . . . before . . .

"This is a family you can trust," Kopec told me. "I suppose the
village holds some bad feelings for you, but—"

"You do not know what the village holds for me," I interrupted,
no longer fearing to hide my anger. "You do not know my feelings.

You do not know what happened before you saw me crawl out from under my father's body or what cost my father his life."

Lucky for me, Kopec was not put off by my anger. When he responded, I was surprised how soft his voice had become. "I know more than you think. I was at the train station long before I came up to you and carried you back to my house. And give me some credit, will you, kid? I always make it my business to know what goes on around me."

I calmed down a little. Now I was unsure exactly *where* to direct the angst that had built up inside of me.

"Tell you what," he continued. "Get it off your chest. Tell me about Grabiny, how you ended up . . . how things happened the way they did."

I must have looked at him rather skeptically, for he said, "Right now. Spill it. I want to hear it all. Then you will deliver the goddamn package like I told you, understand?"

Long before I met Kopec, German soldiers and their informers were everywhere: on the roads, in the villages, and by late 1942 in the forests as well, conducting random hunts with trained Alsatian shepherd dogs. Alongside the Germans were the infamous blue police and yet another dangerous enemy—the NSZ, the National Armed Forces. This was an extreme right-wing group of virulent Polish fascists and anti-Semites. They knew the places Jews were likely to hide far better than did the Germans, and from everything we heard, they eagerly murdered every Jew they could find. Needless to say, Papa and I were constantly on the move, living each day in fear.

Although we had little need to know the day or date, we were pretty sure the new year had come some weeks before. One thing we did feel with absolute certainty was the persistent, numbing cold in our extremities and the emptiness in our stomachs. The barns were locked tight at night, and while I had recently figured a way to break into the church barn by jimmying a window, we knew it would be foolhardy to return again too quickly.

The last time we had eaten had been two days earlier—a few raw potatoes, which we found in a winter storage area under earth and straw. Papa and I were growing weak.

My father, however, had been turning something over in his mind, and he must have decided that it was time to act. Late one afternoon he said quietly to me, "Tonight we're going into Grabiny." The village was only a short walk away.

I looked uncertainly at him. "What will we do there?"

"I had—have—a friend there. You may remember him: Pozniak, his name is. It's been a long time; you were young when you last saw him."

The name meant nothing to me. I remained silent.

"Look, I've known him since we were children," Papa went on. "I'm not going to ask him to hide us, just to give us some food, this one time only. Moishele, we have to trust *someone*. We're going to starve by staying here, so we might as well take our chances in the village. Pozniak will help us; you'll see."

It wasn't fear of being caught in the village that made me feel apprehensive. Truth be told, I was tired of the forests and eager to venture outside, if only for a short while. There was something else that bothered me—a premonition, looking back on it—but I would never question my father's decision.

"I'm ready, Papa," I said finally. "Let's go into Grabiny."

My father was certainly aware of the dangers. Grabiny—unlike our home village of Straszęcin, a stone's throw to the northeast—was directly on the major west-to-east rail line that connected Kraków to Lwów on the eastern front. This increased the probability of German soldiers passing through the village. Papa chose what seemed to be the safest route to Pozniak's house, allowing us to remain hidden by the forest for all but a short distance. It would be foolish to count on the unfolding darkness alone to conceal us.

We approached from the east, emerging from a dense stand of birch trees, then crossing two fields that lay between us and the house of his friend. The frozen ground crackled beneath our feet, reminding me of breaking glass.

And there, just ahead, stood the house. I noticed the weathered wood siding was coming loose from the frame in one corner. The house looked much like my own former home, although the Pozniak residence appeared considerably larger.

Papa rapped on the door. A moment later it opened a crack, the hinges obeying with a strident, grinding noise. Peering through the opening was a man of about my father's age, staring with a look of surprise into our drawn, haggard faces. Pozniak, I assumed.

"Goldner, it's been a long time," he said in a monotone, looking warily at my father.

It seemed to me that the words came out cautiously, more as a statement of the obvious, certainly not with a ring of any overt enthusiasm. The man's eyes darted to me, but they revealed nothing. The brief silence was awkward.

"Please, my friend, I'm asking you a big favor," Papa finally stammered. His breath materialized in great clouds of steam. "We haven't had so much as a piece of bread in months. If you'll sell me a loaf, I'll pay you anything, anything you want, when the war ends."

Pozniak remained silent, as if thinking over the request. The tension was palpable. Then I noticed the man seemed to relax a little, the corner of his mouth turning up in what might have been the faintest hint of a smile.

"Of course, come in. Looks like you and—your son, is it?—can both use a good meal."

Pozniak opened the door and led us toward the kitchen. He was tall, I remember, with a working man's calloused hands and a wiry build that seemed somewhat contradicted by a full face. There was a scar over his right cheek, not a fresh wound, but one that had not completely healed. And he sported a mustache, neatly trimmed, showing no signs of gray. None of these facts made much of an impression on me when I first saw the man. But in playing the scene over and over in my mind later, it's strange how many seemingly meaningless details had somehow been imbedded in my memory.

Curiously, Pozniak asked no questions of us when we came in, made no inquiries as to our welfare. Perhaps no questions were necessary, I thought. Could the man have any idea that this was our first time inside a real home in nearly two years?

I had thoughts of my own home just a few miles away. I wondered if it still stood empty, or if by now it had been "acquired" by another Polish family in search of more land, eager to take advantage of the Jews' losses.

Pozniak set two chairs for my father and me at the table. We sat in grateful silence while he brought out a loaf of bread, then busied himself cutting off a small piece of cooked chicken. I looked closely at my father's friend, tried to remember him from long ago. Perhaps I was very young when the man had last been at our house, for he was a stranger to me now.

At the back of the main room an alcove led to two bedrooms. In one corner of this alcove a chubby gray cat lay dozing on a pile of warm clothing, and I keenly eyed both the new-looking apparel and the obviously well fed animal. I felt momentarily embarrassed at my own deteriorating clothes. They weren't much more than rags anymore, reeking of barns, of the forest, of my own fear and misery. I wondered where Pozniak's family was at this moment, for the house was quiet. They were probably asleep in the back rooms, I guessed, though I had no idea of the hour. Time was for people who had places to go, schedules to keep.

"This war is tough on everyone," Pozniak finally offered as he set the scraps of chicken down in front of us.

Gazing around the cozy house, with its warm hearth, abundant clothing, and stocked larder, I wanted to say, *Obviously the war is not so tough on* some *of us.* But I held my tongue, and ate in silence with my father.

Maybe it was the food in front of us, or the comforting fire, or the hospitality of a former friend of my father's, but as we ate, we were completely unaware that our host had slipped out of the room. Nor did we notice that when he returned, he was carrying several lengths of thick rope.

Before Papa and I realized what was happening, Pozniak had come from behind and pinned my father to his chair with savage determination and lightning speed, lashing him tightly to it with the rope. It took me a moment to understand what was going on, and for reasons I will never understand, I must have simply frozen, because in the next moment I was being tied to my chair as well.

"You son of a bitch!" Papa cried out. "What are you doing?"

Pozniak was breathing hard. There was a sense of duty, not remorse, in his reply. "I'm in charge of the village now. The mayor. It's my responsibility to take you in."

"Your responsibility?" Papa was incredulous. "You were at my wedding. We were friends, or have you forgotten?"

"Times change. People change." Pozniak bound my father's ankles together. "Friendships change."

"I trusted you with my life. With my son's life. And this is what you do?"

Pozniak shrugged. "I do what I have to do. I, too, am trying to stay alive. If you hadn't come here . . ." He paused but apparently decided not to finish the thought.

One final tug at the rope, then Pozniak turned toward the door, grabbed a coat that was hanging on a peg, and walked out into the dark void to make arrangements, as we would soon learn, for our disposal.

I looked at my father, felt his helplessness. I wished I had not eaten the piece of chicken. It left a bad taste in my mouth, a taste of fear. I berated myself—and still do, even today—for not reacting differently when Pozniak lunged for my father. If I had acted, we might have escaped. In the forests we were always alert. Here our guard was down. It was, after all, supposed to be the home of a friend.

My arms were already getting sore from being stretched behind the back of my chair, and my wrists were chafing from the tightness of the rope. But the only pain that mattered at that moment was the hurt and fury I saw in my father's eyes.

I wish I could recall what we said to each other that night, our last night together, as we sat bound to our chairs. I play the scene over and over in my mind. I can make out our faces in the dim flame of memory, but I cannot hear the words.

Except this: "Papa, he was your *friend*," I cry out. A spark from the fireplace dances past my ear; I can visualize that. It lands on the table in front of us, quickly changing color from a fiery yellow red to the sullen ash gray of a dying ember. But my father's response, whatever it might have been, is lost to me forever.

Did I tell him how much I loved him as we sat there, waiting for that bastard Pozniak to return? Did he say the same to me?

I cannot hear him in those interminable moments, but I can still see him as he turns from me, a fraction of a whole, unable to do what was expected of him, what any man would want to do: find a way to protect his family even in the face of such adversity. In the end, I am certain, he had few words to say, for words must have failed him, just as he most certainly felt that he failed us all.

He must have known it then, my poor Papa. He must have known beyond any question of a doubt what the price of that failure had been for Mama and Gita, what it would soon be for him and for me.

Throughout the long, hopeless night, my father and I sat tightly bound to our chairs. From time to time we each struggled to twist and maneuver our wrists in an attempt to loosen the rope, but Pozniak was obviously accomplished at holding his prisoners; the bindings would not come loose.

I had experienced fear before, but my feelings that night extended beyond simple terror to reach a realm that touched on near madness: a melange of panic and hatred and defiance and utter helplessness, all consuming me in unison, chewing off little chunks of reason, pulling together to divide my emotions and scatter them in different directions. Death was beginning to look like an exalted release, except I had vowed that I would not willingly embrace such an easy way out.

All too soon the darkness began to lift. Another promise of a new day. This one, however, would be overcast and bitterly cold. Not that it mattered.

Pozniak had returned during the night, silently walking past Papa and me into his bedroom. There had been whispers from behind the closed door, muted communion of husband and wife, I suppose, although we never saw her. *Does she know what sort of fiend her husband is?* I wondered. *Is she any different?*

Shortly after daybreak there appeared at the door one of Pozniak's cronies: a heavy-set, unsavory character whom Pozniak called Grychowski. The two men lifted my father and me and carried us, bound hand and foot, to a waiting horse cart.

We had traveled less than a mile when the cart stopped. We were in front of the Grabiny train station. The same station where—a lifetime ago, it seemed to me—Papa detrained, most every Friday, after selling his cattle in cities to the west.

As Grabiny was one of two stops in the short distance between the major Tarnów and Dębica stations, the little station itself was nothing much to look at. It was a small wooden structure along the tracks, a place of shelter for waiting passengers. It had once been painted a steel blue, but the color had grown faded and sullied, giving it a pallor of soiled gray. Like most everything else, the whole structure was greatly in need of restoration.

As we pulled up, I saw just one person at the station—an elderly woman. She glanced at the cart, at us, then averted her eyes, and hurried on.

In sheer terror, I must confess, I wet myself. I felt helpless, like a baby.

Pozniak and Grychowski sat silently up front, waiting. Papa and I were positioned back to back, where we also sat, waiting. How the end would come we were not exactly sure.

The horse gave an impatient snort. In the distance the chugging sound of an approaching train broke the silence.

They're waiting for the train, I realized. *They're waiting for the Germans to do their dirty work.* I wondered what was going through my father's head at that moment. *"What will be, will be"?* Now *you know what will be, Papa. Now you surely know.*

The disgusting hands of Pozniak and Grychowski grasped roughly at us, dragging us out of the cart, pushing us against the side of the station house. Papa turned toward me, started to say something . . .

"Shut up," commanded Pozniak. He slapped Papa hard across the face. "No sound from either of you. And stay on your feet."

The train had stopped with a huge hiss of steam. The doors opened, but just one passenger got out: a young soldier, fresh-faced with a smartly pressed uniform. Pozniak walked over to meet him, while Grychowski watched over us.

The German was a sturdy young man of about twenty-five, but in spite of his stiff demeanor, there seemed to be a softness about his eyes. He conferred briefly with Pozniak, then the two of them walked over to Papa and me.

Grychowski grinned with anticipation, undoubtedly thinking of the reward Pozniak would share with him: a few kilos of sugar perhaps, or even better, several liters of vodka. No doubt he had seen the posters put up by the Germans. He knew what a Jew was worth.

"Kill them," Papa's good friend Pozniak said coldly.

The soldier looked at Papa and me, looked directly into our eyes, lingering an extra moment on my own frightened face. Then he turned back to the village leader who had summoned him. The inconceivable words that the soldier spoke next were not often uttered, I imagine, by a Nazi in occupied Poland. I will never forget exactly what he said to Pozniak.

"You know," the German began, "these two may be Jews, but what I see in front of me are two human beings. And you make me come here to kill two innocent people? One of them just a boy?" He lowered his voice, then continued. "It's just possible that Germany won't win the war. Keep that in mind. And if the Third Reich is not victorious, do you know what could happen to you?"

Pozniak, the cold, cowardly bastard, was unmoved. "Just do your job and kill the damn Jews," he growled. "Kill them like all the others and be done with it." Then he added, "Start with the boy. Let Leap— let the father watch."

The soldier stared deep into Pozniak's eyes. If he was looking for some indication that the Pole might retreat from his position, he found none. This was not an act of war; it was cold-blooded murder, and from his own words, the young German soldier knew it. But he also must have known he could not escape his duty, regardless of any sudden dictates of conscience. Pozniak was a powerful man, I learned later, well connected at high levels in the Wehrmacht. Perhaps the SS as well. Poles as cooperative as that one, the soldier might have thought, must be cultivated, played, until the day when they no longer proved useful . . .

Pozniak pushed Papa and me closer together.

I looked at my father helplessly. His eyes were wide in terror as the German unshouldered his rifle.

Behind the soldier Grychowski licked his lips, not unlike a wolf cornering its prey. Then he muttered, to no one in particular, "I wonder if the boy will fetch as much as the father?"

"Shema Yisroel . . . " This I also remember: Papa's lips moving almost imperceptibly, in prayer, I supposed. I noticed it but was too paralyzed with my own fear to speak, too angry with God to join Papa in prayer. All I saw was the barrel of the rifle, pointed directly at me. I am ashamed to say I lost control of my bowels.

The soldier hesitated, then squeezed the trigger.

I closed my eyes.

"Adonoi eloheynu . . ."

I felt a spasm of pain as hot lead pierced my flesh. *Is this what death feels like?* I remember thinking.

My legs collapsed under me, and I fell to the ground, while Papa, I think, screamed my name.

115

"Adonoi echod."

The officer must have quickly shifted his line of sight to my father, for it was a split second later that he fired again. A single shot. A fatal shot.

Papa fell dead directly on top of me.

And until I crawled away sometime after that and was later carried to safety by the Pole who now watched over me, that is the last thing I remember.

"I can tell you what happened after that," Kopec said to me when I finished telling him everything I knew about that day. "It gets even worse, if you want to hear it."

I had been shaking uncontrollably as I talked, but now I looked up at him and tried to compose myself. "Please tell me. What happened after the shooting? I have to know."

"Understand, there was nothing I could do to stop it. I was hiding from a lot of people who would have liked nothing better than to kill me too. And there was others who depended on me staying alive, like there are now. You included. I can tell you there was passengers looking out the train windows during the . . . incident. They did nothing, naturally, because shootings like that happen all the time. You know this. Everyone fears for their own lives. Not just the Jews."

I let the comment pass.

"I watched as his helper, the man you said was called Grychowski, nodded with approval after the shots were fired. Then he wiped his hands on his pants, can you believe it? As if that cleansed him of all responsibility! He started to walk away, but turned around when he heard Pozniak mutter something to that piece-of-shit Nazi. That's when the Kraut hands over his rifle."

I was appalled. "He gave his rifle to Pozniak?"

"From where I watched, it seemed to me like he was unsure at first, but Pozniak insisted. Remember, Pozniak was a big shot in Grabiny. Still is, from what I hear.

I hated to interrupt again, but I had to ask: "You knew it was Pozniak?"

"I knew the bastard the second I saw him get off the wagon and pull you out. Everyone knows him. That he's an informer."

Turns out, people in the area really did know what my Papa and I did not. The Home Army veteran Tadeusz Kozera, who, as I mentioned earlier, still lives in Grabiny, was not reluctant to shed some light on the man who captured my father and me.

"Everybody around here knew about Pozniak in those days," he said. "He was mayor back then. A Nazi informer if there ever was one.

Turned a great many people over to the Nazis. But that's not all. During the war, UNRRA [the United Nations Relief and Rehabilitation Administration] sent food and clothing to local governments in Poland. Pozniak was supposed to distribute it in this area, but he never did. Many of the goods ended up in the hands of the Germans.

"A Home Army group came in from Tarnów on bicycles trying to kill him, but Nazis were stationed all around his house. The partisans couldn't get to him. For a long time they searched for Pozniak, kept hoping to kill him, but they never succeeded. I don't remember if he stayed around here after the war or not. He's long dead now, I know. Long dead."

Back then, when Kopec told me he knew about Pozniak, all I could say was, "My father thought he was a friend."

Kopec snickered. "Friends, enemies . . . who can tell one from the other anymore?"

For a moment, Kopec seemed lost in thought. Then he said, "Anyway, apparently your father's *friend* was not convinced you was dead. Pozniak took that goddamn rifle and tried to jab the bayonet all the way through your father's dead body. His first blow must have struck the poor man's shoulder blade. There was the sound of metal on bone."

Kopec stopped again, looked to see my reaction. "You sure you want to hear this?"

I nodded. I wanted it to feed my rage, my need for revenge.

"Well, next thing I hear an angry growl, like a dog would make. Even from where I'm hiding, I can see Pozniak's teeth clenched in rage. He pulls out the bayonet and stabs again at your father's body, using all his strength to push the bloodied steel blade in deep, to make sure it hits your body underneath. Something must have led him to believe he done the job, but lucky for you, he only nicked your back, yes? Well, again he pulls out the blade, and for a moment it looks to me like he might kick your father's body out of the way to make sure you're good and dead. But he calmly hands back the rifle to the Kraut, nods to Grychowski, and together the two Nazi-loving bastards get back on their wagon and ride off.

"Me, I thought you was dead just like Pozniak must have thought you was dead. I was still hanging around near the station after the place cleared out, and that's when I saw you crawling over to the bushes. Well, you know the rest."

"There are many things I do not know," I said, coaxing out a meek, shaky voice.

"Like what, kid?"

"Well, for one thing, what about the son-of-a-bitch who shot us?"

"The Kraut? He got back on the eastbound train just as it pulled

117

out of the station. Probably went on to the next stop in Dębica in search of a beer, or a cigarette, or a few more victims. Who the hell knows?"

"No, I mean why didn't he kill me like he killed my father? At such close range, how could he only hit me in the hip?"

"You said it yourself, kid. You heard him say he didn't want to shoot neither of you. But he couldn't back down, not in front of Pozniak. Sounds to me like he took a chance and shot you exactly where he wanted. So you might not have to die, at least by his hand. That would be my guess, but like I said, who the hell really knows?"

That possibility had not occurred to me, but it did make sense. It is what I choose to believe today. Not that I feel an ounce of compassion for that Nazi bastard, even if he did have a twinge of conscience and made a conscious decision to spare my life. Still, it helps me to understand. And that is what I have struggled with all my life. To understand. To comprehend that which defies all reason.

My mind was racing with questions for Kopec. "Another thing. How you happened to be at the station, hiding. Seeing everything that happened. Saving me. What were you doing, what brought you there in the first place?"

I could see his eyes grow steely. I thought his gaze would bore right through me, like Pozniak tried to do with the bayonet.

"I was there, and lucky for you I was. That's all you need to know."

And that is all I did know. At least, until I came across more specific documentation by that Polish historian Jozef Garas. It has helped me to speculate on how fate must have brought Kopec and me together on that tragic day.

Garas writes:

> In the middle of December 1942, the squad [led by Stach and Kruk] was planning to unscrew the rail between Dębica and Tarnów and to ditch a train. The German patrolmen stopped them, and they engaged in a fight for twenty minutes. The partisans didn't have enough ammunition, and they had to flee . . .
>
> In their first [successful] action [January 1943] these same partisans took over the train station in Czarna. They destroyed all the rail equipment, phone wires, and the transport documentation. Traffic was stopped for approximately ten hours. (363)

Understand, there are only two stations between Dębica and Tarnów: Grabiny and Czarna. They are just a few miles apart. After the first failed attempt in that immediate area, according to Garas, the partisans regrouped in January and struck at Czarna. This took place just days before my father and I were shot in Grabiny.

I would be willing to bet Kopec was involved in the Czarna destruction—either as an active participant or as a broker of weapons and explosives. And while I will never know with absolute certainty what brought Kopec to Grabiny days later, think about it: He admitted he was hiding, watching the goings-on at the station for hours. To me that says he was on a similar mission, that he and his cohorts, flushed with success, were planning to disrupt train traffic at Grabiny just as they had done days earlier in Czarna. It was my luck that he happened to be there that day.

But Kopec himself offered me no explanations for any of his actions, including his presence that day in Grabiny, other than to tell me time and again that he was motivated by money, by his need to provide for his large family. What he did when I was not around was none of my business. This he told me more times than I cared to count. I resigned myself eventually to the fact that I would never get a straight answer from him. But that would not stop me from asking again in the future.

"Now it's time for you to take that package of mine into Grabiny," Kopec said, dismissing all further questions. He got up and stretched his legs. "Take it right past Pozniak's German-ass-kissing nose."

I obliged. And by now I knew the routine.

The package was compact enough to fit inside my lightweight jacket and could contain almost anything—small arms, explosives, forged papers—who was to say? Kopec had made all the arrangements, and now the drop was up to me. One reason I went instead of him was because I stood a far better chance of getting in and out without arousing suspicion from the Germans or the villagers themselves. I would once again play the part of an innocent Polish child. It had always worked before.

"The reason I've never been killed," I once said facetiously to Kopec, "is because the bullets all go over my head."

I approached Grabiny well after dark, wary of Pozniak and Grychowski, who would kill me in an instant if they knew they had not succeeded the first time. I did not know it then, but Grychowski was no longer a problem. He had been killed some weeks earlier. Trampled by his own bull in the field behind his house.

Tentatively I approached the designated house for my drop. It was distinguished from others by a brightly painted outdoor oven just off to the side, between the house and a small field.

I knocked on the door, tapping out a simple code. The door opened, first just a little, then wider. I was quickly ushered inside.

Taking stock of the dimly lit room, I found it to be much like my own home had been, only this house had one main room and what I assumed were two small bedrooms closed off behind doors in the back.

The man who let me in was thin and balding, forty to forty-five years old, with narrow, penetrating eyes. He introduced himself as Wladyslaw, using his first name only. Then he summoned his wife to put out something for me to eat. I could hear two small children playing in one of the rooms. They were probably no older than seven or eight, to judge from their squeaky, muffled voices.

Two other men were in the main room, both younger than the man of the house, but I was not introduced to them. Nor could I tell anything about them from the way they were dressed; in those times, everyone's clothing was ragged, whether you hid in the forest or lived in a home.

The man's wife was more than generous with the food she put before me—warm cabbage soup, a heel of sour rye bread, a few *pierogi*—and I ate ravenously. Who knew when I might ever enjoy a home-cooked meal again, let alone one served comfortably indoors?

While I ate, the three men went into the unoccupied bedroom with the package I had delivered. From the looks on their faces when they returned, they were not disappointed.

Wladyslaw had just started to ask me how I came to be in the service of Jan Kopec when we were startled by a loud banging on the front door.

In German: "Gestapo. Open at once!"

The first thing that occurred to me was that I had walked into a trap. Could Kopec have been wrong about this family? I jumped up from the table and looked to my host, who signaled with his eyes and a nod of his head for me to go into the unoccupied bedroom. Seeing no other alternative, I ran into the bedroom and closed the door. From inside the room I could hear the outside door open. I tried to catch the words of the German officer, who was inquiring about a *Juden kind*, a Jewish child who had been seen in the area.

Damn!

I guessed I had been spotted and turned in by a bounty hunter. Was it someone who knew me? I wondered (since my own former home was in the next village up the road). Or did some Nazi lover become suspicious because I was a stranger? Probably the latter, I decided, because anyone who knew me would know I was no child. Not that either possibility mattered much. Those days being known or unknown could be equally dangerous.

"I assure you, the only children here are my own two—" Wladyslaw's words were cut off before he could finish.

"Be silent. I will search," came the reply. I was elated—he said "I," not "we." The German was alone. I gripped my Luger tightly, standing behind the bedroom door. I would not push my luck by hiding again under a bed. Only one of us would leave the room alive, I vowed.

I heard the door to the other bedroom open. The chatter of the two children stopped abruptly.

"Oh, you have the same color hair as my little boy," came the muffled voice of the officer.

I heard a light thud as the door closed. The sound of heavy leather boots approaching. The door to my room, slowly opening . . .

The Gestapo officer easily stood six-foot-three, a full fifteen inches taller than me. I suppose that since he probably thought he was searching for a child, he did not take precautions he might otherwise have exercised. All I know is he walked directly ahead toward the bed, apparently believing the room to be empty. As I moved quickly from behind the door, he spun around.

He had less than a second to register his surprise.

I raised my pistol, firing almost point blank into the startled face of the officer. A hole opened up between his eyes.

My enemy was dead before he hit the ground.

As the three men came running in, I calmly tucked my Luger back into my waistband, stepping over the big man who lay prone on the floor, his third eye oozing. I saw the children's mother run into the next room to quiet their cries.

"Go," Wladyslaw said to me, pushing a small package into my hand to take back to Kopec. "We'll handle things here."

I assumed my host and unidentified friends were partisans or at least supporters, so I knew they would take the Gestapo uniform and weapon before disposing of the body. My shot to the German's head was quite intentional.

I had been well treated by this gentile family during my very brief visit; I hoped they would not be linked to my actions.

Sadly, such was not the case.

I never learned the fate of the two silent men, but I later found out that Wladyslaw, along with his wife and two children, were picked up shortly after the incident and taken from their home, over sobs of anguish and cries of protestation.

They never returned.

10

The Train

AUTUMN IS ARGUABLY the most splendid time of year in southern Poland, but I saw only shades of gray and black each time I peered out from one of Kopec's hiding places. The leaves had turned stunning shades of yellow and orange and crimson, but to me that only meant they'd soon wither and drop, creating a crunching, crumbling sound underfoot, making movement easier to detect by the enemy.

We were on the move again, heading back toward Podkarpacie. From little hints that Kopec was dropping, I had an inkling something big was going to take place in a week or so. Well and good. Better to die over "something big" than in mundane robberies of people who usually had little more than we did.

Along the way we stopped near a small town and spent the night just on its outskirts. Kopec left me in a bunker that was nestled in a cluster of bushes while he took care of some business that he was not about to share with me.

Hours later, though, Kopec reappeared and nudged me out of a light sleep. He held out a small caliber pistol—I thought it was a toy, it was so tiny. It fit compactly in my equally small hand.

"Before we move on," he told me, "I got a quick assignment for you while we're here—just a warm-up, mind you, for bigger things. For this one you'll get to spend some time outdoors in broad daylight."

I listened eagerly while I examined the pistol.

"There's a big farm close by, under German operation. All you got to do is lay on the ground and pretend to sleep next to the front gate."

"That's all?"

"Well, almost. The area is patrolled by a single Kraut. I'll get you to the gate while he's making his rounds in another area. When he comes around and gets close enough to you . . . you know what to do. With that gun he's not likely to see it until it's too late."

"But if he does?"

Kopec shrugged. "That's a risk I'll have to take."

You'll have to take? I almost snickered out loud. You'll *have to take?*

But a few hours later, I was in place, waiting for the guard to discover me. I did not have to wait more than ten minutes.

" '*Rauf!* Get up, kid, get up!" the soldier shouted as he came up to me. I stirred, acting as if I had been startled out of a deep sleep. The soldier poked at me with the barrel of his rifle, thankfully not shooting first and asking questions later, as I would have done had our situations been reversed.

"Why the hell are you sleeping here, anyway?" growled the guard.

The German got his answer quickly, in the form of a soft popping sound, as I fired a bullet into my enemy's brain.

I am sorry to admit this, but getting back at the Germans was becoming exhilarating to me. Me, the quiet young man from Straszęcin, a boy who once could not stomach to watch even the ritual slaughtering of a cow.

As instructed, I ran from the fence at full speed, away from the farm and into the woods. Not once did I look back. There would be others waiting to take the uniform and weapon off the corpse. My part of the job was over.

Tomorrow, I knew, would be another shooting, or another robbery, or maybe just another day in solitude while Kopec was off somewhere doing whatever it was he did.

As it turned out, the following days offered none of the above.

"I got all the details on an interesting assignment for us—actually, for you," Kopec told me that night as we continued our southward trek. "It will be much more dangerous than what you done so far, and you'll be on your own the whole time."

"What will you have me do?" I asked, eager to prove myself again.

"First, we go deep into Podkarpacie, lay low a couple days. Other people who are part of this, they been working already. Soon, my young friend, if everything goes like it's planned to, you're going to take a little trip by rail."

Kopec had been looking away as he spoke, his mind somewhere else, but now he stared directly at me, as if he were waiting to see the reaction his next words would bring.

"You, lucky bastard, are going to see first hand what it's like to be taken to one of them death camps."

We were back in Kopec's underground chamber, the one near Jasło that he had fashioned into the bluffs along the Wisłoka. It was early in November, nearly a week since we had left the village where I took out the German guard. I could tell by my benefactor's frequent disappearances for hours at a time—and by his uncharacteristic excitement and energy—that whatever was going on, it was not routine.

In the predawn hours, as a fierce wind heralded an early start to what would be another miserable winter, Kopec returned to our burrow after an absence of nearly five hours. He cradled a boxlike object in his hands, but he did not let me hold it at first. It was only after I had been thoroughly briefed on the mission that he handed over the instrument—for that's what it was—so I could examine it closely. He lit a lamp to give me some light.

It was a camera, unlike any I had ever seen. Nearly square, about a foot and a half in each direction. It had been specially outfitted with some sort of sheathing to eliminate glares and flashes and to silence the mechanical tripping of its shutter.

I had never used any camera before, so I could not tell how this one differed from an ordinary photographic device. But I obediently practiced looking through the viewfinder and snapped make-believe photos from a crouched position on the ground, even though no film had been loaded.

I wondered if the camera had been Soviet-made, like so many of our weapons, for there was nothing to suggest its point of origin. I did know it had to be extremely valuable, worth considerably more than my own life to Kopec's contacts, perhaps to Kopec as well. It was of little consolation to me when I considered that if I did not come back—a very real possibility—neither would the camera.

After he extinguished the lantern, Kopec sat with me in the dark, going over the details again.

"This will be damn difficult, I promise you. You'll be hidden on a train filled with prisoners—hundreds, maybe more than a thousand of them. *Your* people. Jews."

I thought of my own mother and sister. "I understand."

"There's nothing you can do for them. Nothing nobody can do. Except, for now, find out where they're going, document what happens when they get there. My contacts know the Krauts are closing up a camp that's near here, but where the prisoners are being taken—that's the question, now, yes? Nobody seems to know nothing, not even the Resistance."

It was the first time I had heard him use the *R* word.

"That information is worth a lot of money to Kr—" He caught himself. "To my friends. When you bring back the camera—"

"How do you know the train will be coming back this way?" I interrupted.

"When you bring back the camera," Kopec began again, ignoring my question, "my contacts will develop the film, and then they'll know where the hell the train took them Jews. And they will pay me handsomely for that information."

I could almost hear him smirking.

"Handsomely," he said again.

"Can I ask who came up with this plan? Why they think it can work?"

"No, kid, you can't ask me shit. I keep these things from you for your own goddamn good. Like I been telling you, they can't torture nothing out of you if you don't know nothing."

No, you keep these things from me for your own good, I realized. It's true, I cannot give up names or information that I do not know, but they can still torture me. Of course, I have your name, Jan Kopec, not that I would give it willingly, but I am sure they have ways. Then, if they don't kill me first, you will. Perhaps you will anyway, when the war is over. If we live that long.

These thoughts bubbled away in my mind, churned in my stomach. *Fear is good,* Kopec had told me on our first night together. Very well then. I would have no shortage of it on this mission.

It was not a fear of dying that troubled me; I am quite certain of that. On this occasion, if I am to be honest, it was something I found even more alarming: the fear of disappointing Kopec. Of letting him down if I did not succeed.

It was about 3 A.M. when we set out, the master and his willing apprentice. We followed a route that paralleled the road heading east from Jasło. Several hours remained until sunrise, but we had a lot of ground to cover in order to intercept the train before it began filling with its human cargo.

We moved quickly and silently in the dark. Kopec led the way. I clutched the camera case tightly by my side. It had been loaded with film earlier in the evening—either by Kopec or by one of his unseen co-conspirators—and that camera, along with my ever-present Luger, did not leave my side.

After a time we came upon railroad tracks and followed them for a short distance. Twenty minutes later we saw what we had come for: a locomotive and at least twenty-four boxcars, standing silent and empty, portentously awaiting their fragile payload. Part of the train was dimly illuminated by the flickering light of a small fire on the track, built to keep the switch from freezing.

The train stood on a siding just outside Moderowka station, named for the small, nearby village situated between Jasło and Krosno. I understood I would be on the train for a day or two, depending on its destination. Then, if the train did indeed turn around as anticipated, and if I survived, it would take the same time to return.

Well, I would not be *on* the train, exactly.

I would be *under* it. The plan was as daring as it was dangerous.

"The prisoners will be arriving soon," Kopec said at last. "Any final questions?"

I wanted to ask, *If it were not for the camera, would you even care if I made it back?* But I just shook my head.

It was almost as if he were reading my mind. "Remember, when the train gets to where it's going, if you see dogs patrolling near the tracks, if you sense you're in danger of being discovered, don't be no hero. Stay in your hiding place. You're no good to me if you're dead, understand?"

I nodded. It was not quite the answer I wanted, but it would have to do.

"All right, then. From here on, you're on your own, kid."

He handed me a small package. In it were a few pieces of dark bread, a container of water, and a chunk of *słonina*—the back fat of a pig, salted and cut about three inches thick. Staples of war.

"This food will have to last you for two days, maybe more. Eat it slowly."

I nodded, clutching the camera case in one hand, my food rations in the other. But I had to set down the food for a moment, because Kopec was handing me one more thing: the handsome watch he had been wearing.

"Take this too. If you time how long it takes the train to get where it's going, you'll know when to jump off on the way back."

I looked at the shiny watch in awe. "This is your good watch."

"Bring it back with the camera," Kopec muttered, "and maybe I'll let you keep it when I steal a better one."

Which, I realized, was probably the closest to a considerate gesture I had ever received from him.

I smiled nervously. With my hands full I turned toward the death transport that waited for me, ponderous and still, like a malevolent apparition in the smoky shadows ahead.

As I tentatively approached the train, I took solace in noting it appeared unguarded, at least for the moment. I counted the number of boxcars, then made my way to the center car, crouching low along the ground.

Moving beside the tracks, I stopped directly ahead of the car's rear wheels and peered underneath.

There it was, more ingenious than I had even imagined.

The concealed wooden enclosure was about five feet long, three feet wide, and just over a foot deep. Affixed securely underneath the boxcar and nestled between the front and rear axles, it was only big enough to hold a slight, five-foot boy and a square camera case. Even if you checked underneath the car, it would appear to be merely an extension of the boxcar itself, nothing out of the ordinary—except you wouldn't find anything like it under any other car.

Crawling beneath the boxcar, I quickly found the side panel that served as the door. It was the long plank closest to me. It obediently swung open, allowing me to pull myself inside. I put the camera case by my feet and placed my meager food rations to one side. Then I swung the panel closed and fastened the inside latch that held it securely in place.

Only a small amount of outside air came into my hiding place. It wafted up through the narrow openings between the slats that made up the platform on which I lay. This would have to be my source of light as well. I shuddered to think I would be spending at least two days cramped in this coffinlike structure. If I were discovered, I knew, it would indeed be my last resting place.

Pushing these thoughts out of my mind, I began to marvel at the chutzpah of the men who had built and attached this clever compartment. Someone had obviously affixed this enclosure during the night as the train sat on the side rails awaiting its early morning departure. Of course, the Germans had better things to do than to guard an empty train, but still, my little hideaway could not have been attached without some degree of noise.

And then it struck me. No full-sized man could fit between the axles of this boxcar. The enclosure had been custom-built for me, for my small frame. I wondered if the partisans had come to Kopec with this particular idea, or if it had been conceived the other way around.

The other way around, I decided. The partisans were anxious to document the destination of the train, so Kopec eagerly volunteered me, maybe even cooked up the plan as well. I could practically hear the conversations that must have taken place, perhaps first in that village where we stopped, certainly over the preceding days here in Podkarpacie.

Kopec: "You need to know where the prisoners are headed; I can find out. Can you get me a camera with a silent shutter?"

Partisan: "It can be arranged. But how does the camera record where the train is going?"

Kopec: "It's taken to wherever the prisoners are unloaded. The film is exposed. The camera comes back on the return trip. What the hell did you think?"

Partisan: "And you propose to stow away on a trainload of victims being taken to their death? Then turn around and come back, just like that?"

Kopec: "Not *me*, hell no. It would turn to shit if I tried it. You too. Where would we even hide? But I can give you the kid who's with me. What the hell, he might just pull it off. And if he doesn't, well, that's life. Anyway, here's the plan . . . and whether or not the kid makes it back with the camera, here's what it will cost you . . ."

It was slow in coming to me, but finally I understood how Kopec was operating. How many times had he told me that what he did, he did for the money? That made him a—what was the word?—mercenary? Yes, I had read about such people. Soldiers for hire. And I thought then, as I still do to this day, *What a perfect wartime vocation for a lifelong criminal!*

There was not much around for Kopec to steal on his own by this time, but there were other ways to get goods and money if you understood basic supply and demand. Kopec could supply an intimate knowledge of weapons and how to use them, along with a proficiency in guerilla tactics honed through years of banditry and life on the run. In addition, he could supply something nobody else had: a small, unflinching, and highly trained accomplice named Moniek Goldner. With plans that I could uniquely execute, Kopec could command handsome payments. Supporting a wife and eight children, after all, was no small responsibility, especially for a man on the run all his life.

I realized that since none of the payment went to me, Kopec was using me for financial gain, of course. But you know what? I did not care in the least. I had no use for money myself—as a Jew in hiding, where could I spend it? If I were to stay alive a little longer, Kopec was my only ticket. He had molded me into an ideal co-conspirator, and by doing this, he had given me the tools I would need to survive. In fact, to my way of thinking, I was using Kopec in return. And if this mission he was sending me on, or the next, should cause my death— I was certain it was just a matter of time, remember—well, what better way to die than by fighting to live?

Moniek Goldner and Jan Kopec: a match made in hell, it occurred to me. *Had to be, for clearly there was no heaven.*

Suddenly the car above me shuddered and creaked, interrupting my introspection with the abruptness of a pin piercing a balloon. The heavy wheels to my front and back began to grind on the track as the train slowly lumbered forward, switching over from the side rails to the main line, heading toward the loading platform at the station up ahead.

There it stopped. And sat. And waited. A long, mechanical beast, yearning to be fed.

I began to hear the chaos of at least a thousand plaintive voices in the distance, along with the trudging of twice that many feet. Coming closer now, growing louder. Making their way to Moderowka station, to the beast, to whatever horrible fate might be waiting for them at the end of the line.

They were coming from Szebnie, a concentration camp that covered a twenty-six-acre site less than two miles away from the station.

It was a camp that had started, from what I've read, with a purely military purpose. About a dozen barracks had been built as a staging point for the German army. Apparently Szebnie had been expanded into a full-fledged concentration camp back in March 1943, barely eight months before I came to my hiding place under the train.

Throughout that summer prisoners were taken to Szebnie from all over the district. Then, in October, came the remaining Jews from Bochnia, Rzeszów, Przemyśl, and Tarnów—the last four surviving ghettos in occupied Poland. But the camp had become grossly overcrowded. It appeared the Germans felt it was time to thin the herd, the first step in liquidating the camp altogether.

So while Kopec and I made our way to the Moderowka station from our hideout just to the west, several thousand Jews must have been standing for hours during roll call in the camp's muddy *Appel-platz,* waiting to learn their fate. The vast majority of them were ultimately gathered together and marched the two miles to the station. Final destination: uncertain.

If I had not already been tightly enclosed in my compartment under the train, I might have seen the first rays of daylight carve away great sections of night along the eastern horizon. I might have looked in despair as a thousand or more shattered and broken Jews, flanked by a few Germans and a greater number of vicious Ukrainian guards, were forced toward the station with heavy machine guns and blazing flood-lights mounted on trucks. And I might have witnessed the consternation and anguish on their faces as all the men, women, and children were ordered to remove most of their remaining clothing and stand nearly naked in night air cold enough to see one's breath.

129

As it was, I saw it all, but not with my eyes. I saw it through the sounds that enabled me to visualize what was happening only too well. It made me sick with realization: Sędziszów, all over again.

I picked out disconsolate cries of the suffering humanity lined up not three feet away from where I lay hidden, their pleadings in Yiddish interrupted by staccato bursts of German and Ukrainian, spat out like bullets from a machine gun.

I could even hear their clothing drop to the ground, where it was snapped up by guards as soon as the train had been loaded. "Why let the soldiers at the other end get it all?" said a guard who was close enough for me to hear. "Besides, it's easier to take clothing from the living than off the dead," chortled another.

I felt dizzy. Disconnected.

Soon the doors above me slid open, and I knew each car was being filled far beyond capacity for any living cargo. There was the shuffling of bare feet, along with shouts in German ordering them to press tighter as more Jews were packed in. I could picture the scene above me as clearly as if I were up there with them. I was certain that anyone who died on the journey would not even have space to fall down.

I heard the cry of a toddler. And more: the frightened, questioning voice of a teenage girl. An older woman, sobbing. The comforting voice of a man, trying to calm a female relative. A woman, screaming for a child who had been taken from her. The crush of human bodies, surely beyond shame in their nakedness. Cries of being cold, of not being able to endure the suffering, of prayer, of pain.

And from somewhere off to the side, more sounds of laughter, and, in a language I wished I could not understand, the word *Judenfrei*. A soldier was cheering that soon there would be no more Jews in the village. Except for a small number of Jews remaining in Szebnie for what would be only a week or so longer, this train was taking away the last of them.

Up and down the line of cars, the doors were sliding shut, then being fastened in place with wire. I heard the sound of the steam whistle. A lurch, followed by a metallic groan, heralded the train's departure from the station. It gradually picked up speed, although with its heavy load of nearly two thousand Jews, based on the twenty or so cars the engine was pulling, it never reached a top speed of more than, say, thirty or thirty-five miles per hour. Still, as I lay in my hidden box, inches above the rail bed, the miles of track seemed to fly by beneath me.

I cried silent tears.

I cried for my mother and father and sister. I cried for my grandparents and for the shopkeeper Moishe. I cried for the babies I had seen murdered in Sędziszów, for the babies and children who lay dead throughout my homeland, and I cried for the families and shreds of families I heard in the car above me, many still trying to convince themselves that the worst they would endure might be some long hours at hard labor.

But I did not shed a single tear for myself. Perhaps there would be time for that later.

In the Rzeszów Yizkor book—one of many Eastern European memorial publications that trace the Jewish history of a town—there is a short memoir titled "I Shall Not Die but Shall Live," by survivor Lotka Goldberg. As one of the Jews in Szebnie who was *not* evacuated that day, she describes the march to the very death train under which I was hiding:

> As we stood in line on 3rd November 1943 as usual, we were suddenly surrounded by Ukrainian sentries with heavy machine guns. . . . We were several thousand ragged and broken Jews. . . . Jews mostly young and strong were put into the railway trucks at the Moderowka railway station. . . . Next day we found heaps of clothes, boots and pots. . . . These were the only belongings that a camp prisoner had. We recognized the possessions of our closest companions who had been expelled the night before. We were sure that they had all been killed. A long time later we learnt that they had been taken out in nothing but their shirts, so that they should be unable to escape . . . in Szebnie there remained a group of Jews numbering 500. Our fate was sealed. (104)

Less than half an hour after leaving the station, the train slowed considerably for a short time. It was full daylight by then, and I could see through the narrow slots at the bottom of my platform that we were passing a number of railroad crossings, one right after another. This meant we were going through a fairly large town, and I guessed it was Jasło. So we were heading west. In my head I pictured the towns along the way: Gorlice would be next, then Nowy Sącz, unless the train changed direction.

After a time I allowed myself to consume a small portion of the bread and water. As for the *słonina*, it was never to my liking, this disgusting pig's fat, but I knew it would help curb my hunger, so I ate some of that too. As I chewed, the forbidden pork by-product triggered another flashback, a poignant memory of my sister that made me forget, for the moment, the discomfort of my small chamber and the danger that lay ahead.

131

We are out by the cowshed, Gita and I, whispering and giggling about nothing and everything, about all manner of interests and concerns that affect all twelve-year-olds. We are supposed to be going over our lessons—that is what Mama thinks we are doing—but the afternoon is balmy and the waning hours of sunlight after school are too inviting to tempt either of us to bury our noses in school books. Still, I am making a noble effort.

"I'm supposed to help you with your arithmetic," I am saying to my sister. I am not a great student, not by a long shot, but I do have a head for numbers and for taking things apart and putting them together again.

"In a couple months you'll be going to school in Dębica, and I'll have to study alone anyway," Gita says. "I may as well get used to not having your help."

"I'll be home on weekends. Besides, I'm here now. You don't want to do your numbers, that's all."

"I just don't see why a girl needs to know them anyway. I have more important things to fill my head with than silly old numbers."

"Like boys, I suppose," I chide. "That's all you've thought about ever since you started growing those . . . things." I glance down to her bosom.

Gita gives me a light slap on the shoulder. "Is not." Then a barb occurs to her, for she says, "At least I'm growing."

I ignore the comment. My size has never really bothered me. I had decided earlier that if I was not going to be as tall as the other boys, at least I would be tougher. Stronger. No one would bully me and get away with it. And for the most part I succeeded.

"Boys," I continue, baiting my sister. "You know it and I know it."

But she is as stubborn as I am. "Like you don't think about girls. Tell me your biggest desire isn't to kiss a girl."

I become serious, all of a sudden, and look directly at her. This is all before I begin to take notice of Anna Reguła next door, mind you.

"To be perfectly truthful, Gita, that's not the most important thing to me. There's nobody in this stupid village I would even want to kiss. My dream has nothing to do with girls."

"What is it then?"

"I'm not telling you."

Gita shrieks in exasperation. "But Moishe, we tell each other everything!"

"You'll just laugh."

"I won't. I promise. Come on, what is it? You have to tell me."

I am silent for a moment, then I say, softly, "I'm dying to taste *traif.* Pork, especially."

Gita starts to laugh, then quickly catches herself. "Why?" she asks.

"Because I've never tasted it. Because I'm not supposed to. I don't know. I just wonder what it tastes like. I dream about it."

"Then you must try it," Gita says. Her mind, I can see, is working furiously.

"If Mama and Papa find out, they'll never talk to me again."

"They won't find out. It will be our secret."

"No," I say. "I just dream about it, but I can't really do it."

"I dare you."

"What?"

"I said I dare you. You can't back out of a dare. I'll think you're a coward."

I just stare at my twin. How did our silly conversation ever get to this point?

But Gita has already worked it out. "Here's what we'll do. After school tomorrow we'll stop by K——'s store. He sells pork sausage. Kielbasa. You'll buy a piece, you'll eat it, then you'll know what *traif* tastes like and you can concentrate on girls."

Now I am grinning. "Okay, I'll do it. But you won't tell?"

"Dear brother, have I ever told any of your secrets?"

The next afternoon I walk into the gentile-owned store with Gita right behind me. I have never shopped for *traif* before, and I discover the kielbasas are all uncooked.

"What do you sell that I can eat on the way home?" I ask.

"Hungry, yes?" responds K——'s wife, a buxom woman with the reputation around town of being something of a tart.

"Do you have any, uh, cooked pork sausage?" I ask nervously. Gita can barely control herself. She's biting her lip in the doorway of the store.

Mrs. K—— takes down a hard salami. "There's this," she tells me. "How much you want?"

I count out three zlotys on the counter. It's the only money I have. "Whatever this will buy," I say.

The woman slices off a chunk of sausage about three inches long. "Don't spoil your dinner now," she calls after me in a motherly fashion. But I have already run outside the door, holding my forbidden treasure.

Gita watches anxiously as I bite off a small piece. I chew carefully, slowly, waiting for lightning to strike me dead.

"Well . . . ?" she asks, impatient for a response.

I say nothing. I take another bite, nearly choking on the texture. Finally I exclaim, "It tastes wonderful. Want to try some?" I hold it out to her.

"I dared *you*, remember? I don't want to be turned into a pillar of salt or anything!"

I take a third bite, then I throw the rest of the sausage into a field as we pass by. "Actually," I admit, "it tasted a lot better in my imagination."

We giggle all the way home, and when Mama asks us what's so funny, we both say "nothing" and give each other knowing looks, then break out again in gales of laughter.

I was jolted back to the here and now when the train ground to a stop at some switch point in order to let another train pass. At the time I assumed the right-of-way went to a train carrying more important cargo, like German officers or artillery bound for the eastern front. I've since heard that, to the contrary, Hitler insisted that highest priority be given to trains carrying Jews to his death camps. We Jews were a greater enemy to the Third Reich, it seems, than the Russians.

As the hours marched on, I was quite certain that several people above me had already died during the journey; I could hear the wailing cries of loved ones, make out words from the Kaddish—the prayer for the dead—intoned in anguish. It occurred to me that they probably had less space up there than I did in my tight little compartment and most likely even less fresh air.

Were it not for the black oiled-cloth jacket Kopec had insisted I wear, by afternoon my shirt would have been soaked through with urine that was leaking into my compartment from the car overhead. As it was, my pants were eventually soiled with my own wastes. But the situation was undoubtedly multiplied a hundredfold up above, so I felt no shame or pity on my own behalf.

At some point it seemed that the train had changed direction, switching onto a track possibly headed toward the north. But I could not be sure, and besides, my pictures would tell the story, I figured, if I ever found my way back.

It had to be well past four in the afternoon, for the light that filtered into my hiding space was dimming. I ate a bit more food and closed my eyes, trying to tune out the doleful sounds coming from above. The clackety-clack of the wheels, just inches away, became my lullaby. I must have dozed a little, because when I opened my eyes everything was black as coal.

More than sixteen hours after we left Moderowka station, the train slowed to a final stop. The doomed cargo—of which I counted myself a likely member—had come at last to our destination, whatever it was.

I reached for the camera and held it tightly, trying to summon the courage to open my cramped compartment. In a moment, I knew, I would have to step outside, alone and vulnerable, into the terrifying night.

"Out! Out!" they were screaming in German. Not one utterance, or two, but dozens of shouting voices, hateful and shrill, followed by the heavy scrape of the doors above, sliding open, ready to disgorge the wretched shipment.

I breathed deeply, unlatched my own narrow door, and dropped to the rail bed beneath the boxcar. I made sure to cradle the camera case against my body. My muscles ached from being cramped for so long in such a tiny space, but I tried to ignore the discomfort. I lay still for a few moments, waiting for my eyes to adjust to the light, which penetrated even here, under the train. No wonder. The unloading platform was lit as brightly as day by wide, sweeping floodlights.

Good for the photographs, I thought. *Not so good for the photographer.*

From my unusual vantage point, I saw that the train was being unloaded on the right side, where a wide ramp led down from the tracks to a broad staging area. My line of sight was limited to a sea of thin, naked legs, shaking uncontrollably as the prisoners were forcefully pulled and pushed out of the boxcar above me.

Looking to the left side of the train, I saw no signs of any activity. I could not be sure of this, however, for it was mostly in shadow. I removed the camera from its case, putting the empty case back into the compartment I had just vacated. Then, by both rolling and crawling, I maneuvered myself out from underneath the train on the side of the tracks away from the ramp, where it appeared to be deserted.

My legs wobbled uncontrollably as I tried to stand. Gripping the camera tightly, I steadied himself by extending my other hand to the side of the boxcar. Using it for support, I pulled myself up. I moved my legs up and down for nearly a minute, walking in place, until the circulation was restored. I shivered, from both tension and the cold night air. My damp, stinking clothing did little to protect me from either.

Crouching low, I made my way through the shadows, up the line of cars toward the locomotive in front. I had to be particularly cautious as I skulked between the cars, but still I moved quickly, for it appeared that the entire train would be unloaded in less than twenty minutes.

What I witnessed, in my brief glimpses as I passed between the boxcars, was complete and utter pandemonium. The camp SS detail was removing the new arrivals from the train, it seemed to me, as if they were trying to break some speed record. Prisoners in grimy striped uniforms were also on hand, unloading dead bodies—of which there seemed to be a fair number—and helping to clear the ramp quickly. Men and women were being separated, and the new arrivals were being forced into position on the platform in long lines, perhaps five abreast. People who stepped out of line to call to loved ones or seek one final embrace were beaten back with heavy blows. I saw several who were shot. Some kind of grim selection process would take place next, I knew, from what I had experienced in Sędziszów more than two years earlier. At any rate, I soon lost track of the emaciated new arrivals. I had a job to do.

After several more minutes I reached the locomotive. I looked up, saw no one inside. Perhaps the engineer had climbed down when we arrived to take a break or simply to distance himself from the screams and cries that had been reverberating from the train in a steady, dirgelike wail.

I came around to the front of the locomotive—cautiously, cautiously—to where I had a relatively clear line of sight. At that moment my heightened anxiety was displaced by disappointment, for in terms of identifying landmarks, there was not much to see. Behind the unloading ramp and platform stood an ordinary-looking train station. On the road leading up to the station, trucks were lined up . . . for what? To transport the prisoners somewhere? If so, did that mean the camp was some distance away?

But I had no time for questions. I raised the camera to my eye and realized my hands were shaking. Beads of sweat trickled down my neck, pooling beneath my already sodden collar.

Crouching in the shadows, facing directly toward the bright artificial light, I held my breath as I released the shutter in a steady rhythm that nearly matched the beating of my own heart.

I snapped away at the station, at a guard tower, at barbed wire fences, at the lineup of trucks, at low-lying buildings I could just make out in the distance. And then I turned the camera toward the human drama that played out a short distance away: the throngs of trembling people, stripped to their soiled underwear, wailing in the cold night air as they awaited the unknown.

While I was busy with my camera, thankfully, the guards and ss men remained preoccupied with their prisoners. They were well away from where I stood. Behind me all remained dark and quiet. The bullets that I half expected would cut me down at any moment never came.

Minutes later I was finished. I had shot all the film.

I crept back along the dark side of the train, moving toward the middle boxcar. On the other side the unloading of prisoners neared completion. The sound of my pulsing blood pounded in my ears as I reached my compartment between the axles. I crawled back inside,

then put the camera in its case, and gently closed the door closed behind me.

Although I was undoubtedly still in danger, a feeling of relief swept
over me. I had taken sensitive photographs practically right in front
of the Nazi beasts! I lay back and waited impatiently as a short while
later the locomotive was moved to the opposite end of the train. An
hour passed, maybe more, and then I felt the train lurch in the opposite
direction. It moved slowly for a while, then stopped. I panicked for a
moment as I heard footsteps and noises nearby, and then suddenly I
was getting wet. They were hosing down the empty cars. I will not
begin to try to describe the smell as bodily wastes seeped past and
over me, forced from above by the pressure of the spray. I lay there,
trying to think of something else, anything to distract myself, but every
place my thoughts turned to was just as foul.

A short while later the train jerked to a start once more, and this
time it began its return journey, moving faster since it now carried
nothing more than me and the specters of those who had died along
the way.

While I could not be sure the train would cover exactly the same
route or even head back in the same general direction, I had little choice
in the matter. So after about sixteen hours into my return, as the train
came to one of its many erratic stops, I opened the latch to my compartment and looked out.

In the dim light of evening I could see there was a steep ravine
alongside the tracks. Taking yet another chance, I grabbed the camera
case and jumped out, hoping the train would not start up as I crossed
between the heavy metal wheels.

Thankfully, it did not. I was able to get away by rolling down the
steep embankment, coming to a stop in the shelter of the ravine.

It took me the better part of that night to figure out where I was
and which direction I needed to go. As it turned out, I was west of
Jasło, only several hours' walk from the bluffs along the Wisłoka where
Kopec was hiding. Waiting.

I proceeded slowly. No use in getting killed now, I figured, after
everything I had just done. So it was not until early the following morning that I located the mound that marked Kopec's hideaway.

"K," I called in a loud whisper—I had been ordered never to use
the man's full name—"it's me, Moniek. I'm back!"

I could hear the wood strips being removed from below. Then the
mat above began to move. Out popped Kopec's head, like a curious
gopher, and when he saw both me and the camera, he beamed—just
for a moment. Then his smile vanished, and he arched one eyebrow
as he regarded my weary face.

"What took you so damn long?" he asked.

I was not sure if he was joking or not.

And while I had no idea where I had been, or what exactly I had taken pictures *of*, when the film was ultimately developed, it must have pinpointed the destination of Szebnie's Jews as clearly as if I had drawn a road map. Because that particular station with its immense ramp— the *"Alte Judenrampe,"* I know now—was the end of the line for prisoners going to the Auschwitz complex. It was situated midway between Auschwitz I and Birkenau, no more than a mile from each. At that time Birkenau was just months away from getting its own spur line to conveniently deposit prisoners right at the door of its insatiable gas chambers. I wonder if I would have had any chance whatsoever of returning alive had I been under a train that unloaded inside the camp gates.

What my clandestine photos could not reveal, of course, was the fate of the two thousand Jews who rode in the boxcars above me. I learned that grim information at the same time I discovered where I had been. It seems two-thirds of the prisoners on my train, maybe more, had been sent to their deaths before I had even made it halfway back to Kopec's lair.

May they rest in peace.

After that mission I felt more self-assured, more alive than at any time since my father's murder. I had proven my courage and ability (or dumb luck, if I were to be honest) not only to Kopec and his co-conspirators but, more importantly, to myself.

And while Kopec never verbally expressed any sense of relief upon my return, I do not think it an overstatement to say that he was elated to see me. For one fleeting moment, in fact, I had the distinct feeling he might hug me.

For this is what I believe to this day: In his rational mind, Kopec may have told himself it was really the camera's return that mattered; the exposed film, after all, was his money ticket on this operation. But I am convinced—I truly want to believe this—that something deeper in him stirred when he saw me standing there. Something human and caring.

He must have found it to be a strange and uncomfortable feeling indeed.

11

Let My People Go

ANOTHER BITTERLY COLD winter—my third consecutive winter without a home, a family, a roof over my head. Jan Kopec was my only family now. The irony never ceased to amaze me: betrayed by one Pole, saved by another. As if that could even things out.

We sought shelter during the cold winter days just as we had the winter before, by hiding out in Kopec's remarkable string of lairs as well as in numerous haylofts. But one night, when the temperature threatened to dip well below zero, we came upon a modest house outside a tiny village east of Dębica. The smoke rising from the chimney told us there was plenty of wood in the stove. In spite of the warm clothing we had stolen over the previous months, the cold air had permeated right down to our skin. We could not walk another step.

So we knocked loudly on the door, and when it was opened by a slightly built man in his fifties, we walked in right past him, guns drawn. Kopec did all the talking.

"We're spending the night here, and you're going to give us whatever food you got. Don't give us no trouble, and who knows? Maybe I'll pay you something for your hospitality."

Kopec, it seems, had collected a generous sum for my photographs. So lately he had been leaving a few small coins to help compensate for the food and clothing we demanded at gunpoint. *Was that not robbery just the same?* I reflected.

"If, during the night, you try to leave, I will kill you before you get out the door. And if tomorrow, or any other time, you tell anyone we was here, I'll come back and kill you. Got that?"

Although Kopec was well known throughout the area for his prewar exploits, if the peasant recognized him, he didn't show it. Rather, he looked incredulously at Kopec, then at me and back again. And all he could say in response to his armed houseguests was, "You'll *pay* me?"

He lived alone, which made it easier for Kopec and me to keep an eye on him. The man, however, made no effort to be uncooperative. As promised, when we left the warmth of the cottage at nightfall, Kopec left behind a few zlotys.

A few days later, after a short respite from the sub-zero cold, the temperatures dropped once more. This time Kopec and I were near Bobrowa, and again we commandeered a house for the day, giving the same warning to the young owner and his wife. It looked to me like there was a glimmer of recognition in the couple's eyes when they stared at Kopec, though the daylight hours passed without incident.

During this period Kopec continued to meet with his wife from time to time in the forests. The Germans were preoccupied with their eastern front, and it seemed that their concern for Kopec's whereabouts had diminished. Stefania would arrive by various circuitous routes and often in the company of one of their children. As always she brought her husband news of the war along with home-cooked food. What she took in return depended on Kopec's payments from the underground and on whether he had found anything worth stealing since her last visit.

One day in February Kopec came back from one of their clandestine meetings bubbling over with news. A rumor was circulating that top-secret military experiments were going on in the village of Ociecka near the Pustków death camp. Its success, the gossip went, could quite possibly garner a major victory for Germany.

In point of fact, we knew that the rumor was not unfounded, for we had seen unusual streaks of fire against the dark sky on several occasions while hiding in the Blizna Forest in that very area. It was only after the war that I learned we had witnessed test firings of the secret v-2 rocket, which was being assembled just a few miles away from where we hid.

Stefania's other news—of more immediate concern to Kopec—was that the owner of the home we invaded in Bobrowa had indeed run to the authorities, exclaiming that the infamous Jan Kopec, along with a young accomplice, had held them hostage for a day. As a result, we feared the Germans might redouble their search efforts.

Armed with this knowledge, we left that night and headed once more to the southwest, wandering through the bleak forests that followed the banks of the Wisłoka River. This time we did not stop at daybreak to hide. There were patrols everywhere, and Kopec's winter hiding places in this area were limited. Better to push on and put some distance behind us, Kopec insisted.

When we reached a wooded spot that was perhaps one or two miles outside of Dębica, we stopped abruptly. We could hear sounds coming from somewhere up ahead of us.

We crept closer. The sounds grew louder, more distinct: the guttural barking of German commands. One voice? No, two—dominating a chorus of more subdued voices, joining together in dissonant cries. And one sound more: shovels, digging into the frozen earth.

We had stumbled upon a massacre about to happen.

Kopec and I watched from a distance, hidden within a protective stand of pines, as two German soldiers oversaw about fifty or sixty people, mostly men but also a few women, who were being forced to dig what was obviously intended to be their mass grave. A few had been given shovels for the task. The others were forced to claw at the unyielding ground with their bare hands. The soldiers were part of the Einsatzgruppen, the special death squads, which had been operating in the area with increased frequency.

At first I thought the victims might be prisoners from Pustków, but upon closer look, I saw they were dressed in decrepit civilian clothing, not prison uniforms. And each was marked for extinction, wearing the familiar yellow armband with the Star of David. While one soldier trained his rifle on the group, the other shoved, kicked, and beat the weak and sickly laggards, who apparently were not digging fast enough.

The news through Kopec's grapevine was that the nearby Dębica ghetto had been liquidated the previous April, with nearly all its inhabitants sent to the Belzec concentration camp or shot in the surrounding forests. Could these poor souls have survived until now as part of a labor force in Dębica? Or were they remnants of a Jewish partisan group or groups, just recently captured? To me, of course, it did not matter who they were or how they got there. There were just two soldiers, and two of us. I was sure we could rely on the element of surprise to take them.

"We got to do something," I whispered to Kopec.

The stocky Pole shrugged. He wasn't being paid to stick his neck out here, I guess. "Why should we help them?" he said. "They're just Jews; they're going to die anyway."

Just Jews. The remark hit me like a fist, and I'm sure my face must have reddened. "I'm a Jew too," I reminded the man who had saved my life. "Am I just as insignificant?"

141

Kopec was silent for a moment, then said, "It's too late for them and too goddamn risky for us."

But I ignored his response and informed him, "What we do is wait until the prisoners finish digging the pit. Then we wait a little longer while the Krauts line them up alongside the hole. When the bastards are ready to fire, they will be concentrating on their victims, right? That's when we make our move. You go for the son-of-a-bitch on the left. I'll kill the other one."

Kopec looked at me in amazement and growled, "You telling *me* what to do, kid? Nobody tells me what to do. Why, I was stealing guns while you was still shitting in your pants!"

I stood my ground. For once I did not give a damn how he might react to my insolence. I knew what had to be done. "This time, yes, I'm telling *you*. If you don't want to help me, fine, you can go. I'll take my chances and try to kill both Krauts myself."

Kopec, to my surprise, started to grin. My guess is he had to admit to himself that I was right. Maybe he also thought better of his remark about their being "just Jews." I will never know.

Still grinning, he said, "You know, kid, our time together has made you tough as nails. And me, I must be getting soft."

As I think about it now, he was correct in that perception. Many traits of the uncaring, violence-addicted bandit and the sensitive, thoughtful young boy he saved had rubbed off on one another. Neither one of us would ever be the same again.

But I did not dwell on any such observation at that moment. I just looked to Kopec and waited for his answer.

"You win this one," he finally said. "We'll do it like you want."

We did.

We sat tight for another half-hour, until the German guards apparently decided the pit was deep enough. That's when they shouted for the group to stand in front of the wide-open hole. Having no other choice, the captives complied, no doubt too weak and tired to run, too broken in mind and spirit to care. My heart ached as I watched them line up together for what they must have believed would be their last breaths.

Just as the two soldiers raised their weapons to begin firing, so did Kopec and I. We each took careful aim.

I fired first. "My" soldier took a German-made bullet right through his icy heart.

A split second later Kopec squeezed the trigger of his gun. The other bastard dropped like a turd into a bucket.

I have to admit I took particular satisfaction from my marksmanship; for once I was able to cut down the enemy and see firsthand the lives that would be spared a while longer as a result.

But Kopec and I did not stick around long enough to see the expression on the prisoners' faces. We made fast tracks out of the area, not stopping until we were well to the south of Pilzno, some twenty miles away.

I will never know how many Jews we truly saved that day. In the grim retrospection of history, I have to assume that many were eventually recaptured and killed. But possibly one or two or more of them made it through the war, perhaps found their way to Israel or Canada or Australia or America. I can only hope.

Still, my feeling of jubilation at freeing that doomed group did not last long. For a short while later I despaired to learn that the Germans exacted strong reprisals for the death of the two soldiers at our hands. From what Kopec and I heard, more than fifty Polish citizens were rounded up at random in nearby Dębica and shot.

It was actually small-scale punishment, as reprisals often went. For any German officer with the rank of captain or higher had the authority to shoot between fifty and one hundred Poles on the spot for every German who was killed. From what I understood, that number frequently went significantly higher.

At the time I gave a lot of thought to the consequence of my actions. At first I wondered, *If I save the life of fifty or sixty Jews by killing two Germans, and as a result an equal number of innocent people are shot in retribution, did I do the right thing?* Then I asked myself, *Suppose a* hundred *innocent people are shot in return—or two* hundred*—what then?*

Part of me wanted to argue, *What's the difference how many? I'm trading Jewish lives for Polish lives.* But then I had to acknowledge that sort of thinking—diminishing the worth of one group of people below that of another—would make me no better than the Nazis.

Ultimately I convinced myself that to do nothing was never an option. Innocent people were already dying every second of every day, for being in the wrong place at the wrong time, for being a Jew, for hiding a Jew, for being a Gypsy, or a cripple, or an intellectual, for looking the wrong way, for being on the wrong side of the street, for being on the street at all, or for just *being.*

Still, while I felt no remorse for stealing food and clothes or for harming those who would kill me, given half a chance, I was feeling guilty—and still feel some culpability today—for the deaths of innocent people at the hands of the Nazis in reprisal for my actions. But what else could I do? Did I have any choice?

As it was, my need for vengeance was growing along with my confidence, and with every new mission came the opportunity, directly or indirectly, to do to my enemies what they had done to me. The only consequence that mattered, I was convinced, was to hurt as many adversaries as possible and stay alive another day to do it again. There was no point in thinking further ahead than that.

Around the same time that Kopec and I stumbled upon the *Einsatzgruppen*, another incident occurred involving the death of one particular Jewish man in a nearby village. Kopec had been told by his contacts that this man had been turned over to the Germans by people in the village, who got new suits of clothes as a reward. Now, I did not know this murdered man myself, but he was apparently very well liked by the partisans, even by Kopec. More important, he was probably one of the group, for I was aware that there were indeed a number of Jews among the partisans in the forests.

"We're going to teach that village a lesson," Kopec told me. "How would you like to come along?"

He did not have to ask me twice. That evening the two of us joined up with several others—people I had never seen before—and we crept into the village carrying matches and rags soaked in brandy or vodka. They became excellent torches. Working in unison, we set fire to a number of houses, then fled into the nearby woods. I looked back for a moment to gaze at our handiwork, the flames leaping skyward, jumping from house to house, the entire village ablaze. We were long gone, of course, by the time the townspeople put out the fires and glumly surveyed the damage, but I would have loved to have seen the expressions on their faces when they discovered the sign we left behind.

"Next time, leave your Jews and dogs alone," it read.

As for Kopec, he redeemed himself in my eyes, making up for his "just Jews" comment days earlier. For I had to admit he was certainly adamant about taking revenge on the Poles who turned in this Jewish man, whoever he was. And to the best of my knowledge, no money changed hands either. What Kopec did in this instance, he did for free.

By this time I found every act of retaliation was sweet. So when we finally returned to our home area along the Wisłoka, I was almost giddy when Kopec announced that our first destination would be Bobrowa. This is the town, remember, where weeks earlier a boastful homeowner ran to the Germans with the news that Kopec and an accomplice had robbed him.

Shortly after nightfall when everything was quiet, we approached that house. Kopec took a stick grenade from the pouch inside his jacket, removed the cap, pulled the cord, and lobbed it through the window.

"I always do what I say," he muttered to no one in particular as the house trembled and partially collapsed in an explosion of flame.

Something gelled at that moment in the back of my mind, a hunger that had been there all along but had just now been given light and substance, like an image materializing on a sheet of photosensitive paper. From that moment on, it would remain in my consciousness, fixed indelibly, until my own plans for retribution could be put into action.

12

Shoeshine Boy

IN THE WANING MONTHS of the German occupation, the three most challenging missions Kopec sent me on all involved the destruction of trains.

The first of these adventures was another operation created specifically for me, as it required someone who could pass as a youngster. Once it was underway, I knew I would be completely on my own, just as when I hid under the boxcar. Only this was not simply a feat of reconnaissance. This required my close personal contact with German officers.

Chutzpah, in other words.

I wondered, as I had during my previous assignment, who had dreamed up this dangerous plan. In this case I am guessing it was not Kopec, but rather a member of Kruk's underground unit—or the leader himself—who conceived the operation. Or maybe the two of them came up with it together.

For from what I have heard, the People's Guard—by this time calling themselves the People's Army—had been gaining strength ever since the Red Army's offensive in late 1943. In southeastern Poland the People's Army was particularly active east of Dębica, and most aggressive from there southward, in and around the forests of Podkarpacie, where Kopec and I had been spending increased amounts of time.

By the spring of 1944 it was apparent that the Russians were dropping weapons by parachute in record numbers. Russian paratroops were also landing with supplies and large sums of money. What's more, People's Army units in our area had amassed additional money by pulling off daring robberies at mills, large farms, breweries, and other businesses under German management. So there were certainly ample funds to pay the rapacious Kopec for my services. After my success with their camera, I imagine they were eager to use me again.

This time, the mission involved a worn-looking rectangular shoeshine box, carefully crafted by unknown hands. At least unknown to me. Kopec brought it one evening to our newest hiding place back in the forests near Blizna.

"You understand this will make crawling under a train with a camera seem easy?" Kopec asked me after he thoroughly explained the operation.

I nodded.

"And that even if you pull this off, you might not get away in time, or if you get away in time, the jump alone could kill you . . ."

"Look, I could get killed doing nothing too. At least this way I have the chance to take some Nazis with me."

Kopec was silent for a moment, perhaps wondering if my bravado was genuine. I can assure you it was.

"It's all right to be afraid, you know," he said. "Like I told you before, you can use it to your advantage."

I looked up at Kopec, fixed my gaze directly on his face, and said, "Why should I be afraid? You're going to drill me and work with me over and over again until I know the mission backward and forward. You're not going to send me on a mission you don't think I have any chance of returning from."

It was a question disguised as a statement, but I have no idea which way Kopec took it, for he made no comment in return. To be frank, I really was not sure whether he wanted to keep me around or not. Why else would he send me on a mission this dangerous? I was filled with doubts; one moment I was sure he cared for me, the next, not quite convinced. And I wondered, if he were to be completely forthright, did he really know the answer himself?

Two days later the time and place of the operation had been decided. Kopec, I guess, felt I was as ready as I ever would be.

The day was pleasant and mild—it was spring once more—as I walked alone toward the train station in the town of Ropczyce, along the main Kraków-Lwów railway line, which transversed my dangerous little part of the world.

Ropczyce had been selected, if I remember correctly, because it had more activity than the small villages in the area along the railroad line, places like Czarna and Grabiny. Yet its station was not as busy as the one in Dębica, a couple miles to the west. The word was out that the Russians were moving closer every day. This meant the eastbound trains were filled with German soldiers being sent to shore up their lines along the pressing Russian / Ukrainian front.

It had rained the night before—a fresh, cleansing rain. In its aftermath small, muddy puddles collected in the rutted ground beneath my feet. Good. That meant dirty boots, an affront to German neatness and order.

I crept into the city limits of Ropczyce during the night and narrowly missed being caught in the headlights of a speeding car carrying ss officers. Kopec had decided I would leave my Luger and grenades behind. I felt naked, unprotected without my weapons. But I would play my role like a consummate actor, carrying only the little shoeshine box, with nothing hidden beneath my clothing to give me away if I were patted down or searched.

It was strangely exhilarating, walking through a town in broad daylight, wanting to be noticed rather than hiding in the shadows. Not many people were milling about, and those who did pass me, it seemed, were anxious to get on with their business and draw as little attention to themselves as possible.

"Shine, mister?" I would say whenever a man passed by.

To my great relief, I either got no answer or just a grunt in return. Street urchins were common enough in all the towns and villages. I appeared to be just one more impoverished little ragamuffin, too young for the work force, simply trying to pick up a zloty here or there. I would act disappointed each time I got no response, for that was the part I had to play.

It was still early when I arrived at the station. Two hours remained until the eastbound transport was expected to come through. I looked around for likely candidates, found none. *That's all right,* I thought. *There's time.*

As I sat down on the nearly deserted platform to wait, my stomach began to growl. How long had it been since I had eaten something? Too long, and it could be quite a while longer still. Before being rescued by Kopec, I had known them well, these pangs of hunger, but I would never get used to the feeling. I would never forget what it was like to go for days at a time with an empty stomach.

After about twenty minutes my patience was rewarded with the sound of a conversation in German coming from the side of the station house, around the corner from where I sat. Listening in, I picked up enough to confirm that the speakers were waiting to board the train. They grumbled about being reassigned to the front. I hoped they were officers, not rank-and-file soldiers; it might mean there were others of similar rank on the train.

I picked up my shoeshine box and began walking toward the sound

148

of the voices, swallowing my hatred like bitter medicine. My heart fluttered a bit. I guess I felt a little nervous after all. Kopec would approve.

Turning the corner, I pretended to act pleasantly surprised at stumbling upon the two men—they were ss—who were leaning against the station wall, each smoking a cigarette. They were in their mid-thirties, blond and fit, except for one who coughed nearly every time he inhaled. At first they seemed to take little notice of me, dismissing me as they might a cockroach.

"Shine, sirs?" I asked in Polish, pointing down at their long brown boots.

"These miserable kids are a bigger nuisance than the fucking rats," said the first officer to his partner, his muttered German punctuated at the end with a loud cough.

"Gutsy little guy, you have to give him that," came the other's response, letting me know this man would be the easier mark.

"Shine, sirs?" I repeated again, this time in German, with the same sweet innocence and look of expectation.

The two officers glanced at each other with a look of surprise.

"What's your name and where are you from?" asked the one officer. The other merely glared suspiciously, until he was seized with another coughing fit.

I knew my life depended on my response to such questions. My mind raced with possibilities as to how I could answer. The scent of wildflowers growing near the pavement, an unexpected fragrance in an ugly time and place, filled my senses, momentarily distracting me.

Focus now, I told myself. *Channel your fear.*

"I'm called Jan," I said, taking Kopec's first name. It was common enough for a Pole. "I live on a farm in Chechly, not far from here. My father is very ill. We have no money."

The lies came smoothly. Still, I was apprehensive as to where this questioning might lead.

The surly officer frowned and said, "I'll bet this kid is a Jew."

I nearly wet myself.

"He must be a Jew," the bastard repeated. "He speaks German."

I was ready for that remark. I just hoped the answer I used once before—that while my father was a Pole, my mother was German—would work as easily as it had then.

After dispensing this lie, I mustered my best anti-Semitic smirk and added, "If I were a Jew, I would not be here, would I? This town is *Judenfrei,* like all the others. And better for it, my father says."

I prayed they would not pull down my pants to check for further evidence.

149

The friendlier officer seemed convinced, but I could not read the other officer. He just grunted. He took one last drag on his cigarette and then tossed it on the ground inches away from my shoeshine box. I held my breath. I watched the stub continue to burn, a bit of ash catching a breeze and floating gently upward. The heel of the Nazi's boot came down hard on the butt, crushing it into the ground.

"This brat's a pest," he said, not softening his position on the matter.

His friend chuckled and said something to the effect of "Weren't you ever a kid yourself, Franz?"

I decided it was time to try again. "Can I shine your boots now?" This time I specifically addressed the kinder officer.

"I have no occupation currency," he said to me. "But I can give you some candy." I nodded agreeably, amazed that he was amenable to payment of any kind. I opened my box, took out a brush, a cloth, and some thick brown polish.

Ten minutes later I looked into the polished leather, which captured, then reflected, the bright midmorning sunlight. In the mirror of that Nazi boot I saw the face of a boy who belonged to a group that numbered in the millions, all destined for extinction at the hands of men like the one who stood before me.

"There you are, sir," I said respectfully, as I swallowed my loathing and looked up at the face of my enemy. "I trust they are polished to your satisfaction."

"You're too damned generous with this scum," grumbled the coughing officer when his companion handed me several pieces of candy. Then he looked down at me.

"For all that candy, you need to do *two* pairs of boots. Lucky for you, mine are also dirty."

I wanted to kill him on the spot, kill them both. But I politely said, "I will be happy to clean them, sir. They will shine like your friend's."

They did.

I thanked the two officers profusely for allowing me the honor of shining their boots. Then, in what I hoped would appear to be an afterthought, I turned to the more agreeable officer and asked, "Could I shine the other boots as well?"

"Other boots?"

"On the train. Could I come on the train as far as the next stop and offer to shine the boots of the other soldiers?"

"There are enough Polacks on the train already," the surly officer snapped, referring to the laborers who serviced the cars and their passengers.

"What's the harm in one more?" the first officer responded. "The

150

kid's got determination, you got to admit. Willing to walk back home from the next miserable stop if it means a couple coins or a few scraps of food."

I knew the next town on the line was Sędziszów. I had walked back from there before, more than once, right out from under the German sons-of-bitches. I could do it again.

"You can board with us, but then you're on your own," the German said to me. "Keep in mind not everyone's easygoing like me."

That, I knew, was an understatement. Still, it had been relatively simple to get invited onto the train. The real dangers lay ahead.

An hour later the train chugged into the station. An old locomotive, spewing smoke and coal dust, pulled about a dozen passenger carriages that had been conscripted to carry German soldiers to the eastern front. Three other soldiers boarded along with the two who sported newly shined boots. One very anxious Jewish shoeshine boy followed close behind.

You're not going to send me on a mission you don't think I have much chance of returning from. My words echoed in my head. And I thought of Kopec. The look on his face, before he turned away in silence.

The car stank of stale smoke and the sweat of two dozen soldiers. Most of them regarded me with disinterest. Some dozed; others looked out the smeared gray windows with bored expressions. I studied their faces. I delighted in knowing they were doomed men, every one. Most undoubtedly had families waiting for their safe return. If all went well, I would take them from their families just as my family had been taken from me.

"Shine, sir?" I asked, starting with a middle-aged officer in the car's front seat.

"Go ahead. The kid does a good job," said the German who invited me on board, having taken the seat directly behind.

I opened my box and went to work on the officer's boots.

By the time the train left Ropczyce behind and began to pick up speed, I had worked my way several rows back. Nobody questioned my presence on the train or asked to see papers. I was a nuisance to some, an industrious urchin to others, but I am sure it never occurred to any of them, at least not until it was too late, that inside my box, underneath the rags and brushes and polish, a false bottom held a powerful explosive and a crude but effective timer. I would have no more than fifteen seconds to escape once I flipped the lever concealed beneath the tin of black polish that remained unused among the sea of brown boots.

I had been on the train for maybe fifteen minutes, packed in with some of Hitler's finest. The train was eating up track at full steam,

151

racing through forest on its way to Sędziszów, Rzeszów, and the front beyond.

It was time.

I had just started to shine my third pair of boots when I looked up at the pleasant-faced soldier who sat before me. The man was young, perhaps only a few years older than me.

Grabbing my stomach, I grimaced as if in pain, although I did not know if the soldier noticed me at first.

"It's my stomach," I said, in response to no question that had been asked.

"What?"

"My stomach."

"What about it?"

"Hurts. I have to shit."

"You can't finish my boots first?"

"I'll shit right here if I don't get to the bathroom fast."

"Christ. Go, then."

"I'll be right back," I lied, picking up the brown polish and putting it back in the box, back on top of the black polish. My index finger deftly found the lever beneath them both.

Pushing the shoeshine box under the forward seat and out of the way, I got up and walked, doubled over as if I had cramps, as fast as possible toward the tiny bathroom at the rear of the carriage. It was unoccupied, but that made no difference. I walked right past it and grabbed the handle on the heavy door just beyond.

It was stuck!

The train shot forward through the forested countryside, a speeding time bomb, while I struggled to implement my only chance to escape. Straining, I tried again. And again.

Clackety-clack, clackety-clack, clackety-clack sang the train. Eight seconds, nine seconds, ten seconds . . .

My adrenaline surging, I gave one more, desperate try. This time the door gave way and slid back with a loud slam. Out of the corner of my eye I saw several heads turn, including, I think, that of the ss officer who had brought me on board. He must have wondered where the hell I was going. I could only hope that in the seconds remaining, he would begin to put things together, would start to understand his complicity in what was happening, just a beat or two before he was consumed by eternal darkness.

Clean, fresh air filled my lungs. The rushing wind almost knocked me over as I stood in the open space between the carriage I had just left and the one behind it.

The train was flying past a forest in a dizzying fury. Oblique rays of sunlight flickered between the trees as if someone was sending a message in code. The sound of metal on metal pounded in my ears, momentarily eclipsing the sound of my own heartbeat.

Without any further conscious thought, I jumped from the speeding train, hitting the embankment and rolling away from the tracks. I felt sharp pain in my ribs and shoulder—worse pain, possibly, than when Pozniak had me shot and bayoneted two years earlier—but I continued to roll over and over until I came to an abrupt stop against the trunk of a tree.

It was at this moment the explosion blew apart the carriage I had just left. Projectiles of mangled steel splayed in all directions, destroying the carriages both immediately in front and behind, overturning several of the remaining cars and scattering others off the track.

I pulled myself deeper into the forest, wincing in pain from my bruised ribs and torn shoulder. I could have easily been killed three times over: by the force of the nearby explosion, or the carnage of flying glass and metal, or in my jump from the speeding train. This time I did not even try to understand why, once more, I had escaped with my life.

In the distance behind me, I thought I heard screams in German. Soldiers undoubtedly trying to help their injured comrades.

Only the officers in the carriage I boarded would have understood the source of the explosion, and I was quite sure they were all dead. So without any sense of fear, I walked away, slowly and with great discomfort, eventually finding my way back to Kopec and the now familiar Blizna Forest.

And as I walked, I thought back to my audacious act. In spite of the pain, I actually began to smile. For I imagined the two ss officers whom I had approached at the station. I saw them clearly now, rotting in hell, holding their shiny brown boots high in the air, away from the flames that licked cruelly at their pale-fleshed heels. But it was not long at all before the flames grew higher and hotter, consuming their legs, their torsos, and finally all of them, their boots being the very last to burn.

Somehow Kopec had heard about the success of my mission even before I came stumbling in, bruised and weary, to our hiding place in the forest. It was nearly evening; the sky was shimmering with an opalescent glow.

But until he saw me, Kopec could not have known how I had fared—whether I survived the explosion, or the jump, or the ensuing search that must have invariably followed. Did he care? Certainly, Kopec would be amply remunerated by Kruk whether I returned or not. Still . . .

Still, the sight of me—bruised but very much alive—nearly brought tears, it seemed to me, to the irascible bandit's eyes. Like a proud papa he listened intently as I related my experiences at the station and on board the train.

"I prepared you well," Kopec declared when I had finished. "You done better than I ever expected." It was a rare compliment, self-serving though it may have been.

I allowed myself to smile. He could not have been sure I would survive the mission but seemed genuinely glad that I had. I still wondered if he was capable of turning on me some day, perhaps at the end of the war, but I had to acknowledge a strange affection for him. You get a strong feeling of security, for one thing, by staying with someone like Kopec who has eluded capture himself for more than two decades. But during my transition from quiet little boy to criminal's accomplice, I saw something in my benefactor that most others, I am sure, did not see: under the man's ruthless, often violent exterior, there beat a heart that could be kind and compassionate. Really!

The two of us sat together in silence for a time. But my mind quickly turned to the most vexing of my many unanswered questions. This seemed to be as good a time as any to probe more deeply.

"That day you found me at the Grabiny train station . . ." My voice trailed into a tiny squeak, waiting to see if Kopec would cut me off.

"What about it?"

"Why did you put your own life at risk to save me? Why didn't you just leave me there?"

Kopec looked down, saying nothing. He picked up a branch that had been lying nearby and began to poke at the ground with no apparent sense of purpose. The air was unusually still, almost stifling. I waited patiently.

Finally he responded a little, though his words were measured.

"I won't deny that you been convenient in helping me make some money off this miserable, goddamn war. I suppose I guessed how useful you might be almost from the first moment I saw you lying there under . . . well, you know."

Then he grinned and held out a handful of zlotys—the down payment, perhaps, for my recent exploit. "I got to say, you been proving far more valuable than I ever thought."

I practically stopped breathing, not daring to interrupt, waiting for Kopec to continue.

"But I suppose that's not the only reason I picked you up back then. You was gushing blood, you would have died without no help, and at any rate, any Krauts who found you there would certainly have finished the job."

"Or Pozniak would have," I added.

"Or Pozniak, yes, or any other goddamn informer. Our villages crawl with them. Look, I been no saint. I done my own share of . . . hurting people. But no children. Never no children."

Kopec looked at the random pattern of holes he had made in the ground as if he had just become aware of them. He tossed the stick aside, sighed deeply.

"If I left you there to die, the fascist Kraut pricks and their informers would have won another little victory. They must never win. Not after all I seen . . ."

He stopped abruptly.

I looked at him impatiently. "Go on," I implored, anxious to hear more.

But the moment had passed. "It don't matter now. Nothing matters except getting through this war. And putting an end to the running, if I can ever do that. And seeing my family again, in my own home."

"Yes, you have a family to come home to." No rancor in my words. Just flat statement of fact.

Kopec stared at me. Was he reminded of the vast differences between us? He shrugged, "Who knows, kid, all sorts of things can happen between now and the end of the war, and after it's over too. A lot of people been looking a long time for me. But since you got nothing holding you here, you could get out of Poland, make a new life for yourself, some place where you don't have to hide no more."

In all innocence I asked, "Why should I hide in Poland after the war is over?"

Kopec looked surprised that he had to state the obvious. "You better be damned careful if you ever go back to Straszęcin or Grabiny or, what the hell, most anywhere else in this godforsaken country. There's people like Pozniak everywhere, people who want to finish up what Hitler started. The Russians, too, for all I know."

The thought had really not occurred to me before. The words sent a chill through my body.

Kopec still had not taken his eyes off me. "You asked me something not too long ago. You asked why you had the bad luck to be born a Jew. You remember what I answered you?"

"Something like, 'that's life, kid.'"

"Yeah, that's what I said, all right. It's how things are, and you can't do nothing about it. The war will end some day, and the Krauts will rot in hell." Kopec sighed and put one hand on my shoulder. "But you, my young friend, will always be a Jew."

155

13

Two Bridges

NOT TWO WEEKS WENT by before Kopec came to me with news of another major operation.

"We're going to hit a second train."

"We?"

He ignored this. "Preparations are going on right now. My contacts want to keep pressure on them Krauts, distract them from reaching the front."

The People's Army, it has been documented, called this the "battle of the rails": a concentrated program of sabotage geared to disorganize German troop movement to the eastern front. At least this is what most of the rank-and-file membership believed they were fighting for, even though it was not necessarily the sole objective of the group's high-ranking Communist leadership.

In the area where Kopec and I moved about and hid, commanders Stach and Kruk were being hunted relentlessly by the Germans—unsuccessfully, at this point, although many individual members of their units had been killed. As a result, it was apparent that direct military activity had been greatly curtailed for these leaders since February 1944.

But it was also clear that their restrained activity did not eliminate all opportunities to strike. The pipeline of money, weapons, and intelligence information had never been better. So I can only conclude that the idea of paying Kopec to risk his neck—and me along with him—must have appealed more than ever to these partisan leaders.

"This job involves the destruction of a bridge," Kopec told me.

My eyes, I am sure, opened wide. I asked which bridge he had in mind.

"It's near Tarnów, on the main Kraków-Rzeszów line. We can get there in less than a day."

I was astounded. That bridge was under heavy guard at all times. It seemed crazy to attempt sabotage there, and I told Kopec so.

He waved his arm in a dismissive gesture. "We can do anything we damn well choose to," he said with unmistakable arrogance.

The old doubts came back to me. Did he really mean, "There is no risk too great where your life is concerned?" Still, I could not help but grin. "Let me guess," I said. "My part of the operation depends on someone just my size."

"And your speed. You're going to set off the explosives."

He handed me a small wooden box, with two wires that hung loosely from one side and a lever that protruded from the opposite end.

"What do I do with this?"

Kopec pulled out a crumpled sheet of paper and penciled a diagram. "I'm going to show you exactly what to do and when to do it. Just hope everything else is in place. Less chances for things to go wrong."

I looked down at the wooden box in my hands. I should have died over and over again before now. I figured what's one more try at cheating death?

As with all the previous missions, this one was carefully explained to me and rehearsed, step by step.

Several evenings later, after dark, we approached within sight of the bridge from a point just a little downriver. I was not sure where exactly we were, but if Tarnów was as close-by as Kopec led me to believe, this would be the Biała River. The half-moon overhead, peeking in and out of impatient clouds, helped to reveal a bridge that differed from others I had seen.

Instead of the familiar trestle construction, this bridge was supported by a single arch, which spanned the river in a graceful curve. Left and right of center, rigid vertical spandrel columns rose to transfer the load of the rail bed to the arch itself, which was constructed of large stone blocks tightly and skillfully wedged together.

Augmenting the off-again-on-again moonlight were blazing searchlights, sweeping in sometimes overlapping circles across the surface of the river. As I had expected, the bridge was under guard. At least two soldiers, looking jaded and bored, paced near the bridge on each side of the river. We hoped there were no unseen backups. Kopec carried his submachine gun, alert to the possibility.

The two of us scrambled down the steep embankment some distance from the span, well out of sight of the guards. I wore a thin, dark covering over my jacket. It was made of some new kind of material I could not identify, intended to help camouflage me in the water.

We crouched at the river's edge. Kopec removed a watch from his pocket and synchronized it with another watch he wore on his wrist. Then he handed me the first watch and wished me good luck.

I nodded, then slipped silently into the icy water. With one hand I grasped the side of the riverbank as I moved along it toward the bridge. My other hand held the little wooden box just above the waterline.

Although it was a mild evening, the cold, murky river started my teeth chattering almost instantly. In the waist-high water, it took me about five minutes to get within range of the searchlights, where the real danger lay. I knew I would have to make faster time getting back and wondered how accurate the timer was in the box I carried. While I now trusted that Kopec would not knowingly send me on a suicide mission, I had no idea how expendable either of us was to the people behind this operation. To them, I assumed, Kopec was merely a supplier.

Next came the hard part. I had to wade over to the footing of the arch, which was about a hundred yards ahead. But if I got caught in the beams of the roving searchlights . . .

Each time a light swept over the water in my direction, I was instructed to quickly submerge myself, keeping only the wooden box and my fingertips—blackened with coal, as was my face—out of the water. The box would appear to be a piece of driftwood or discarded lumber. Or so I hoped.

The first time I dodged a searchlight by plunging under water, I began to sputter when I came up for air. I caught myself, fortunately, and stifled the sound. On eight or nine more occasions when I inched forward, I had to dive each time to hide from the lights. Once, two beams crisscrossed, one slightly behind the other, throwing off my timing. I came up too soon. I could only hope I was not spotted in the split second the light revealed a form behind the "driftwood."

A few minutes later—it seemed like hours to me—I reached the footing on the east side of the river. Protected from the searchlights by the shadow of the arch itself, I pulled myself and my precious box up onto the riverbank. I had grown numb to the cold after being in the water for a while, but now the brisk air slapped at my wet skin. I started to shake.

I checked my watch, amazed that it was still keeping time even though it had been in the water. It was unlike any watch I had ever seen, unlike any we had ever stolen. I was sure no ordinary Pole had a timepiece like it. *Where did it come from?* I wondered. It told me I had just a few minutes until I needed to pull the lever.

158

Meanwhile, I still had to find the wire leads. And hope that, in the time remaining, the guards remained up above by the tracks.

I closely examined the stone blocks that made up the support, nearly panicking at first, when no leads turned up. Then I saw them: two slender wires, inconspicuously pressed into the cracks between the stones, snaking down from somewhere high above.

I had to marvel at the accomplishment. Somehow, over the preceding few days, a small team of resistance fighters had wired and attached explosives to the spandrel columns or to the track itself without being detected. All for this moment. It seemed to be an impossible task, especially since the bridge was always under guard. Yet here they were, two wires, as promised, waiting for me to finish the job.

I set the box down firmly on the ground and connected its wires to the two leads, which dangled from above. My shaking had stopped now. I was all adrenaline and intensity, counting the seconds that remained until the exact moment when I would pull the lever.

Three . . . two . . . one . . .

I depressed the lever fully, setting the timer in motion. Slowly the lever began its upward return to its apogee, at which point it would close the circuit and detonate the explosive.

I did not plan to stick around and watch.

Jumping down into the water, I headed back along the riverbank, again dodging the searchlights. This time I did not have the box to worry about. I could propel myself forward by swimming under water, staying submerged for long periods until I could no longer hold my breath. It occurred to me how lucky it was that Papa had insisted I learn to swim as a youngster, spending many Sundays with me in the Wisłoka River until I no longer feared the water.

Papa, how I miss you! I thought, then pushed aside my yearning for what was long gone. I needed to concentrate on the dangerous task at hand.

With the searchlights far behind me, I stood in the waist-deep river and walked as quickly as I could, fighting the resistance of the water, which slowed me down. As I put distance between me and the bridge, I could hear the chug-chugging of a train from somewhere behind and up above, growing louder every second as it sped on its way toward a destination it would never reach . . .

Had I looked over my shoulder, I would have seen what Kopec, from his vantage point, clearly saw: a locomotive pulling nine or ten flatbed cars of tanks and heavy artillery, bound for the eastern front. I would have seen a section of the rail bed give way in a tremendous burst of light and fire, a span of the bridge collapsing along with it, as

the TNT detonated in high-speed waves just moments before the locomotive reached the opposite side. And where the bridge broke up like
a house of cards, I would have seen four cars of the train, along with
their machines of war, plunge into the river below.

I was scrambling up the embankment when the force of the explosion hit me, the blast echoing through the night. I never looked back.
I just kept running and running, my clothes wet and stinking, my lungs
gasping for air, until I caught up with Kopec, feeling far safer under
the protection of his submachine gun.

Together we ran a bit further. Then we collapsed for a brief moment
on the ground, almost giddy with the excitement of our success.

And while I was the one who had done the dirty work, Kopec had
a look of exhilaration on his face that seemed almost to say, *Hell, I'd
do this again even if I wasn't getting paid.*

In short order, we were given two more opportunities to do it again,
although the first of these operations was suddenly aborted. The Germans must have been tipped off, because at the last minute, guards
had our target completely surrounded. There was no way we could
get through. Kopec and I had to retreat immediately. The next day my
mentor disappeared for a few hours to get new instructions.

He returned filled with excitement. "We lay low for a few days;
then we hit a different bridge. This one you know. It's practically in
our backyard, over the Wisłoka."

I did know it well. It was a high trestle railroad bridge that spanned
the river between Grabiny and Dębica.

"And this time you'll be carrying the whole works, not just a deto-
nator. Also, you'll be doing a little climbing. You afraid of heights?"

"Do I have a choice?"

Kopec smiled.

After a few more days everything was ready. Kopec had left me
alone for almost a full night, returning with a fairly large box, which
he strapped to my back. It was a mine, he told me, which would be
detonated by the pressure of a train passing over it. I was surprised
at how heavy it was. I had never carried explosives before, at least not
as far as I knew.

The operation took place the following evening. Although the
bridge was less than an hour away from where we were hiding, we
started out early, skirting Grabiny as we made our way toward the
river. Kopec carried the mine himself on this part of the trek to conserve
my strength.

"No sense tiring you out before you even start, right?" he said
magnanimously.

160

I merely grunted in reply.

Once we were within sight of the bridge, Kopec put the mine on my back, strapping it in place over my shoulders and around my waist like a knapsack. I again wore the same black covering over my clothes, and once more my face and hands were darkened with coal.

The sky was cloudy, as I recall, which was just as well; it would help keep me hidden. As for Kopec, again he stayed safely behind, at the edge of the river, giving me a good-luck sign as I began walking toward the bridge that spanned the river high ahead of me.

This railroad bridge was supported by four tall iron trestles, spaced equal distances apart across the riverbed. The track above was brightly illuminated and patrolled by several soldiers on each side. A couple of searchlights were directed down into the river immediately below the bridge, but the trestles themselves remained in the dark.

Are the Germans stupid or just careless? I wondered. I decided I could stay on the riverbank without being seen. I crouched low as I walked, ready to drop to the ground and freeze if I thought anyone above noticed me, although by that point it would probably be too late.

There was just one moment, before I reached the wide base of the trestle closest to me, where I had to cross an area brightened by the peripheral gleam of a searchlight trained on the water. I paused at the dark edge of the area, waiting for the light to pass, knowing I would have only a second or two to scurry past before the light swung back. This I accomplished easily, and moments later I waded a few steps into the murky water directly under the bridge. When I reached the trestle, I began my careful ascent up the side.

Summoning all of my strength, I began to climb. To my amazement I found the experience exhilarating; the heavy bundle on my back seemed more a nuisance than an obstacle holding me back. Using the structural crosspieces as my ladder, I advanced higher up the trestle, hoping that the soldiers above were watching only the track and not the dark trestle itself.

At last I reached the top, where the trestle narrowed like an inverted *V*. My head could almost touch the horizontal crossbars that framed the rail bed above. The soldiers who guarded the bridge were close, standing where the bridge joined with the track leading from Grabiny. I had climbed up the opposite side of the trestle, quite out of sight, I was fairly certain. But any sound—a sneeze, a cough, a scrape of my boots—could carry on the gentle breezes and give me away.

If anything was likely to go wrong, a prime moment would be when I wedged my small body in between the structural crosspieces. Here at the top there were vertical spandrels, each bar spaced at two-foot intervals. I sat between two of them, on a wide horizontal bar,

161

legs dangling inside the hollow trestle. It was dark here, but enough light spilled over from the floods on the track above to allow me to work. The river was far below, but I knew not to look down.

I held on to a spandrel with one hand, while with the other I removed the straps that were fastened around my waist. This accomplished, I pulled my free right arm out from under the shoulder strap, so the mine hung loosely over my left shoulder. Then I changed hands, sliding the left strap off my shoulder until it rested securely in my hand. Now I had to move fast, as the box was heavy. I had to keep my balance as well.

The mine fit perfectly between the vertical support on my left and the one just to the left of that. Straddling the horizontal bar, I tied the loose straps of the mine to the iron supports, then reinforced it even more with rope I had brought. I was finally satisfied that the mine would not go anywhere until it blew into thousands of pieces.

What I had to do next was to affix a small metal device—a pressure plate of some sort, I assumed—beneath the rail bed above my head. I did this slowly and carefully, feeling for the track with my fingers while I practically held my breath. The thought occurred to me, *What if a train were to come right now?* I did not want to be inches below the rail bed, hanging onto an iron support, when it rumbled overhead. With the plate finally in place, all that remained was to connect its two descending wires to terminals in the mine itself.

By this time I was anxious to get away as quickly as possible. I scrambled down the trestle, feeling light as the wind, going as fast as I thought I could safely move. My hands were cut and bleeding as they grasped at the iron support bars, one after another, squeezing hard in case I lost a foothold and had to hang on to keep from dropping like a stone.

I wondered if Kopec was watching my descent. Was he nervous, or anxious, or concerned for me?

At last I reached the footing of the trestle and dropped into ankle-deep water. I paused only long enough to avoid the searchlight beam that brightened the riverbank as it passed. I ran and gulped in great breaths of air, not stooping low to the ground this time, just trying to put some distance between me and the bridge, the bridge that would blow to kingdom come if the mine worked as it should, and if I had fastened it correctly, and if the guards did not spot it first, if, if, if . . .

But by the time the next train crossed the bridge, Kopec and I were long gone. He had his money, and I had him by my side, and that is really all we cared to know.

The last time Kopec and I headed south to the forested areas of Podkarpacie—it had to be our seventh or eighth trip—we nearly did not get back alive.

We were on foot, both heavily armed. Even I was carrying a submachine gun this time in addition to my Luger and array of grenades. I imagine I looked very much like a smaller version of my able-bodied partner. We were coming into an area just north of Krosno where Kopec had planned to meet with one or another of his coconspirators.

It was then we heard the first bombs drop. Ahead, maybe a mile, a fireball rose in the air, coloring the night sky like blood on coal. We froze in our tracks, listening, listening . . .

"Dogs," I said with alarm. "I hear the barking of dogs."

Kopec heard it too. "Krauts, on the offensive. Maybe they're sweeping the forest. My contacts could be trapped, but we got to save our own necks."

"Do you think they were tipped off?"

"Who?"

"The Krauts—were they tipped off that resistance fighters were in the area?"

Kopec gave a snort. "What do *you* think? Maybe even by another partisan group."

"How can that be?" I asked. "I thought everyone in the underground is fighting against the Germans."

Kopec gave me a look of annoyance. "Don't kid yourself. One group would turn against an opposing group like *that*." He snapped his fingers. "You better understand, it's not about just getting the Krauts out now. It's about who's going to take over when they're gone. That's the trouble with this world, kid—everyone's choosing sides. Me, I look out for myself and to hell with everyone else."

In the distance we heard a new sound: heavy artillery rolling into place. Kopec tapped me on the shoulder.

"We're getting the hell out of here while we can."

We turned back to the north, taking our time once we were out of the area, for there was no reason to hurry to a destination that might be just as dangerous as the one we had left. We followed the Wisłoka, stopping only during daylight hours to lay low and rest in one of Kopec's hiding places.

"It's frightening to think," I observed as we lay in a camouflaged bunker, "that if we had gone south one day earlier, we could have been trapped with the others. Do you think they were killed?"

"Some of them maybe were. Hell, maybe they all were." He sighed audibly. "Like I told you once before, that's another reason I never joined, never became part of no unit. I don't believe for a minute there's safety in numbers. Completely the opposite—there's far more danger. You and me, we come and go, farts in the wind. You got any idea how many big goddamn partisan units have been wiped out by the Germans or the Ukrainians or the blue police or a rival partisan group?"

He was right. In the end a great many resistance fighters—particularly in my area, the broad Kraków district—were betrayed, caught, murdered. As for Chłendowski and Jaskier (Kruk and Stach), the People's Army unit commanders who were apparently behind my missions, both managed to live through the war, it turned out. But just barely.

According to historian Jozef Garas, Kruk died of natural causes four years after the war's end. Stach also lived to see the Red Army drive the Germans from his land, but just days after the liberation he was murdered by "reactionary Poles"—a euphemism for members of the opposing Home Army.

But back in the bunker I was desperate to keep the conversation going. Kopec had seldom given me this much of a window into his thoughts.

"You said that not being part of a large group was 'another reason' you didn't join. As if I knew the first reason."

Kopec snickered. "Of course you know it, kid. I couldn't support my family if I was in a unit, even if I was a paid leader. I come up with plenty more money my way."

Finally, in a rare display of candor, he added: "Let's face it, you couldn't of done what you done without my planning and training, and I couldn't of got involved in some of it without you. Finding you was lucky for both of us, yes?"

"I'm alive because of you. I know that."

"That's true; you are. But never forget you're also alive because you got balls. Otherwise, you wouldn't of ever come back from taking them pictures at the camp. Or from the train where you shined all them Kraut boots. Or from any of the other jobs you pulled off so good. Hell, I sent you places that would have got anyone else killed. Me too, no doubt."

So he admitted it at last. He sent me to places that "would have got anyone else killed." Somehow I was still around.

Why did I have the luck to stay alive when most others did not? I wondered, not for the first or the last time.

But what I said was "I did what I had to do," and left it at that.

14

Out of the Fire

THE RED ARMY WAS on the move.
By mid-July 1944, Lublin, to the north, had been liberated and designated as the temporary headquarters of the Russian and Polish armies. Closer to home the Russians had already advanced to within fifty miles of Dębica. The German retreat was underway, and it seemed like it would be only a matter of days—weeks, at most—until the Russian front came through the area where Kopec and I were biding our time, sweltering in the above-normal summer heat.

My protector and I had been keeping a low profile ever since returning from our nearly disastrous journey to Podkarpacie. We ventured out of the forest at night only to steal food from the fields, nothing more. I yearned for another opportunity to strike out against the Germans, but even Kopec admitted it was getting too dangerous. We were right in the middle of intense fighting that was going on between the retreating Germans and Poland's two major partisan groups—as well as fighting between the two groups themselves.

Since the spring of that year the rival Home Army had amassed an impressive supply of arms, and for the first time during the war the group was advocating their widespread use. From what I learned much later, this was part of a large-scale operation code-named Burzha, or Tempest.

From a military standpoint Tempest appeared to embrace Home Army units fighting alongside the Russians and their armed underground, the People's Army. One would think that the mutual objective of these two organizations would have been to defeat the Germans. But that was just a smoke screen.

Politically the Home Army's operation was directed *against* Russia, and understandably so, I suppose, for the Polish government-in-exile was determined to prevail over the Soviet army in the liberation of major Polish districts. It also hoped to force Russia back to prewar borders.

At the time, however, such strategies were far beyond my grasp. I cared nothing about politics. I was just trying to get back at the Germans and make it through the war at the same time, amazed with each new day in which I drew breath.

As things turned out, of course, Operation Tempest failed to stop Stalin from taking over after Hitler's defeat. Tempest actually hastened the demise of both resistance groups—the Home Army *and* the People's Army. Squads on each side began to disband, one after another, throughout the summer months.

Meanwhile, the Red Army had pushed victoriously to the west. On August 24, the last Germans were driven from Dębica, and the town came under Russian control. There, along the banks of the Wisłoka River just across from my home village of Straszęcin, the army's westward push stopped in its tracks.

Immediately to the north, though, between Ropczyce and Baranov, heavy fighting was still going on. I know, because I was there. In this area a fierce battle took place around September 12 or 13 in the Blizna Forest. This was very close to the newly deserted Pustków camp and the grounds where they had assembled and tested the v-2 rockets.

Kopec and I had been hiding in that forest on those fateful days, and before we knew it, we were caught directly in the middle of a firefight between a German battalion and a Red Army division. I have since read that a Home Army unit was also involved, but I know nothing of that.

What I do know is this was a battle not just of guns and bullets, but of heavy artillery—German tanks versus Russian *katyushas*. Mounted on the bed of a large truck, the *katyusha* was a formidable weapon: a multiple rocket launcher that, in just seconds, could deliver tons of ordnance over an area of up to ten acres. We heard that the Germans called it "Stalin's Organ" for the terrifying howling sound the rockets made when launched in a salvo.

Terrifying was the word. Throughout the night bright fireballs of devastation flew above Kopec and me in a nearly continuous fusillade. But as long as the artillery made loud and sustained whistling or howling sounds, we knew the shells would pass over our heads, heading for the front lines on either side of the forest. At least twice the intensity of sound began to diminish in pitch, suggesting that the shell was off its mark and would land dangerously close. On those occasions we ran like the devil to another part of the forest.

By dawn these errant shells had turned the forest into a blazing inferno. Flames shot up into the early morning skies like eruptions out of hell.

A cleansing fire, it seemed to me. *Let it burn all of Poland, for all I care.*

Kopec shouted, "Time to get the hell out of here, kid!" His voice was strained, urgent. For the first time ever it sounded on the verge of panic.

"Which way do we run?" I asked anxiously, realizing how quickly the fires were spreading. The flames were getting closer now, fanned by the breezes that were blowing out of the northwest.

"Which way?" I asked again, screaming this time, still hearing no response. I began to feel the heat on my face, hear the crackle of burning trees, smell the pungent odor of smoke and decay. I was suddenly aware that my eyes were stinging.

Hearing no answer, I operated solely on instinct. I started running, searching wildly for a hole in the advancing wall of fire. I headed in what appeared to be the only direction that offered a way out of the burning forest. And as I ran, I looked back, expecting to see Kopec right there behind me, loaded down with weapons but keeping pace nonetheless, as he had done so many times in so many places over the past eighteen months; Kopec, my rescuer, my protector, my teacher, and, strangest of all, my friend.

But he was nowhere to be seen.

I was running alone.

Stumbling through dense underbrush, I could barely see through the thickening smoke. My Luger remained securely tucked in my waistband, and I carried a submachine gun over my shoulder. A shell whined overhead. I was aware of a frightening diminuendo in sound level, but I kept running straight ahead to where I thought there might be a way out of the forest. The shell hit somewhere behind me, too close for comfort, and the ground trembled with its impact.

I could not imagine what had happened to Kopec, or how we had become separated that morning. It occurred to me, *Does he think I'm somewhere back there, right behind him?*

My instincts regarding direction were right, for soon I came to the edge of the forest. Straight in front of me was a large, open wheat field, pockmarked with the craters of artillery shells where recently a sturdy crop had been harvested. I did not like the idea of running out into the open, but I saw no other alternative. Behind me the forest was burning. There was no place to hide.

Except one. For on that pitted field, far in the distance, stood a solitary, burned-out German tank that must have been disabled by a Russian rocket. It dawned on me that I might find some protection if I could crawl beneath it.

I ran across the field, expecting a bullet to cut me down at any moment, although I saw no soldiers. The sun, which had risen high above the eastern horizon, glinted savagely off the steel plate of the tank that loomed ahead. Two lifeless German soldiers lay sprawled on the ground beside the tank; there were undoubtedly more dead inside. I did not stop to consider whether any might still be alive, hiding, waiting.

With my bare hands I fervently dug away at the earth beneath the rear of the tank, between the stilled wheels. Without much rational thought I tunneled far enough to get beneath the disabled vehicle. There the ground gave way to a large bowl-shaped depression created by earlier shelling. I collapsed within it as the roar of artillery continued to rage nearby.

And while Stalin's Organ played its percussive opus, I passed out from sheer exhaustion.

Sometime in late afternoon the artillery fire finally gave way to silence. Intermission? Finale?

I opened my eyes, aware of some pressure on my back, along with a feeling of moisture and warmth. Then I saw blood, sticky and dark, congealing in a damp pool all around me.

Thankfully, it was not mine.

Right next to me lay two dead German soldiers. While I was unconscious to the world, they must have somehow crawled under the tank toward me. Perhaps they were mortally wounded and simply tried to hide, as I did. But they were not so lucky. For a moment I was back at the Grabiny train station, and it was my father's lifeless body that pressed against me. A fresh wave of fury and revulsion swept through me. I vomited, I think.

The bodies blocked my exit from under the tank, so I had no choice but to crawl over them. My face passed just centimeters from their vile uniforms, their puffy, blue-tinged flesh. My stomach continued to churn as the dead Germans rolled under my own advancing body. Covered with their blood, I finally reached a point where I could see daylight.

For a long while I listened cautiously for any words of German, heard none. I reached behind me, grabbed my submachine gun, and put it on the ground ahead as I prepared to emerge into the open.

Then I did hear voices, two of them. I froze. Could one of the men be Kopec? I listened carefully. No, the words were unmistakably Russian. I had been spotted by Red Army soldiers.

"Get out," one of the soldiers shouted as he approached.

The Russian's baggy khaki pants were covered with mud, and his entire uniform—such as it was—looked like he had slept in it for days. His submachine gun was aimed at my head as I peered out at him from underneath the tank.

I scrambled out, relieved that the victors of this battle were Russian. Still, I was unsure of what might happen next. I could speak and understand Russian fairly well; I always had a good ear for languages, after all, and I had grown up not very far west of the Russian border.

"*Evrei! Evrei!*" cried the second soldier, when he saw that I wore no German uniform. "Jew! Jew!"

I tried to stand on wobbly feet beside my own submachine gun, which lay on the ground.

"Partisan, eh!" exclaimed that same soldier, sizing me up and gesturing to my weapon. The fact that it was a Tokarev model just like his was not lost on him.

"Yeah, I'm a Jew, all right, and a partisan too, I guess." Truth is, I had never thought of myself as a partisan. I was just a boy trying to survive in the forests. "What are you going to do about it?" I asked. My voice was more challenging than questioning.

The soldier appeared startled by my reply in Russian, or maybe it was my directness. He had no answer at first. Then he said brightly, "We're going to help you. You come with us!"

"Mister, I got no place else to go," I replied, relieved but dazed. I felt lost without Kopec. But I regarded my new captors and said, "Give me some food and a place to sleep, and I'll do whatever you say." It was an attitude—a resignation, more exactly—that had served me well up to this point.

Soon I found myself heading toward the temporary Red Army headquarters back in nearby Sędziszów, of all places, where I had witnessed the murder of my grandparents, where I last saw my mother and twin sister, where rain barrels once held the blood of innocent babies. Only now Sędziszów was just behind the Russian front, no longer hostage to Nazi horror. But the smell of evil, of death, was still there, and even the chill autumn rain could not wash it away.

My first night behind the Russian lines was spent in a cottage near Borek Wielki, along the road to Sędziszów. Once a simple farm home, the cottage had been appropriated by the Russian army when the front came through. Its occupants were told to relocate to another village well behind the lines until the area was secured and the army continued westward. This time the word *relocate* was not a euphemism for something darker.

I saw more than a dozen soldiers of both sexes packed into the one room farmhouse. Many were already asleep on the floor when I arrived in the company of the two soldiers who had found me.

Although my clothes were bloody and foul, no one seemed to notice. They must have either known or guessed at my involvement with the Soviet-backed partisans, for I was treated with a great deal of deference. To my amazement, I was even allowed to keep my weapons.

Frequently my thoughts turned to Kopec. I wondered if he had made it out of the forest and if so, whether the Russians were giving him the same consideration.

I never had a chance to say good-bye, I thought. *Or thank you. Or good luck . . .*

As I sat at a small wooden table and greedily ate a little food that someone had found for me, I noticed two soldiers—a man and a woman—standing in a nearby corner. They were staring straight at me, murmuring something back and forth.

"I think he's a Jew they left behind," said the young man to the girl. It was the only part of the conversation I overheard.

I was not sure what he was getting at, but it was enough to trigger my anger. I jumped up from the table and bounded over to them.

"You know," I said to the man, patting the pistol in my waistband, "I may be a Jew, but my bullets don't give a shit who *you* are. They have killed plenty of Germans, and they can kill a Russian just as dead."

The two of them looked at me in disbelief, I think, and the target of my wrath raised his hands as if to say, "No harm meant." Then they both turned and walked outside into the damp night air.

I went back to my food and water, still finding it hard to fully comprehend that in this part of Poland, the war was really over. I was free! But freedom, I discovered, was relative. Free to do what? To go where? I had nothing. I had nobody. As long as the war raged on in the west, I decided, I would take my chances with the Russians.

The following day I was brought to a grand house in the center of Sędziszów, accompanied by the gangly Russian soldiers I had met the previous day. At first I had no idea why they had brought me there, but once inside, I could see it had been set up as a provisional office.

In the main room was a large desk of heavy dark wood, flanked by a number of uncomfortable-looking chairs. There was a wooden file cabinet on either side of the desk and next to the cabinet on the right, a Russian flag. On the wall behind the desk, slightly askew, hung a picture of Joseph Stalin. I guessed that until recently a painting or icon of Jesus Christ had hung in its place.

I looked around apprehensively, wondering what was coming next.

170

After a few moments a middle-aged man entered from one of the back rooms, his nose deep in a dossier. Looking up and noticing me, he smiled, then waved off the soldiers, who quietly left the room. The man's crisp gray army uniform was not faded and ill fitting like the uniforms worn by most of the others. And on his chest and shoulders an array of ribbons and medals was emblazoned like a flag. He was clearly a high-ranking officer; beyond that I could tell nothing more.

The Russian officer moved to his chair behind the desk and not so much sat down as dropped into it. He motioned for me to have a seat while he continued to examine the file.

I selected one of the chairs in front of his desk, sitting straight and rigid on the edge, never taking my eyes off the officer. The man seemed to be in his forties, with thinning black hair and a bushy eyebrow—it floated above both eyes in an almost unbroken line, like a hairy cater-pillar—that undulated up and down expressively as he read. A thick, short neck seemed to just barely hold his head above his shoulders. The man was solid, but not heavyset. Built somewhat like Kopec, I observed.

Finally the officer put down his file and gave me his full attention. The Russian's eyes were bloodshot from lack of sleep, but they were soft, gentle eyes, and they seemed to look not just at my face, but some-where . . . deeper.

"Do you speak Russian?" he asked.

"Enough."

"I know a little about you," he said slowly.

I thought, *You may know more about what I have done and where I have been than I know myself.* I wondered if the dossier on the officer's desk had a reference to me—and if so, whether it also mentioned my associ-ation with Kopec. Would I be punished for being with the bandit, for doing what I did?

The officer, to my surprise, smiled warmly. "I'm very happy you survived the terrible German atrocities and that you found your way here. I want you to know you're safe with us, and I'll personally do whatever is within my power to help you."

"How could you possibly help me?" I snapped back, unprepared as I was for gentle words. "I lost everything. There is nobody left."

The officer was silent for a moment. I wondered if I had responded too sharply to what were probably good intentions, then decided I did not much care.

"You may not believe it now," the officer continued, "but you'll be all right. You've made it this far; you'll go on to recover your life or start a new one."

171

I said nothing, felt nothing. I was numb to any such promises.

"Your name is"—the officer glanced down at his file—"Goldner, is that right? Moniek Goldner?"

I nodded. I had nothing else, but I still had a name.

"They call you 'Moniek' in Polish, but I'm guessing your given name is different. 'Moishe,' perhaps?"

My jaw dropped, and I leaned forward, my right hand grasping the officer's desk for support. *How could he know?*

The officer smiled again in response to my look of shock. Slipping easily into Yiddish, he said, "I'm a Jew too."

I sank back into my chair, letting the impact of this revelation pour over me.

"I didn't realize," was all I could say.

The Russian officer regarded me solemnly. He spoke rapidly now, Russian again, in a low voice. I leaned forward to catch his words.

"There's no reason you would realize I'm a Jew, nor do most of my comrades know it either. Only the Fascists made our people proclaim our heritage in a symbol to be worn on our sleeves; the Communists did not. But those who know never let you forget. I would be no more a Russian in their eyes than you are a Pole in the eyes of your countrymen. We are Jews. Just Jews. And in Russia that can be every bit as dangerous as it has proved to be in Poland or Germany. More dangerous, actually, these days."

I listened, spellbound. I did not say a word as the officer leaned forward, half rising from his chair.

"I know what it's like to have nobody. My family, too, was killed."

He paused, momentarily lost in some cherished memory. Then he settled back in his chair and looked once again at me.

"You want to hear a story?"

I nodded.

He told me he was born in a small village in Lithuania. When the Red Army was being organized in 1918, he joined—underage—as a volunteer. He later graduated from a military academy in Moscow. At some point after that, he was arrested, if I remember correctly, then released for unknown reasons. But by this time his family had been lost in one of Stalin's purges. A year or so after his release he was wounded at Stalingrad. When he recovered, he was assigned to his present post in the southern flanks, western front. Sędziszów was to be a very temporary headquarters.

The Russian got up from behind his desk, put his hands on his hips, and stretched in a backward arc, as if trying to drive away tension. For the first time in several minutes, I also relaxed and sat back in my chair.

"It's ironic," the officer concluded, "that here I am fighting for freedom from Fascist tyranny and the megalomaniac at its head, under the leadership of yet another megalomaniac. At this moment I think I'd rather be in your shoes, with the war behind me and the opportunity to build a new life upon whatever memories and fragments of the past might still be in your heart.

"Me, soon I'll move out with my unit to challenge the Nazis once again. The Soviet army is all I have, and I'm reminded daily that it's my duty to serve in any way that's asked of me. Stalin won't be around forever, but hopefully Russia will. I can't envision a world where Jews are hated forever."

I became filled with awe for this man, who was taking a bewildered Polish teenager into his confidence in this way. The last thing I ever expected was to be rescued from the Nazis and then immediately befriended by a Russian officer who was a Jew!

Before I left his office, he gave me papers that granted the bearer, one M. Goldner, safe passage and hospitable treatment anywhere that fell under Russian authority.

My care and feeding by the Russian army continued almost immediately, when I was issued an army jacket and military coat, including a roomy pair of *valenki*—felt army boots with soles of real leather—to replace the threadbare boots I had been wearing. The sleeves on the coat and jacket were too long for my small frame (what else is new?), but I pinned them up and wore them proudly.

Happily, there was no diminution of hospitality when new soldiers came into Sędziszów. These men replaced some of the others who had accompanied my unexpected new friend and confidant to the front lines a few miles to the west.

For the first time in three years I was able to eat and sleep regularly, even enjoy little luxuries like having a bowel movement, pardon my frankness, where I could sit down in safety and in surroundings of relative comfort. As a civilian I was treated almost like an affectionate mascot by the soldiers. They told me they were sure I would bring them luck.

And when the terrible news reached me, months later in Katowice, that this Russian Jewish officer had been killed in action during the bloody January offensive, I was overcome with anguish. Not since witnessing my father's death had I felt so distraught.

Even now, after I have long forgotten the Russian's name, I remember his penetrant words and the compassion we shared for that very brief time in the late summer of 1944. And with this remembrance tears still manage to well up in my eyes.

15

Liberation

FOR THE REST of the year the front lines advanced no further. I continued to be fed and cared for by the Red Army in Sędzi-szów. Food was not always in plentiful supply—we sometimes ran out of bread and groats—so I, along with some of the soldiers, resorted once more to stealing whatever rations we could find.

After a while I stopped checking on a daily basis to see if Kopec might have come looking for me. It could be he was still hiding from the Germans, for Straszęcin was just on the other side of the Wisłoka River, still under German control. Or perhaps he was hiding from the Russians at that moment. It was possible—he had many enemies. Maybe he never made it out of the forest, or if he did, might he have been killed? I forced myself to stop thinking such things, for I did not want to face the possibility of never seeing him again. Even if we could be together just one more time—long enough for me to express my gratitude or to say good-bye, if it came to that—I would be grateful.

But there was no word from him. The Red Army was my new family.

The troops were uneasy, awaiting the inevitable winter offensive. I listened as they were indoctrinated with stories of the many heinous crimes the Germans had committed against civilians on Russian soil. Their outrage was further fueled by the gruesome discoveries of death camps—Maidanek and Treblinka being the largest—which their forces had overrun along the way.

This organized propaganda effort was supported by retellings of harrowing personal experiences among soldiers and officers. Sędzi-szów was heaped with signs, posters, articles, and leaflets demanding vengeance, and their inflammatory message, I must admit, had not been lost on me. I grew increasingly anxious to help the Russians destroy everything German.

I soon got my chance.

The early hours of January 12, 1945, brought the kind of weather in which nothing moves. According to an account I've read, temperatures at the nearby Baranov bridgehead were barely above freezing. Roads were icy. And along vast areas of the Vistula River, blizzards and fog reduced ground visibility to near zero.

So the Germans clearly were not prepared, at 4:30 A.M., for the incredible devastation they sustained from Russian artillery, which had been massed wheel to wheel, their targets accurately registered. After just five minutes of heavy shelling, the first Russian infantry troops moved forward in swarms of mini-battalions. But the main assault was yet to come. By the end of the first full day, the first two German lines had been overrun. Their third line collapsed the next day, just twenty-five miles west of the starting point.

Red Army flanks achieved similar successes, overwhelming the Germans at nearly every turn. Much of this news reached us daily in Sędziszów as victories mounted in the west and south.

First we got word of the liberation of Tarnów. This meant my home village of Straszęcin was also out from under German control. On January 17, the Podkarpacie region was secured by the Red Army, although reports said Jasło had been almost totally destroyed by the Germans in revenge for defeats on the eastern front. On January 19, the Germans were driven out of Kraków, leaving in such a hurry they never had time to set off the explosives they had planted throughout the city.

And on January 27, in perhaps the most emotional moment of all, came news that more than seven thousand remaining prisoners at Auschwitz-Birkenau had been liberated by the horror-stricken Red Army. Of the people who first heard this report, myself included, very few realized that the officer leading the Russian troops into Auschwitz was a highly decorated colonel by the name of Grigori Elishawetzki.

Elishawetzki, a Jew.

Until the January offensive I remained behind the front in Sędziszów, staying in a house with low-echelon Russian soldiers. Perhaps they were released prisoners of war or newly conscripted peasants; I never made it a point to ask.

Whoever they were, they had adopted me in a way, for I was not only the lone civilian in the group but also the only non-Russian. They called me "little Pole," which I took to be an affectionate nickname. If word had spread that I was a surviving Jew, it never came up.

For the time being I felt so at ease with the Red Army, my easiest decision about the future was to make no decision. As long as the Russians provided me with shelter and food, I decided, I would stay put. What else could I do? Where else would I go?

So when I awoke one morning in mid-January to find the house and streets nearly deserted, a mild sense of panic set in. It was ironic: For years I had harbored a fear of being discovered. Now came the anxiety of being left behind.

I ventured out into the cold, snowy morning, having quickly thrown on my army-issue clothing—padded pants, quilted coat, and fur cap with fold-down earflaps. I tucked my old friend, Luger, into my waistband. Then I wandered down the nearly deserted street in search of a familiar face.

Minutes later an American Jeep pulled up, driven by a ruddy-faced Russian soldier whom I recognized immediately.

"The offensive has started!" he exclaimed, shouting with excitement. "The First Ukrainian Front has overtaken the *fascista* at Tarnów. Soon we'll be in Kraków. If you're still with us, hop in, little Pole. We'll have Germany in flames before you know it."

"I'm with you, all right," I replied. Without a second thought I jumped into the Jeep.

Seeing Dębica free from German control—it had been liberated more than four months earlier—elicited no emotion other than renewed resentment and anger. It was not the Dębica I had known before the war, nor would it ever be. The synagogue had remained standing, but it was hollow. There was no Torah, no Jews, to give it meaning. The city could be restored, rebuilt, repainted, but her soul was another matter. I sensed it was dead forever, buried in unmarked ash pits and ravines and mass graves in Pustków and Belzec and the surrounding forests.

I was in Dębica for no more than a few hours, for my new comrades were merely passing through on their way to the western border. On this journey I did not leave the side of my Russian friends for a moment. Heading west, we bypassed my village of Straszęcin. It was Kopec's village too, of course. I felt pangs of regret at not being able to stop and see if he was all right. But Straszęcin was not on the main road to Tarnów, which was my unit's next destination along the route. I would have to come back another time.

We traveled in Jeeps and trucks and cars and transports, along roads strewn with burned-out German tanks and overturned trucks, always on the lookout for hidden mines that could end our lives at any moment. We remained just behind the advancing front lines, with the insistent sounds of gunshots and artillery constantly booming from some point up ahead. At night I often saw the blur of *katyusha* shells, their fiery arcs like shooting stars against the ebony sky.

As we traveled, we frequently came across terrible reminders of the war. These became indelibly etched in my memory, much as I wish I could empty out the images like yesterday's garbage. I saw bodies that were piled as high as eight or ten feet: lines of soldiers, some German, some Russian, cut down by machine-gun fire. They had climbed in waves apparently, one after another, over bodies already dead until they themselves were riddled with bullets. There they remained, a frozen tableau, stiff and cold as the wintry winds that blew over them. Here were thousands of nameless men and boys, stacked like potatoes—no, more like grotesque sculptures carved of ice. Soon would come the thaw, and then they would lie rotting all across the Polish countryside, a foul potpourri of death and decay. I had seen plenty of killing, but never before had I smelled and tasted death of this magnitude. The sheer enormity of it overwhelmed me, as it does still when I think about it.

We passed through Tarnów, much of which lay in ruin, and continued on to Kraków, traveling along roads packed with refugees, some in carts, many on foot. The soldiers who were with me were eager for action and revenge, so we passed straight through Kraków as well, continuing westward, headed toward the town of Katowice and the German border just beyond.

We came into Katowice in early February, just days after the Soviet front had liberated the city. I was surprised to see no sign of battle. I had no idea at the time that the Russians had simply stood by while the Germans fled in retreat over the border. They did this to spare the city from otherwise certain devastation. The Russians wanted to catch their prey on German soil; it was there they planned to exact their vengeance.

Once we crossed the border just west of Katowice, I saw large posters that had been put up along the road by troops on the front lines. The words that had been printed on them were carefully chosen to goad their second-line comrades: "Red Army soldier! You are now on German soil! This is your hour of revenge! Kill all Germans! Kill! Kill! Kill!"

The towns and villages in this area—once part of Poland before the invasion—had been heavily colonized by German civilians. Now they found themselves overrun by an out-of-control Red Army.

I shudder to recall the atrocities I witnessed at the hands of the Russians: looting, rape, plunder, dismemberment, murder, and other horrors of unimaginable cruelty and depravity, all directed against the

177

German population. I myself had the chance to shoot several fleeing German soldiers, and I have to be honest, I felt no hesitation about eliminating them. But the heinous barbarity I witnessed all around me as the Russians shouted "Kill, kill the *fascista*," or "This is for my father," or "Here's for what you did to my family" was something else again. Revenge against the German military was one thing, and while I was with Kopec, I had participated readily. But the murder of civilians trying to flee the onslaught, along with the wholesale rape of females from little girls to grandmothers—that turned my stomach.

In German-occupied homes the Russians spared no one, including the family pets. Men were forced to watch as their wives and daughters, screaming for mercy, were savagely raped by Russian soldiers—who, after having their way, slashed each German throat. From what I could tell, the Red Army authorities made no effort to reign in the barbarity. Stalin himself, I have since heard, shrugged off the rape and looting as "having some fun" and "taking a few trifles."

Entire families who lived in aboveground apartments were rounded up. Then, accompanied by the sounds of their own screams and the shattering of glass, they were thrown through their windows onto the pavement below. This happened day after day, in one village after another. I could not help but see the barbarity unfold, and I was certainly powerless to stop it. All I could do was mentally record the total breakdown of law and morality as my Russian liberators did to the remaining Germans what they knew, or had been told, the Germans had done to them.

And when the Americans and their western allies put an end to this wholesale slaughter a short time later, I knew for certain that the Russians felt tremendous animosity. Many of them wanted nothing short of the total destruction of Germany and her people.

Yet in spite of the deplorable savagery, I must confess I would have stayed on with the Russian army a while longer, to avoid making decisions about my own future. The Russians had already reached a point along the Oder River less than sixty miles from Berlin.

But one brisk morning in late March, as I waited for marching orders with my group, a high-ranking officer came over to me and said, "You've done your share." There was a gentleness in his voice that belied the brutal enthusiasm with which he personally had killed German families. "Hitler will be defeated soon, and we can't continue to look after you. It's time you were back with your own people."

"My own people are dead." The words flew out of my mouth, as if I had bitten into a rancid piece of meat.

The Russian wasn't flustered. "You know what I mean. It's time for you to be on your own. Go back to Poland. Find your destiny. You can keep the uniform. It will help keep you safe wherever you go."

"All right, I understand." There was nothing more I could say.

For the remainder of that day, I said good-bye to my Red Army friends—words of farewell that I never got to say to the man who made my survival possible. The soldiers acted genuinely sorry to be moving on without me. Together we shared a last meager meal of buckwheat groats studded with pork fat. Soon I would go back to being hungry, I figured, stealing food when and where I could.

The war is over in most of Poland, I thought, *but how much will have really changed for me?*

And for the first time since my earliest missions with Kopec, I felt a vague sensation of uneasiness seeping down into the pit of my stomach, like water eroding rock. But this time it was not the anxiety of being caught, or tortured, or killed, or failing a mission that unnerved me so. It was something much less definable and far more paralyzing:

The consternation of having survived, with no idea, no idea at all, of what to do about it.

Confused and bewildered, I headed back east toward the area I once called home. I had a burning need to find out what had become of Kopec in the seven months since we had somehow become separated in the Blizna Forest. All I wanted was to see him once again, and after that—well, after that there was one more thing I needed to do. I was too disconcerted to plan any further ahead than that.

For the first leg of my journey I hitched a ride on a horse cart into Kraków. Wandering alone through the city, I walked along the winding Vistula River. I passed Wawel Hill, with its storybook castle that until just weeks earlier had been appropriated as the private residence of Governor General Hans Frank and his Nazi henchmen.

Will it now fall into the hands of the Russians? I wondered and then realized that I could not have cared less.

South of the castle I stumbled through the Kazimierz district, its synagogues empty and in various states of ruin. Across the river, in the Podgorze district, I came upon two-meter-high walls, which were all that remained of the cramped, filthy ghetto. A young refugee, passing in the other direction, told me the ghetto had been uninhabited for two years. The only sound remaining behind these walls was the whistling of the fierce March winds.

After a night of uneasy rest in an empty building, I continued south on foot and came upon what little was left of the Plaszow work camp. From what my Russian companions had told me, the camp's German

179

guards had dynamited it two months earlier, in January, just moments before the advancing Russian line reached the area.

I wondered if my mother and sister had been sent to a place like that. My rational mind held little hope that they would still be alive; nobody could survive four years in a German work camp, I supposed. Then again, I reasoned, by all rights I should be dead too. So was it so foolish that a part of me should still hold out a tiny speck of hope for a second miracle in the family?

From Kraków I hitched rides much of the way back to Tarnów. The city was chaotic; Jewish refugees who had spent the war years in Russia were pouring back in. Some of them, I imagine, were men who originally fled at the same time as my father, back in the autumn of 1939.

The voice in my head replayed a familiar lament: *Papa, Papa, what did you come home to? Why didn't you stay in Russia?*

But it dawned on me how different circumstances might have been if my father had stayed there. Papa would likely be alive right now, not me; for if not for the shooting in Grabiny, I would never have wound up with Kopec, to be safely tucked away in his many hideouts. I felt another pang of guilt. Then I jumped on a wagon that took me as far as Pilzno. From there I began walking north, toward Straszęcin.

It was the beginning of April, and the weather, while turning more temperate, was still chilly enough to make me turn up the collar on my coat and lean forward into the wind. So I was not paying much attention when two men approached me, less than a mile outside my home village, as I trudged through the gloomy morning.

"Hey, boy," one of them called to me. "Where you heading?"

I stopped right where I was and turned to look at them. They were both Poles, somewhere in their forties. Probably farmers, to judge from the mud on their shoes and pants. Either that, or they had been in a hurry, cutting through the fields. I did not recognize either of them. But if they were local farmers, I had undoubtedly stolen their food at one time or another.

I remained silent as the two men approached.

They looked me over, clearly curious about my Russian uniform. The heavyset one of the pair whispered something to the other, who grinned, then addressed me.

"I see you survived the war. Aren't you that Jew kid who lived just up from the bridge in Straszęcin?"

My heart began beating faster. The way the man said it, with a sneer, let me know they were up to something from which no good would come. The two men gave each other a knowing glance, then grinned again, waiting for my response.

"What's it to you?" I replied belligerently. Then I reached into my coat and pulled out the Luger, pointing it directly at the man who spoke.

"This says that who I am and where I'm heading is none of your goddamn business. Don't you think there are enough dead Polacks for one war?"

Given the slightest provocation, I would not have hesitated to fire, believe me. One thing I learned from Kopec was to shoot first and ask questions later. That approach had kept me alive up to this point. Even though the war had ended in the area, it seemed too soon to act otherwise.

"That's just the thing," said the same man, glowering at me. "There *are* too many dead Poles. And all because of . . ." His voice trailed off, as he decided not to finish his sentence. Not that it mattered. I could fill it in.

Then he held up his arms in a supplicant gesture. "But take it easy, my little friend," he said, with all the condescension he could muster. "No harm done."

"We're going; you can relax," said the other, speaking for the first time. Then the two men looked at each other and gave me plenty of room as they briskly walked past me. Soon they broke into a run.

Is this the way it's going to continue? I wondered, as I watched them grow smaller in the distance. *Is there never going to be an end to the hatred and accusations?*

Little did I know then that in the first year after the so-called liberation, hundreds of Jews returning from the camps and various hiding places were killed by Poles, individually as well as in mass pogroms. No part of Poland was exempt from this renewed violence, including places like Kraków and Rzeszów in the district where I came from.

Even after the Germans had been driven out, it would seem, the war against the Jews was not over. Not in Poland. Not by a long shot.

When I reached Straszęcin, I headed straight for the home of Jan Kopec.

I pushed aside earlier fears that he might kill me now that the war had ended in this part of Poland. It was still a remote possibility in my mind, but my need to see him one last time outweighed any irrational doubts about how the man would react to seeing me.

It was midday when I knocked at Kopec's door. I waited anxiously as I heard approaching footsteps from inside. Soon the door opened a crack, and Stefania Kopec peered through. To me she looked heavier. Older. And more than a little startled to see me standing there.

"Moniek."

She said my name in a flat tone of voice. There was no exclamation point at the end.

What a strange and unresponsive greeting, I thought. No "Jan will be glad to see you," or "It's good you're alive," or even "What a surprise!"—pleasant or otherwise. I could see that she regarded me warily. Maybe it was the uniform, I told myself.

"I was wondering . . . that is, how did . . ." I was nearly stammering, my brain working faster than my tongue. I began again. "Is your husband . . . is he home?"

I could hear children in the background. Stefania looked over her shoulder for a moment, then returned her gaze to me, and replied sharply, "He's not around now."

After a brief silence it became apparent she was not going to volunteer any further information. At least her response indicated to me that Kopec had made it back, was still alive. I was thrilled.

Meanwhile, something about my expression or bedraggled appearance must have softened her, because her next words were more compassionate.

"Are you hungry?"

"Yes."

"Wait a moment."

The door remained slightly ajar while Stefania went, presumably, into her kitchen. I stood waiting, wondering why she did not invite me to come in. A moment later she was back with some water and bread. I drank the water, handed back the cup, put the bread in my pocket.

"Don't come back here again," she admonished, looking not at me, but past me, as if I were no more than a pane of glass. Then she said it once more. "Don't come back ever again. Your ties with my husband are over now. We don't want trouble."

Trouble? I did not know what to make of that. I just stood there for a moment, hurt and angry. *Was turning me away her idea or his?*

Finally I stumbled with some words, although they were nothing like what I had imagined saying to Kopec himself. "Just tell him I asked about him. Tell him . . ."

My mind raced while I tried to sort out what I was trying to say. Stefania continued to look at me, patiently waiting for me to finish. I wished I could read her thoughts, but her expressionless face offered no clues. Then I remembered something Kopec had told me. They were words that stayed with me because they revealed more about Jan Kopec than the taciturn man might have ever imagined.

If I left you there to die, the fascist Kraut pricks and their informers would have won another little victory. They must never win.

"Tell him," I said softly, "that I will never let them win. The informers, that is. Tell him . . . I will never forget him, what he did for me, even if what he did was also for himself."

There was confusion in Stefania's eyes, which said to me her husband would never get that exact message. Or any message at all. And maybe it was just as well.

"Look, tell him I wish him well," I said finally. Then I turned and walked back to the road, crushed not only at being turned away but also at not even being asked about my own well-being.

It was almost ironic, as I thought about it. Since the day he had found me, I wondered if Kopec might try to kill me after the war was over. But it had never occurred to me, not once, that he might just simply treat me as if I had never existed.

Could Kopec still be in hiding? I asked myself. *If so, from whom? Or could he be evading only me, and if so, why?*

I still puzzle over those questions, more than a half century later. At the time, though, I came to the reluctant conclusion that Kopec simply did not want to see me again, that Stefania was just following her husband's instructions. It felt like he had slapped me in the face, as if he were telling me, "Get lost, I don't want no part of you now that I don't need you no more." And the only reason I could think of for him to treat me that way, after all we had been through together, was this: he may have decided I knew too much, that I could connect him to people and events he would rather keep to himself.

As I have mentioned, I did not have a clue as to who his contacts were in those days, other than hearing a few code names like Kruk. I certainly had no idea his money was coming from the Russian-backed partisans, a fact he presumably concealed from his family and certainly kept from his Communist-hating Home Army acquaintances like Kryzak. My guess was Kopec had his own story of what he and I did during 1943 and 1944, and that interpretation did not include any activities in opposition to Home Army dogma. Without me in his life, there could be no one to contradict his version of events.

Frankly, I continue to lean toward this explanation today, that he wanted no further contact with me after the war because of what he thought I might reveal about him. But there are other possibilities, I realize now.

Perhaps it was Stefania who did not want me to see her husband. She had made it clear from the beginning that she disliked his hiding with a Jew. While she could not influence Jan regarding whom he spent his time with in the forest, her own home would have been another matter. There were her neighbors to consider, after all, many of whom lived in fear that we Jews would return and reclaim our property—

property they had taken for themselves. Or, as the thought once occurred to me, she could well have been put off by my uniform. The military jacket might have made her wonder if I had ties to the Russian secret police, whom most Poles feared (often with good reason, I understand) even more than they feared the Germans.

Finally one additional possibility has come to light: that they might not have wanted me around, either of them, because they were getting ready to change houses. Of course, I did not know this at the time.

You see, after raising eight children in the cramped quarters of their run-down, multifamily dwelling, the Kopecs, it seems, were weeks away from moving up the block and across the bridge to a large, single-family home. It was a Jewish-owned home, at that: the residence (and former store) of Moishe the shopkeeper. Poor Moishe, who undoubtedly perished when he walked into the arms of the Germans after wandering away from Papa and me in the forest.

How did the Kopecs come to acquire that particular house? Ah, that is the question. According to a cousin of Kopec's children, Moishe's house was bequeathed to a close relative of the shopkeeper, a man who lived in Grabiny. Right after the war that man sold it to Jan Kopec for *bubkes,* for a symbolic figure, "because of all Jan had done for the Jews," in her words. Kopec's children also believe this to be the case.

Had I heard such an explanation back then, I do not know what I would have done. For while I did observe signs of generosity on Kopec's part—like a Polish Robin Hood, he sometimes robbed from the poor and gave a portion of his take to the even poorer—I must say, in the year and a half I was with him, he did not give any indication of even *caring* about Jews. "You're different from the rest of them," he told me once, as if to explain why he kept me with him. And as I will never forget, this was the man who said to me (when we came upon the prisoners digging what was to be their mass grave), "Why should we help them? They're just Jews."

Do not get me wrong—I am eternally grateful for Kopec's tutelage and protection. And hiding a Jew certainly complicated his existence and increased his danger. But "helping the Jews" does not explain how he came by Moishe's house any more than if someone said "the Pied Piper gave it to him."

Continuing this line of thought, I think it possible that the Kopecs did not want me around simply because of the circumstances, whatever they were, surrounding their upcoming takeover of Moishe's house. Of course, all this is conjecture on my part, but it remains a real possibility as I've tried to deal with why I was turned away without even so much as a "be well, Moniek."

Never again did I return to Straszęcin to look for the man to whom I owed so much. When people make it clear they do not want you, you have nothing further to gain by pushing yourself on them. But for a long time to come, I did inquire about Kopec—with no success, I might add—every time I came across someone from southern Poland.

How could someone who saves your life, who teaches you how to survive against insurmountable odds, ever be far from your thoughts?

Back on that April day in 1945, immediately following my dismissal by Stefania Kopec, I wandered along the dirt road that paralleled the "palace," which stood undisturbed behind a high fence on my right. Disconsolate and alone, I crossed the wooden bridge. I passed Moishe's house, which stood empty, never dreaming it would soon belong to Kopec. Then, instead of turning right to follow the road leading into Dębica, I abruptly changed plans and continued straight ahead for another block. There I stopped in front of another familiar house.

My house. Mama's and Papa's and Gita's house. Or what was left of it.

For it was now a vacant shell, standing forsaken and disemboweled of all interior furniture and cabinetry. The whole structure was in such disrepair, it looked as if it might fall down at any minute.

For a moment I thought I would cry. I looked away.

I saw the lady who lived across the road. She was feeding her chickens. The slanting rays of late afternoon sun backlit her golden hair, which stuck out from the scarf that always covered her head. I thought about going up to her, then decided against it. *Trust no one*, an inner voice directed me.

I was tempted also to call on Reguła next door but was not sure I could trust him either. I was still bitter that he had sent me and my father away the last time we had come for food. I believe now that he was being truthful when he told us that others lived with his family who might turn us in, but for years I did not understand. It has taken time for me to realize that not all Poles were eager to sacrifice their Jews. You must understand, my limited experiences revealed so many who did just that.

If I am to be honest, there was possibly another reason why I did not knock on Reguła's door that day—his daughter, Anna. I thought it would not be a good idea to see her again. I was not the same person. I did not feel like much of a person at all.

I took a final look at my childhood home and then continued walking to the northwest, not toward Dębica, but along the road to Wola Wielka, where my beloved grandparents once lived. I had no idea why I was walking in that direction. I had seen my grandparents lying in their own blood—could four years have passed already?—and slowly it occurred to me, what would I gain by going to their house? I had no desire to see who had taken over their property, possibly even torn the beautiful mezuzah off of their doorframe.

It was foolish, such aimless wandering. I was just getting farther away from Dębica, where I had some unfinished business. After that, who knew what I would do or where I would go next?

I saw a large farm just ahead of me, set back from the road. It would be dark soon, and I felt too tired to face another two hours of walking to reach Dębica. Besides, I figured it would be more comfortable to spend the night in the country than to head immediately for the city, with its chaos of Russians and refugees. I would have to spend enough nights there as it was.

My stomach gurgled, reminding me that Stefania Kopec's bread would not keep me going much longer. Once that would have been enough, but my recent months with the Red Army had reacquainted me with the luxury of two or three meals a day.

I walked up to the farmhouse and knocked on the door. I would use my gun, if necessary, to get what I wanted. A man answered, thirty-five or forty years of age, tall and slender. He wore a cap, which he removed as he stood in the doorway. With his sleeve he wiped away a bead of sweat that had collected behind where the rim had pressed on his forehead. It looked as if he had just come in from his field.

"Do I know you?" he asked before I could open my mouth. He eyed my Russian jacket and the handle of the Luger sticking out from my waistband. Then he looked back at me.

"I don't think so . . . I don't know. I used to live near here, in Straszęcin. My grandparents had a farm in Wola. It was a long time ago. I was wondering . . ."

"What's your name?"

"Goldner. Moishe, uh, Moniek Goldner."

The man's face softened. The gruffness melted away from his voice. "I know . . . knew . . . who your grandparents were. I heard what happened."

I nodded, then got right to the point. "I need some food."

"Of course." A smile now. He introduced himself and invited me in.

He must have noticed I was hesitating. For a split second, when I looked into his face, I saw Pozniak staring back.

"It's all right. I liked your grandparents, and I don't like what Hitler did to your people. He was bad enough to my own people, but what he did to the Jews . . ."

He finished by shaking his head from side to side, making a clucking sound with his tongue.

I entered and stood quietly while he summoned his wife, a pleasant, dark-haired woman of about the same age as her husband. Her eyes immediately dropped to take in my pistol, but her face showed no reaction. If the couple had any children, they were nowhere to be seen.

The man invited me to sit at the table while his wife put out some bread and *słonina*. I wondered, rather cynically, whether they really were compassionate or simply afraid because I was armed.

As I ate, I told them a tiny bit about what I had been through. Not my activities with Kopec, but earlier—how my father and I had been betrayed. The man's eyebrows went up when I mentioned Pozniak's name, and I noticed that he exchanged a quick glance with his wife.

"What does that look mean?" I asked.

"Pozniak's a dangerous man," he said. His wife busied herself by going through the motions of cleaning the stove, which as far as I could see was already spotless.

"You know him?"

"Grabiny's not far from here."

I sat up straight. "Then you do know him!"

"We're aware of who he is and what he's done. Some of it anyway. And not only against the Jews. He turned a few of his own people over to the Germans too."

The man glanced again at his wife, who hovered quietly in the background. "Look, I don't think he's the mayor any longer, but as far as I know he still lives there, and if he realizes you're alive—which he probably does or soon will—he could kill you. The war is over, but he'll likely as not try to kill you just the same."

Not if I kill him first, I thought.

At least I knew for certain that the man was still alive. I had hoped maybe the Russians would have already made the bastard pay for what he did.

"I can take care of myself," I said. "But thanks for your concern."

The man shrugged and changed the subject. "If you'd like to spend the night in our barn, even stay on a few more days, you're most welcome."

I thanked him, said I would be leaving in the morning.

"I don't have much, but it looks like you could use this." The farmer held out his hand. In it were five zlotys.

I was surprised at the gesture. Food was one thing. But money . . .

"I cannot accept that."

In my mind taking a handout of money as an orphaned refugee was to betray my family's memory. It seemed to me as if I were profiting from their loss, illogical as that might appear. I could rationalize the charity of food and clothing and shelter. But not money. That was one thing I could never accept.

As I turned and began to head for the barn, the man called after me. "It's none of my business," he said, "but when are you going to get rid of your weapon?"

I stopped and looked at him with a blank expression. After a moment's pause I turned away and continued walking toward the barn.

I had no answer.

16

Revenge

OON AFTER SUNRISE I began the familiar walk into Dębica. Along
the way I stole a cow.
The opportunity presented itself as I walked past a small farm
just across the Wisłoka River, outside the city. I spotted four cows inside a low barbed-wire fence that ran alongside the road. With no humans in sight, it occurred to me that I might liberate one of the cows,
to use the expression of the times, which might fetch me a few zlotys
at the market.

It was paradoxical, and I knew it, that while I would not accept
money as a gift, stealing in order to *get* money was another matter
entirely. *Perhaps too much of Kopec has rubbed off on me,* I thought. It
triggered new pangs of regret that I would never see him again, that
he presumably did not want to see me.

I had nothing with which to cut the barbed wire, but there was a
locked gate, and the lock offered no resistance to the 9 mm bullet from
my pistol. I grabbed the cow nearest to me, pulled her out, and led
her along the road toward town. I arrived at the cattle market just in
time to find a willing buyer, who offered me a paltry sum. I took it
eagerly. No proof of ownership necessary.

I found that Dębica, like everywhere else, was teeming with refugees. There was little food, and whatever could be bought was exceed-
ingly expensive. What I did with myself for the first few days is a blur
to me now. I do know this: For reasons I cannot fully explain, I declined
to register as a survivor. Neither did I take advantage of help from
international organizations like UNRRA.

In part I was reluctant to call attention to myself because of my
long alliance with Kopec. After all, he had been hiding from the police

and other enemies since long before the war began. Did that make me an accessory? Who knew? I reasoned I had better be careful in any regard. Not only that, but during the eighteen months I had been with Kopec, innocent Poles had been killed in retribution for our actions. Might that not make me a target still?

Then there was one other matter: *The war will end some day, and the Krauts will rot in hell. But you will always be a Jew,* Kopec had warned me. Better to remain detached, I decided, even from the other surviving Jews who were coming into the city.

I did, however, visit the Red Cross to inquire about my mother and sister, as well as my Aunt and Uncle Silverman. Their home, I noticed, was now occupied by strangers.

No information. No surprise.

Then I asked about Mama's brother from Mokre. To my astonishment, my Uncle Isak Flam was on a list of survivors, and he was reportedly right where I was, in Dębica! His last known address was temporary housing that had been provided for some of the refugees. I made a note of the street number.

My next visit was to the Russian authorities. I demanded they take action against Pozniak for my father's murder. Although I had charitably decided to let the police deal with him, it quickly became an exercise in futility. I was passed from one person to another, then sent to another building entirely, from which they administered the villages like Grabiny. Here an officer listened politely (after asking how I came to own my Russian military jacket), then looked through a dossier on Pozniak.

He told me Pozniak had helped the people in his village temporarily relocate behind the lines when the Russian front came through. Yes, he may well have been a Nazi sympathizer, but he gave the Red Army no trouble. A chameleon, that man, one of many. No, there's nothing we can do about that now. Yes, of course we understand how you feel. Perhaps you should talk to someone over at district headquarters across the city in the old section. Good luck, young man.

I was getting the runaround and growing angrier by the minute. I headed for the district headquarters, which was more than a mile away, but stopped suddenly after two blocks. Coming my way was a solitary man, walking with his shoulders hunched, eyes downcast.

"Isak Flam? I can't believe it's you, Uncle Isak!" I practically shouted when I recognized the familiar face.

He squinted his eyes and carefully looked me over. Then he lit up like a bonfire. Calling my name, he stopped dead in his tracks as I ran up to embrace him.

Tears streamed down Uncle Isak's cheeks as the joy of finding me

190

mixed with the anguish of reporting that there was no word about my mother and sister. Most certainly they were dead. I told him about Pozniak's betrayal of Papa and me and of my attempts to get the Russians to go after the son-of-a-bitch.

"Don't be consumed with vengeance, Moishe," Uncle Isak said. "Pozniak will get what's coming to him. As for the Russians, they're not going to lift a finger unless it's in their own interests."

I told him also about Kopec, how the man had looked after me and trained me to be useful to the partisans and therefore to him. I mentioned how Kopec's wife had turned me away. I asked if he had heard anything about the notorious resident of Straszęcin. He had not.

"Just be glad he didn't turn on you," Isak said. "He doesn't need you anymore. And now you certainly don't need him, so forget about that ganef."

Well-meaning advice, certainly, but things were more complicated than that. I had changed too much as a result of Kopec's influence on me. What I had become—forceful, fearless, more determined—had been shaped, to no small extent, by the man who had saved me. Like it or not, he was a part of me now.

Uncle Isak and I chatted a few moments more, making a pledge to spend time together, to try to figure out some kind of future. Before we parted, I asked him about his brother, a man whom I seldom saw and scarcely remembered.

My uncle began to shake uncontrollably. "It was all so stupid," he sobbed. "So damned unnecessary! He lived through the war, hiding in the forests, as I did. He never let the Germans find him. For four years he suffered and hid and lived, by luck and sheer force of will, to see the Germans driven out and sent to hell."

I did not understand. "What happened?"

"He didn't know the Germans were gone completely. How could he know? My brother remained hidden in a bunker in the forest. A friend tells me this; he saw it from a short distance away, with his own eyes. A group of Red Army soldiers come across the bunker, can tell someone's hiding inside. They order him out; he doesn't respond. They shout again—in Russian, of course—'Get out, get out *now*, hands in the air.' They don't know who's in there, a Jew, a German, a Home Army soldier . . . my brother, he doesn't understand. He's afraid. Maybe it's a trick, maybe—who knows what the hell he's thinking? 'Get out,' they holler one last time, and still he ignores them, so what can they do? They fire a hail of bullets into the bunker. They got him out all right."

"My God," I replied in a barely audible voice, and in hearing my own words, thought: *How can God let this happen? How is it possible?*

Uncle Isak was silent for a moment, then regained his composure.

"So you see," he concluded, "three in our family lived through the war. But now only two of us are left, as far as we know. You be careful, Moishe. Don't do anything foolish. I don't want to lose you too, now that we've found each other."

I nodded half-heartedly and promised to stop by my uncle's apartment. Then I continued on my way to the district headquarters building.

It never occurred to me, not then anyway, that I had not asked where my uncle had been hiding or how he had managed to survive the war.

"I can't help you," said a dour officer with the Soviet secret police. I had found my way to a run-down office in the dingy old building that served as headquarters of the district. The smell of mildew was almost overpowering.

Needless to say, I was livid. "You guys send me running around the city, from one place to another, and meanwhile the man who killed my father is walking around free!" I was on the edge of my chair, almost shouting.

"What are you complaining about?" said the officer. "He's free, that's true, but so are you. You finally *can* run around the city, go from place to place. Isn't that enough for you?"

But I heard it as "isn't that enough for *you people*?" It took great self-restraint to keep me from leaping up at the man and grabbing him by the throat. I visualized myself choking him until his face turned the color of moldy cheese.

I waited a moment to calm down, then said to him, "My freedom means nothing as long as that bastard is alive. If you don't do anything about it, I will gladly do it myself."

The Russian got up from his desk chair and walked over to me. He leaned wearily against the front edge of his desk.

"Look, the war's over," he said. "You can't just run around killing people."

I let the comment pass, although I thought, *Your comrades sure as hell didn't mind running around killing people when they pushed into Germany. Or, from what I've heard, when they rounded up thousands of Home Army leaders in Poland and either shot them or sent them to Russian POW camps.*

But what I said was, "What would *you* do?"

The Russian looked away, as if thinking it over. Then he turned back to me and replied, "I feel for you; I really do. There's just nothing we can do about this man in Grabiny. And if you're smart, there's nothing you will do either. Forget the past."

The urge to strike the man down, perhaps snap his neck, came over me again. Instead, I turned toward the door.

"Thank you for your time," I said with venom in my voice.

I left the building as the afternoon sun filtered down through a hazy veil of sky. A chill breeze was blowing. It felt good to breathe fresh air after nearly an hour in that musty, old place.

Forget the past reverberated through my mind, over and over, like an endless recording on a Victrola that was turning too slowly.

Like hell I will, I said to myself. *As if I ever could.*

I made no effort to look at people on the street as I walked, but I did overhear snippets of their conversations. The talk was about Russian and Allied victories in the east. The forces were just outside Berlin. Within days, it appeared, the war would be over throughout Europe.

But the war was not yet over for me. I should have known better than to expect help from anyone else, I realized. Very well then, I would have to handle this unfinished business myself. I would do it that very night while the need burned white hot within me.

I had an appointment to keep with an old family "friend."

I found it exhausting to trudge once more across the Wisłoka, this time just south of Straszęcin directly toward the village of Grabiny. What I was determined to do had to be done at night. There would be time to sleep when it was over. And when it was over, I realized, I would have nothing more holding me here, and no place really to go. At least my favorite uncle had survived; I was grateful for that. Well, sooner or later I would find some direction, I supposed.

Each step of the way, I relived the night when Papa and I sat bound to our chairs in Pozniak's kitchen. I could still see my father's despair, feel his fury. *I trusted you with my life. With my son's life. And this is what you do?* And the next morning, at the train station: Pozniak's lack of feeling for human life, his utter disdain for any sense of morality. *Just do your job and kill the damn Jews. Kill them like all the others and be done with it.* And how Kopec described Pozniak plunging the German's bayonet through my father's body, scarring my own back with a permanent memento of his inhumanity.

I tingled with anticipation as I saw Pozniak's house up ahead, illuminated by a nearly full moon in a clear sky. Nothing had changed. Even the siding on the side corner remained loose, as if nailing it back in place required too much effort. The barn in back looked like it had been destroyed, maybe when the Russian front came through. But the house was still there. In one room a lamp was burning. I could see it flickering through a side window.

I worked quickly. I carried two RG-42 grenades with me—the

Soviet-made "oil cans"—in the pouch within the lining of my jacket. I removed the first one and pulled the pin, squeezing the handle to keep it from detonating until seconds after I released it.

"This is for my father," I said aloud, the same way the Russians had shouted as they sought their vengeance in Upper Silesia.

I moved to the front of the house, then stood before a window, and threw the grenade. Glass shattered. The grenade dropped to the floor inside. I ran to the side of the house and pulled the pin on my second grenade, shouting, "And this is for me, you bastard." I sent this one flying through the side window, into the room lit by the lamp.

The explosions, one just after the other, shook the ground beneath my feet. I could feel the heat of the resulting fire on my back as I ran from the house, from Grabiny, from the ugly need for revenge that had driven me there.

At that moment, if I am to be honest, I no longer cared about Pozniak's house or who might be inside it. If Pozniak was not home, so be it. If, on the other hand, the man's family was injured, well, that would be an eye for an eye, would it not? It seemed to me—at least it did then—that I could wash any blood off my hands as easily as I might clean away a streak of mud.

Washing away any remorse that would eventually settle deeper within me, however, would prove to be another matter entirely.

On the second day following my attack on Pozniak's house, I was arrested.

I was picked up on the street in Dębica by two agents of the Russian secret police and put behind bars in an old building, not far from the cheder I attended as a boy. It was a dank, foul-smelling cell, redolent of sweat and urine—the collective ripeness of human beings kept in captivity by Poles, then Germans, and now Russians.

The irony did not escape me. For four years I had evaded capture by the Germans, only to be caught and imprisoned by Russians, who had befriended me. All for an act I committed myself only after the authorities refused to see justice done. Of course, it was those earlier efforts to goad the Russians into taking action that led them directly to me.

They put me in a cell by myself, taking my military jacket and remaining weapon—the Luger and several rounds of ammunition. They would not or could not give me any information as to the length or nature of my incarceration. It looked as though my luck had finally run out. I imagined that Kopec would be ashamed of me if he only knew. "After everything I learned you," he might say, "you go ahead and get yourself locked up. Didn't you take away nothing from our time together?" Here it was, months after he had rejected me when I came to his house, and I was still seeking his approval.

"Why did you arrest me?" I screamed to the men who brought me in. "The bastard killed my father!"

They were unmoved. "Because you committed a criminal act. The war is over, yet you run around throwing grenades. There's been enough lawlessness here. It's time we have some respect for authority."

"Who ordered my arrest?"

No answer.

"What am I accused of doing?"

"You know what you did. By the way, the man you were after, he wasn't home. He was out playing cards, we found out. Playing cards, can you believe it? At a friend's house."

So I didn't get him after all, I cursed to myself. Then aloud: "Well, I gave him something to come home to, that's for sure."

"You did that," replied the guard as he slammed the cell door shut on me. "You most certainly did that."

For two weeks I languished in my prison cell. I had bread and water twice a day, but little else. No word was forthcoming as to what the Russians planned to do with me. I was allowed no contact with anyone except the guards who brought my food.

I did not ask whether Pozniak had a wife or other family at home on the night I paid my visit, and no one told me how much damage I had caused, either to property or to people. I chose not to ask because I had convinced myself that I did not care.

On about the fifteenth day of my imprisonment, I was released.

"There's someone here who wants to speak with you," said the guard who unlocked my cell.

"What is there to talk about?" I asked, not hiding the insolence I felt.

The guard merely said, "Maybe you'd rather not go free?"

Free! My inclination was to jump for joy. But still I was wary. What would anyone possibly want to talk to me about?

I got my clothes back, including my Russian military jacket. I was led to an office one floor above the holding cells.

It was like every other administrative office I had been in—gloomy and musty, sparsely furnished. Other than two chairs and a cabinet, the main piece of furniture was a plain, cluttered table, which served as a desk.

I paid no attention to the name on the door. But the man who sat behind the desk was another matter. I assumed he was with the secret police, but I was not sure. He cut an imposing figure, with his tall, athletic build and light brown hair that lay in an unruly tangle above his thin face. He was maybe thirty years old, no more, to judge by his smooth, youthful face. He motioned for me to sit down.

"I know all about you, Mr. Goldner," he said, speaking slowly in Russian. I was surprised that his voice was rather soft.

I could not recall anyone calling me "Mr. Goldner" before. That was my father's name. For some reason it made me angry.

"If you know so much about me, you can tell me who had me arrested. And why."

"The 'who,' I don't know."

The Russian, I am sure, saw the skepticism on my face, for he added, "I can assure you I had nothing to do with it. I only found out about you a few days ago. As for the 'why' . . . well, the war is over, Mr. Goldner."

"So I've been hearing."

The officer got up from behind his desk. The man stood six-feet-two, maybe more. He came over and sat in the empty chair beside me.

"Your uncle was here a week or so ago. Isak, is that right?"

I gasped audibly. *How did my uncle find out I was here?*

"Luckily, he wound up talking to me and not to someone else," the officer continued. "He told me what you've been through."

"He knows very little about what I've been through."

"What he told me was appalling enough."

The Russian was silent for a moment; then he said, "Look, taking the law into your own hands wasn't the answer, but you've suffered enough without spending who knows how long in one of our cells. I was able to . . . let's say I took care of things. You'll be free to leave."

I did not know how to respond.

The officer got up and walked back behind his desk, opened a small drawer, reached in. I could not believe my eyes—the man took out my Luger and ammunition.

"I believe these are yours," said the Russian. He held them out to me. "The man you were after—he's looking to get you, I understand, and he's got friends eager to help him. Do yourself a favor; get out of this area. You've had your revenge. Don't give him his."

"Let me see if I understand. If Pozniak succeeds in killing me after all these years . . . *then* maybe you'll arrest him?"

The Russian shrugged.

I stood and put the cartridges inside my jacket but held on to the Luger. An old friend, back again. I stared at the man standing before me. "You trust me not to use this on you right now?"

"I said I knew all about you. That includes knowing you're not stupid."

He interlocked his fingers, cracked his knuckles, then walked to within inches of where I stood, forcing me to look up into his face. Once my eyes met his, he added, "Besides, why would you want to kill me for no reason? A fellow Jew, no less."

You could have knocked me over with a chicken feather. A second time!

"Like I said, it was lucky your uncle wound up talking to *me*. By the way, he asked me to give you this." He reached back and fished a scrap of paper out from under a file on his desk. "He left this past week for Katowice. At the time I didn't know how much longer you would be . . . staying with us. Here's an address he wrote down for you. It's the Red Cross there. Said he'd leave word with them as to where you can find him."

"I came back here from Katowice, and now you're telling me to go back again? What would I do there?"

The officer glanced past me to the door and the empty hallway beyond. In a low voice he replied, "*I* know what to do. Look, we can't talk here. Where can I meet you, say, tomorrow night?"

I thought it over. I was not sure I trusted this Russian yet, but if the man really was a Jew . . .

"The *targowica*," I suggested.

The Russian's puzzled look reminded me that he was a newcomer to both the town and to the Polish language. I gave him directions to the cattle market, and we agreed on 9 P.M. It would be empty. I could watch him approach, assess the situation from a hidden vantage point. I could not imagine what the man had in mind, but what the hell, I figured, there was nothing left to lose by finding out.

"I don't like being called *Mr.* Goldner," I told the plainly dressed Russian officer in the shadowy confines of a deserted animal pen. "My name is Moishe."

"All right, Moishe, then."

Moishe. It was good to be called by my given name once more.

"And you may call me *friend*. I'd prefer it if you forget my name," said the Russian.

That was easy. I never caught his name in the first place. Getting right to the point, I asked, "You said you knew what to do. What do you have in mind?"

The Russian, I think, liked my directness. "What I have in mind is a journey. An escape. A new life."

197

"To where?"

"Berlin, to begin with. Not now, but soon. To the American sector, once it's in place. From there to Germany's American zone and then, with luck, to Palestine."

My head was swimming. "I don't understand. Berlin?" It was the last place I wanted to go.

The Russian smiled. "Germany surrendered to the Red Army. Haven't you heard? Two days ago it happened. Eastern Germany is fully under Russian control now, and that includes all of Berlin, or what's left of it. But there's word that the city will be divided between the major powers, just as they'll divide the rest of Germany. The Americans should be in Berlin next month. July or August at the latest.

"What about Hitler?" I asked. I had not heard any news.

"Dead for over a week, may he rot in hell. Killed himself." He dropped his voice to a whisper. "Unfortunately Stalin is alive and stronger than ever."

Now things were fitting into place. I remembered fragments of an earlier conversation, with an even higher-ranking Russian officer. *Here I am fighting for freedom from Fascist tyranny and the megalomaniac at its head, under the leadership of yet another megalomaniac. At this moment I think I'd rather be in your shoes.*

"You're planning to escape from Stalin?" I asked. It was more of a statement, really, than a question.

"Stalin . . ." he whispered the word bitterly, as if it were poison. "It's a name he gave to himself. Do you know that Russian word, *stalin*? It means 'man of steel.' The arrogance of that bastard! Believe me, Hitler has nothing on him when it comes to Jew-hating. But then Stalin hates nearly everyone, including his own people."

"Not just the Jews?"

The Russian squatted down so we were nearly eye to eye. "Did you know that repatriated Russian POWs are being killed on Stalin's orders, because they surrendered or were captured, instead of dying gloriously in battle? Did you know that liberated Russian civilians— even those freed from German concentration camps—are being sent to Siberia? And Stalin's friends, men who helped him rise to power, did you know he killed many of them? Can you imagine it—killed his own friends!"

"Yes," I replied bitterly, thinking of Pozniak and my father. "That is something I can imagine only too well."

We both looked away toward the darkness. After a moment the Russian spoke again. "Then imagine this: sitting at a dinner table, not being able to carry on a normal conversation. In Russia there are spies everywhere. A child might leave the house, repeat some idle mealtime chatter, and the whole family winds up being sent to the Gulag. It happens all the time. It will happen here."

I kicked at the dirt with my boot. I did not for a moment doubt what I was hearing.

"You see, Moishe," concluded the officer, "neither one of us can feel at ease the way things are. Back in Russia nothing will change. And while Stalin supposedly promised free elections in Poland, you mark my words, nothing will change here, either. We're Jews, Moishe. The only place for us is in Palestine. And the only way we can get to Palestine is to get out from under Stalin." He looked at me with an intense stare. "Are you with me?"

Palestine. Finally a new direction, perhaps even a sense of purpose in my life. No more aimless wandering, that was the promise of the moment. Just one final mission awaited me, a mission not to destroy, for once, but to escape all the destruction. My new Russian friend was clearly educated, highly intelligent. . . . How could I go wrong following such a person?

"I'm with you, all right," I replied. "Just tell me when and where."

"Katowice," the Russian said. "Leave this place; join your uncle. I'll find you there when I can get away."

A fleeting image of Jan Kopec popped into my head, bursting like a bubble. "I'll do it, friend. Because you are right, there is nothing in this part of the world for me anymore."

Palestine!

17

Flight to Berlin

I T WAS EARLY IN July when I left Poland behind, stepping back onto German soil under Russian occupation. It was the first step in my search for a country where I might start a new life. Life—a concept I almost began to believe I could embrace again.

I had left Dębica within days of meeting my new Russian friend, exercising great precautions until I was far west of Pozniak's possible sphere of influence. I was pretty sure everyone had given that son-of-a-bitch too much credit, but I did not care to find out.

Along the way burned-out tanks and transport vehicles still lay helter-skelter by the side of the road. But the stacks of frozen bodies I had seen the previous winter were gone, plowed into the earth to rot, all nationalities and political alliances equal in death.

I slept wherever I could, demanded food whenever I felt hungry. My Luger, visibly tucked inside my waistband, served me well as an unspoken threat. I cared little about the consequences of resorting to violence should that prove necessary. Relying on my gun to get what I wanted was second nature to me, and if I had to use it again as more than a prop, I would. Or so I had convinced myself.

The reunion in Katowice with my Uncle Isak was a joyous one, and the companionship of a family member made the city seem far less foreboding the second time around. I had to give my uncle credit—he was not living in squalor like many of the other refugees. He had already settled into a modern apartment that had been abandoned by its former German owners, then taken over by two female Jewish survivors. Their women's touch showed. The interior had been fixed up and made absolutely beautiful, I thought, complete with linens, respectable silverware, even a delicate vase they filled with fresh flowers whenever they could find them.

How my uncle finagled this living arrangement, I did not know. I felt it would be rude to ask, although I had my suspicions. One of the women was close to my uncle's age, and Isak, I came to realize, had always been a ladies' man. The other woman was much younger, though still a few years older than me. The two women found each other, somehow, and Uncle Isak had found them both.

I was even more astounded to learn my uncle had claimed a second apartment—for him to escape to and for me to live in. At that time empty apartments were scattered throughout the city, all hastily deserted by German families who either fled or were executed as the Russians came through. If I remember correctly, it was just a matter of finding one before someone else did, staking a claim, then being prepared to defend that territory if necessary.

I knew my Russian friend from Dębica would probably not arrive until year's end, so I would need to bide my time until then. My uncle came and went as the spirit moved him. He spent far more time with his new lady friend than he did with me, and I understood completely.

As I think back on my six months in Katowice, they were completely uneventful. I moped around a great deal, keeping mostly to myself. The synagogue and Jewish community center was still standing at 13 Mlynska Street, but not once did I venture there to seek out and mingle with other Jewish refugees. What can I say? I guess I felt more comfortable being alone. Maybe it was my years of solitary living in the forests; all I know is I found it difficult to interact with others— even people who had known similar losses, faced the same period of terror and misery as I had. Countless thousands of people suffered together, yet our anguish, being such a personal ordeal, led some— like me—to endure the aftermath alone.

Uncle Isak insisted on fixing me up with the young woman who lived with his lady friend, and I reluctantly agreed. She was not unattractive, but I found her overly chatty and far too effusive. After our second outing together I mumbled some excuse and declined to see her again.

"Moishe, you've got to get some release, or you're going to burst!" Uncle Isak said to me, but I paid no attention. I simply was not ready.

Even my dream of Palestine took a back seat to the drudgery and emptiness all around me, and by the first snowfall in late 1945, with no word from my Russian friend, I fell into a state of depression. Often I would not leave my apartment for days at a time.

I found myself thinking about Kopec less often during this time, but when I did, I would try to imagine what he might be up to and speculate on whether he ever thought about me. I finally concluded he could never erase me from his mind, because in the end I gave him something beyond the money he earned for my services. Like it or not, I gave him a reason to care for someone else outside his own family. I had managed to burrow beneath his cold, calculating exterior; I was sure of it. Strangely enough, I took some comfort from that belief.

And so the days went slowly by until ten days after the arrival of the new year, on a blustery afternoon, I heard a rapping on the door, followed by hoarsely whispered words of Russian in a voice I had almost forgotten.

"Moishe? Moishe Goldner, you in there? Open up, damn it! It's cold as Stalin's heart out here!"

He danced around my apartment, flapping his arms back and forth across his chest as if he was imitating the mating ritual of some strange bird. For the first time in weeks I smiled.

"You're Russian," I told him. "This weather should be nothing to you!"

"In Russia we dress appropriately for the weather. Which, incidentally, is something for you to keep in mind for tomorrow evening."

"Tomorrow?"

"That's when we leave for Berlin. I've got it all arranged. Not that the trip will be easy. Or necessarily uneventful."

So soon! My gloom lifted, a gray ash carried away on the wind. "I'd better tell my uncle," I said. "Maybe he'll come with us."

"I've already spoken to your uncle. That's how I found you here. He knows he's welcome to come; there's already a sizeable group going with me. But I got the feeling he wasn't ready to leave on such short notice." The Russian winked and grinned as he said, "He seems to be keeping warm enough, no?"

I did not catch the man's intimation. My mind was already focused on leaving. "What will I need to bring?" I asked.

"Your pistol, for sure. A silencer, if you have one. We may need them both. Bring warm clothes and a heavy coat, of course. Your Russian military issue will be fine until we get to the American sector. If you have anything you can change into once we get across, bring it also."

"I don't, but I can steal something before we leave." I shook my head slowly and added, almost sadly: "Who would have predicted the one thing I seem to be so good at?"

"You learned from a master," said the Russian. Back in Dębica, when he had gained my trust, I had told him a little about my time with Kopec.

"Have you heard any news about him?" I asked anxiously.

202

"None. They're keeping an eye on him, I would imagine, because of his crimes before the war. He must be keeping a low profile."

I had no way of knowing, as we spoke those words, that Kopec was dying. He would live only a few more weeks.

"At any rate, whatever you learned from Kopec, you can put to good use over the next few days," said the Russian. He explained that there were several ways to escape into the American zone, which was in southern Germany. From there, according to his plan, we'd go on to Palestine. Some refugees, he said, were being secretly transported directly across Czechoslovakia, by the Bricha Zionist organization. Their exit papers, it turned out, were expertly forged right where I was, in Katowice. What I did not understand is why we were first going north to Berlin, which was still in the Russian zone.

"We think it's a better alternative," he explained.

We? Who is "we"? I wondered.

"Once we get into Berlin's small American sector—and that's where the greatest risk will come in, although arrangements have been made—the Americans can help us get safely to the American zone in the south of that miserable country."

The Russian said it confidently, but it had to have been only an assumption, something *he* had been told, for the area's politics were changing literally every day. Although Berlin's American sector had been established months earlier, it was only weeks before our border crossing—in January 1946—that U.S. authorities had reversed their position against Jewish infiltration and declared the sector a safe haven for displaced Jews. Of course, I knew none of this then.

I said, "Whatever happens, I'm with you. But I know we're going to make it across the border. I have no doubt of it."

The Russian smiled, and he asked me, "Is there anything that frightens you? *Really* frightens you?"

A moment's pause, then: "Yes—the thought that I might never understand why God let almost all the Jews here perish." I looked away, my voice choking with emotion. "And why I wasn't one of them."

It was late afternoon on the following day when I said good-bye to Uncle Isak and walked to the central station in Katowice. My uncle assured me he had no plans to remain in either Poland or Germany much longer but would take his chances with one of the organized refugee programs rather than sneak across the border, as he put it, like a "common criminal, no offense."

I knew nothing about who had planned the border crossing—*arrangements have been made*—or what the arrangements were. Was my Russian friend the leader, or was there someone else?

I had learned over the past few years not to ask too many questions. So I showed up at the appointed time, carrying only my silenced Luger and my remaining ammunition inside heavy layers of clothes. Underneath my military jacket I wore a civilian jacket that had hung, until the day before, on a hook inside someone's open back door.

Shortly after I arrived at the crowded Katowice station, the Russian officer collected a group of around twenty people: a few of them Russians, many of them Poles, all of us Jews. Our ages ranged from my twenty years—my twenty-first birthday was just weeks away—to a couple of men in their forties. There was a woman in the group as well, a mean-looking lady, with a mouth like a sewer, from the little I had overheard. Well, I supposed, she had earned the right to be bitter just like the rest of us.

The train from Berlin finally arrived at the station, more than an hour late. At least they were running now, and with some regularity, if not punctuality. Katowice was the end of the line, the turnaround point for the overnight run back to Berlin. Already the cloudy winter sky had darkened. I was anxious to put this part of the world behind me.

"Will we be able to board soon?" I asked the Russian.

"Board?" He laughed heartily. "I guess I forgot to mention that we won't be boarding this train."

"What?"

"We'll be riding on top."

Well, I thought, *I've been* under *a train. Why not on top of one for a change?*

"Now you know why the warm clothing is so important," said the Russian. "It's going to be a long, cold night."

And it was. The full twelve hours it took us to get to Berlin. Dozens of refugees rode with us on the roof. We were packed together like olives in a jar. Other travelers stood on the running boards; some even clung precariously to the sides. In the carriages themselves passengers were crammed cheek-to-jowl with no heat or lights—the result, I supposed, of Germany's coal shortage. The train carried displaced Germans mostly, whole families of them, but also surviving Jews like those in our ragtag group, trying to escape from continued persecution.

With indifference to us all, no doubt, the train's engineer pushed northward, past Brieg, Breslau, Cottbus, and Frankfurt, then due west into the eastern sector of Berlin.

My traveling companions and I huddled together and sang folk songs in Russian and Yiddish. They insisted I stay between them, in the middle, fearful that my small body might slide off the roof as the train picked up speed. I did not object; it was warmer there. Already this was shaping up to be a terrible winter. The history books say that it was the most severe winter ever recorded in eastern Germany at that time.

About eleven hours after the train left Katowice, it slowed to a crawl, plodding between indistinct heaps of rubble. Eventually we reached the bomb-pocked Stettin station—end of the line. Pandemonium reigned as the rooftop refugees climbed down off the cars, blending into the crowded masses.

It was just past 6 A.M. The rising sun scurried the thousands of rats that ruled the city at night, feeding on refuse that choked the streets and canals.

With the dawn I was shocked to see that nearly the entire city center lay in ruin. Of course, damage was severe everywhere in the city. Only one house in four, we learned, remained habitable, and the best of those had been requisitioned by the occupying armies.

The Berlin that I entered on that cold January day was truly a hellhole, already packed with millions of displaced persons. Thousands more, many of them Jews, came pouring in every day.

"We've got a long walk from here," the Russian officer said to our anxious little group. The walk, in fact, took nearly the entire day. Back then everyone had to walk. No public transportation was running in the paralyzed city.

I marveled at how my Russian friend seemed to know exactly where to lead our group. He had never before set foot in Berlin, yet here he was, following a precise plan, directions apparently committed to memory.

There was little conversation as we trudged along, exhausted and hungry, each step bringing us closer to a point on Berlin's Soviet-American border that someone, somewhere, had selected. Each step of the way we scanned the devastated terrain ahead of us, for this was the direction in which our future lay. There could be no turning back.

A total of eight checkpoints, as I understand it now, connected the Soviet sector of East Berlin to the three western sectors. Through the main east-west crossing, the Brandenburg Gate, you would pass into British control. To the north two checkpoints opened the way to the French-controlled area of the city. To the south five official points of entry provided access to the American sector. All were heavily guarded on the Russian side, with frequent patrols along the wire-strewn border between checkpoints.

As our group plodded on, the Russian officer revealed that someone was supposed to meet us at a prearranged place between the city's southernmost checkpoints. By the time the sun was low in the western sky, we had reached the area, definitely more rural than urban. The place itself looked as if it once might have been a park. The border was just beyond a line of scraggly trees visible in the distance.

The plan was simple: Someone was supposed to bribe the Russian border guards with cigarettes. That was the preferred form of exchange in those days, far more valuable than reichsmarks. In return the Russians would turn a blind eye to our group as we walked across the border. One cigarette for each one of us would have been a decent bribe; one pack per person would have been a windfall.

Who was to meet us? Where would the bribe come from? My questions were meaningless, because after we waited for nearly an hour, it became apparent that no one would be showing up. The Russian leader looked impatiently at his wristwatch, then up at the fading light. Clouds were moving in, full and gray. Soon there might be snow.

"Something went wrong," he said at last. "We can't wait any longer. Help or no help, we're going across the border now."

As warmly as we had dressed, everyone in the group was beginning to shiver again, from the falling temperature, from simply standing around, waiting. We were as ready as we would ever be.

My Russian friend came over to me and spoke softly, telling me what I needed to do. In his hand was a Tokarev TT automatic, a Russian modification of the original Colt-Browning design. He snapped in a magazine of eight cartridges. I reached under layers of clothing to pull out my own weapon, the familiar Luger. It felt good in my hand again. Too good.

Our leader addressed the group. He spoke first in Russian, then repeated his words in Yiddish. "You will follow me to the border, although we'll need to spread out. Our young friend here will go on ahead and meet us there, because a Red Army guard or guards will be patrolling with orders not to let us cross. I chose him"—he pointed to me—"because there's no one among us better qualified or better prepared, and I guarantee, no one with more balls."

I glanced over at the foul-mouthed woman in the group, who glared back. I thought to myself, *Including you, sister.*

My traveling companions wished me luck, for their own chances of reaching the American side depended on my success. They had no weapons, after all. Only the leader and I were armed.

I walked alone toward the stand of trees up ahead. From there I peered into the distance and saw the barbed wire glistening in the rays of the setting sun. The border. The thin wire demarcation that separated oppression from freedom. Cross that line and we would soon be on our way to Palestine. Or so I believed.

There was still a distance to cover before I reached the wire. I did not know how close-by the nearest patrol might be, so I crouched down into the dirt and scattered scrub, crawling forward on my belly. In one hand was my Luger. In the other was a small wire cutter, which our leader had given me. I moved slowly, cautiously, alert to any sound that might signal an ambush or, at the very least, a curious Russian guard.

And as I crawled, I recognized the return of an old, familiar sensation I thought I had outgrown long before. No mistaking it, the feeling was fear. I felt it in the pit of my stomach, in the beating of my heart, the throbbing sensation in my head. It was a level of apprehension I did not feel when I boarded the train with my shoeshine kit, or when I climbed the trestle bridge with explosives, or during any of the other situations that brought me face-to-face with death.

Why had it returned, this feeling? Looking back, I think I can explain it. Since I was so close to freedom, suddenly human life—*my* life—had value. Before, I fully expected to die one way or another, and I probably should have, many times over. But finally I could see an end to the hiding and running. I could choose life over death. I could keep the blessed memory of my parents and my sister alive in me, *in me!* The promise of all this was just up ahead, waiting, on the other side of the barbed wire. But there were Russian guards nearby who were under orders to kill me, if necessary, to keep this freedom from me, and I did not want to die, not now, not here at the border, not after coming so far.

I reached the barbed wire finally and still saw no sign of guards. I cut through the fence until there was a sizeable opening, and without further ceremony I stumbled across to the American side. It looked no different from the Russian side, here in what must have been the outskirts of Berlin. I saw a farm just to the west. And beyond that, a road. I waited by the open wire, crouched low to the ground, as a short while later my companions came through the trees, from the direction I had just come. They did not try to conceal their approach as I had done. There were too many of them to try.

As I expected, their presence did not go unnoticed for long. To my left a Russian guard came into view, a submachine gun in his hand. He was walking quickly alongside the wire fence, and luck was with me once again, for he appeared to be alone. He was a young man, not much older than me, I guessed. No different from the many young Red Army soldiers who had befriended me ever since I crawled out from under the disabled tank outside the Blizna Forest.

I grimaced at the thought of what I had been chosen to do.

Although the guard was still some distance away, had he continued to look straight ahead he might have seen the opening where I had cut the wire. But as he got closer, he was clearly looking to the east, in the direction of the approaching refugee group, and he was veering slightly away from the border fence to meet them. I heard him call for the group to proceed no further, to go back or seek out a legitimate checkpoint, and while his voice was firm, it was also polite. This suggested to me that he had no desire to fire at the refugees, that he just wanted everyone to understand his orders.

I cursed at what I had become, at what I was about to do to a young Russian soldier who meant no harm, all because someone failed to show up with a few lousy, goddamned cigarettes. With all the terrible things I did in order to survive during those cursed years, this is something I especially regret.

But back then there was no time to linger over remorse. Taking careful aim at the unsuspecting young guard, I pulled the trigger and fired my Luger for the very last time.

We walked for nearly half an hour, seeing no one. No American guards congratulating us for getting past the Red Army, no GIS running up to us, welcoming us with open arms.

You made it; we've been waiting for you! Here, eat all you can, and you must try these American candy bars. When you're done, there are private rooms and hot baths for each of you. Rest up, and as soon as you're ready, we'll get you on the next ship to Palestine. Outside cabin, upper deck, I should think, after all you've been through. The American officer spoke in Yiddish, and his voice sounded just like my father's. At least that is the way the scene played in my imagination.

The Russian officer and I stripped off our military jackets and left them on the ground. Our Russian uniforms would be liabilities from this point on. I had an ordinary jacket beneath it, the one I had stolen the previous day. The officer had a heavy flannel shirt, but no jacket. We would be warm soon enough; we were sure of it.

We walked along the road that ran beside the farm I had seen from the border. Each step of the way, we looked for signs of life. All was quiet. And then . . .

We all heard the sounds at the same moment. Gears shifting. The throaty whine of an engine. Tires slipping on cold, damp pavement.

We waited expectantly as the sounds got louder, and then, turning the corner and heading right toward us, there came into view an American Jeep so splattered with mud and grime it was impossible to tell what color it was underneath.

Brakes squealed as the two MPS in the vehicle saw our small group standing on the road. They stopped and trained their rifles on us. We all put our hands up.

"Well, who have we here?" drawled one of the MPs. At least that is what I suspected he was asking, for I understood very little English then.

The Russian officer answered in broken English. I was astounded to realize he spoke the language.

"Jews," he said, gesturing to the group. "Polish and Russian nationals. We come to ask refuge in American sector, please, sir." He then turned to us and repeated his answer so we could understand.

"Jews, huh? How'd you get past the Russian border patrol?" The American looked directly at the group's leader, then glanced at his automatic pistol. He had not hidden it away within his clothing as I had done.

I looked away as the Russian smoothly told the MP about the bribe of cigarettes. He neglected to mention that the bribe had failed and that we had to take out a guard to get to this point.

The American seemed satisfied with the response. Or perhaps he did not care *how* we got there. It was the British, we learned later, who were most intolerant of illegal border crossings, knowing that most Jews were trying to get to Palestine. *Their* Palestine.

While the MP's partner got on his radio and called for a transport, he asked my Russian friend if anyone else in our group spoke or understood English. When the leader shook his head, the American asked him to translate this message:

"Tell them . . . tell them you're all safe. A transport will come shortly and take you to an infiltree camp, to Schlactensee probably, here in Berlin. Then we'll see about getting you to a DP camp somewhere in the American zone."

In Yiddish and Russian the leader repeated the message to us. We asked what is it, this "DP camp"? A temporary holding area for displaced persons, we were told. I did not like the sound of that. How would it be different from what we heard about the Nazi's camps? This was clearly not what I had imagined, but I had to believe everything would be all right. These were the Americans, after all.

Next thing I knew, one of the two Americans walked directly up to our leader while the soldier's partner watched intently. "I'll need you to hand over your weapon, sir," was what the MP must have said.

The former officer of the Soviet Army hesitated an instant, then slowly pulled the automatic from his waistband. Gripping the thick barrel, he handed it to the American. After a sideways glance over to me, he looked back into the face of the MP and said something in English that I could not understand.

"I told him he could have it," he told us later. "I don't want to ever use the damned thing again."

The whole time I remained silent about my own weapon, which I kept well concealed. True, I could have echoed the Russian's sentiment, for I, too, never wanted to fire my gun again. But I would hold on to that Luger and my few remaining cartridges for as long as I could get away with it. Because, well, I figured it this way: you never could tell . . .

18

Displaced

M Y GROUP SPENT less than forty-eight hours in Berlin before being packed into an UNRRA transport bound for the American zone.

Just weeks earlier, according to the Americans, UNRRA had become more involved in managing the DP camps. They were planning to take over administration of the camps from the U.S. Army. As a result, acceptance and transfers had become easy to arrange.

The drive was a long one, nearly twenty-four hours to the southwest, much of it over roads and highways smoother than any I had ever seen in Poland. Our destination was Landsberg, just outside Munich. It was reputedly one of the largest DP camps in Germany.

For the first half of the journey, we were still in the Soviet zone, but this route had been sanctioned for the western powers, and we went unchallenged. Still, when we crossed into the American zone somewhere near Coburg, all of us aboard the transport let out a whoop of joy.

It was only when we arrived at the camp that we became aware of a new reality: the situation in the west was not much better than it was in the east.

The Landsberg DP camp, specifically, was a horror.

It was grossly overcrowded and growing more so every day. It held more than six thousand men, women, and children. Mostly Jews, I think, a majority of whom came from concentration camps, particularly nearby Dachau. Landsberg had also been designated as a reception center for unauthorized groups of Jews fleeing Poland.

Processing and registration took place in the main building, called the Roosevelt House. Registration consisted of a series of questions regarding personal background and information, administered in Yiddish by the few Jewish soldiers and officials there who could speak the language. Some, I understand, had themselves escaped from Europe just before the war and returned as officers in the U.S. Army.

"Name?" a soldier asked me, when I finally came to the front of a long line.

"Goldner. Moishe Goldner," I answered. Moniek had been my Polish name. I shed it as easily as a snake sheds its skin.

"Nationality?"

"Jewish."

"Nationality?" the soldier asked again, louder this time, with obvious annoyance.

"Polish," I said, almost choking on the word.

And so it went.

I was assigned to a filthy barrack that had once housed a Wehrmacht artillery post. Others in my group, for whatever reasons, were assigned elsewhere.

My block was three stories high and built of brick. Bunks were made of rough-hewn lumber, both double- and triple-decked. The mattresses were sacks filled with straw. I was given one shoddy gray blanket, which could have been either U.S. Army or Wehrmacht issue. Who could tell? It was my only possession, other than my concealed weapon and the fresh clothes I had been given—the clothing donated, I suspect, by American Jews. I was allotted a narrow wooden wall locker in which to keep my things. I did not need it.

There was no place in the camp that offered any privacy. Not in the barracks nor in the washrooms or latrines, where more than half of all sinks and toilets were inoperative. The streets of the camp were strewn with garbage. Above the iron fence that surrounded the compound, I could see the remains of barbed wire.

On the day of my arrival I had plenty of time to take note of my new surroundings while standing in line for my first bowl of soup. I stood out in the cold for more than two hours as the long line slowly inched forward. The apparent lack of organization and planning was maddening.

I was not much of a conversationalist; I had little to say to anyone. Eventually, however, I turned to the man standing behind me.

"I feel like I've gone from one hellhole into another," I said in Yiddish. "I was lucky never to have been imprisoned in a concentration camp, but now that the war is over, here I am. The German camps could not have been much different than this one."

The man I spoke to, it turned out, was an emaciated Dachau survivor who was at least fifty years old. He pulled his thin coat tightly around him in a futile attempt to ward off the chill. He considered my words for a moment.

"You're wrong about there not being much difference," he said dryly. "At Dachau, I must tell you, we didn't get a blanket."

I forced a weak smile, then said, "I just got here, but I'm planning to leave soon for Palestine."

The man snickered, "You and everyone else. I've been here a while, and let me tell you, I don't know anyone who's made it to Palestine yet. The British control the immigration, and they're no more partial to us than the Nazis were."

I mused how for the past four years I had lived in hiding, a wanted man. And now, here I was, *un*wanted, like all the other DPs. *Which is worse?* I wondered. *Which is truly worse?*

As unpleasant as I found Landsberg, though, conditions there had actually been improving, from what I heard. Under the command of U.S. Army Major Irving Heymont a plan had been put in place to eventually transform Landsberg into a self-governing community.

Heymont was sensitive to the feelings many of the refugees held—that they were now merely prisoners of a different sort. So he abolished the old system of allowing the refugees to leave the camp only with permission and for just one day at a time. By the time I arrived, we were all free to come and go as we wished. American guards had been withdrawn from the camp, except for one stationed at the main gate. His job was not to keep anyone in, but to keep the starving and desperate German masses out.

While the long lines for food continued day after day, at least I received basic nourishment. From time to time—usually in the mess line—I ran into the Russian Jew who helped get me out of Poland, but over the ensuing months our paths crossed less and less.

Much of my time was spent in the progressive educational system of the camp. Garages had been turned into classrooms and vocational schools where various trades were taught. My schooling was primarily in Hebrew, for the goal was to prepare everyone ultimately for life in the Jewish homeland. In spite of the shortcomings of my childhood education, which ended at age thirteen, I had a great ear for languages. I began picking up English, even Hungarian, which I heard spoken around the camp.

Shortly after my arrival I was approached to join Hanoah Hatzionim, one of the many kibbutzim that had been formed in Landsberg and other Jewish DP camps. I still had little interest in being part of any survivors' group, but the single objective of communes like Hanoah Hatzionim was to facilitate immigration to Palestine. Realizing the importance of being a part of it, I joined.

213

Still, even among the Jews I came to know in my new commune, I remained silent about my wartime experiences. How could I talk about some of the things I had done or the even worse acts I had witnessed? How could I explain my eighteen-month relationship with an infamous criminal, even to fellow survivors who had their own horrible tales? I could not. I felt it was no one's business but my own. I would keep details of my past to myself. It was enough that I should be forever haunted by it.

But the few times I came across refugees from my general area in Poland, I would ask if they knew anything of Jan Kopec, the famous bandit. A few had never heard of him; others knew about him from before the war, when his actions fueled the pipeline of local gossip. Not surprisingly, no one knew what had become of him once the Germans invaded.

One day I met a refugee who had just come to Landsberg, an elderly man originally from Tarnów. He told me he was not certain, but he thought he had heard, through a friend of a friend, that a man from the area—a Pole who for years had robbed and terrified people all over southern Poland—had recently died, leaving a wife and eight children.

If Pozniak's bayonet had pierced my heart when I lay beneath my father, it would not have hurt more. I thanked the man for passing on the news, but my first reaction was disbelief. *It could not be true,* I thought. I had resigned myself to never seeing Kopec again, but I could not believe he was dead. Who knew better than I that he was indestructible! But then I started thinking, *Suppose he really is dead? Could one of Kopec's many enemies finally have finished him off after all?*

Turns out, that is not at all what ended his life.

For according to Kopec's children, their father's health had already begun to deteriorate at the war's end. I do not recall noticing any changes in him during our final days together, but apparently years of living on the run, imprisonment in Auschwitz, exposure to the elements—all this took its toll. Just months after the liberation, his children said, their father's condition worsened. He became weak. Had trouble breathing.

And on February 15, 1946, at the age of forty, he succumbed. Not to the Russian secret police, or to the Polish authorities who had hunted him years earlier, or to any of the victims he had robbed or harmed or threatened during his illustrious life, but to an even more ruthless foe.

Viral pneumonia.

This being the case, he died not at all in the way he had lived— boldly, dangerously, bigger than life—but instead, gently and peacefully.

In his sleep.

In his new home.

The very home that had stood empty the day I walked past it for the last time. The home that had belonged to Moishe, the shopkeeper, the Jew.

After four months in the overcrowded Landsberg camp, I yearned to see what was on the outside. So one morning in late May, after tucking my pistol into my clothes, I strolled toward the mess line but kept on going, straight through the front gates of the camp, toward the town of Landsberg itself.

Rationally I knew I could leave any time I wished. Yet with every step I almost expected to be stopped and ordered at gunpoint to return. It was not until I found myself blocks away from the camp that I got my bearings and thought to myself, *Now what?*

I wandered through the city of Landsberg and began to realize that while the camp I just left was dirty and disorganized, with barely any privacy, at least there had been a sense of belonging, a shared past, a common destiny.

Although I was free to go anywhere at all, I felt a renewed wariness, a vague sense of caution that had greatly diminished inside the camp. For in the German cities and villages a tremendous amount of anti-Semitism still existed against the Jewish DPs. I suppose there was a fear that we might enter a trade or occupation on German soil, or—perish the thought—reclaim property that once was ours. And the town of Landsberg, even with its heavy U.S. military presence, was no exception. Apparently just six months before I arrived, the town mayor complained in a memo to the Bavarian government about the "Israelites" who were infiltrating the community and threatening to convert it "into a ghetto."

By midafternoon, I reached the other side of town, and if I had kept walking down the same road, I eventually would have arrived in Munich. But I was tired and hungry and unsure of what to do next, so I stopped when I came to a large farmhouse.

I walked up to the door and knocked, with the intention of re-questing—demanding, more accurately—food and a place to sleep somewhere on the property. Old habits, I guess, are hard to break.

The door opened and there stood the owner of the house, a German woman who was maybe in her early fifties. She seemed well-to-do, by postwar standards.

Speaking in German, I told her that I would require something to eat and a place to rest. I held the Luger in my hand, not pointed threat-eningly at her but down at my side. Enough to suggest I was not to be trifled with.

"Please don't hurt us," she pleaded. "You can have what you want, and I promise you have nothing to fear from us."

"Us" included her daughter, a stunning girl in her mid-twenties, and another woman of perhaps sixty whom she had taken in. Both of the older women had lost their husbands in the war, I would soon find out. One had lost two sons as well.

I felt no sympathy.

I came inside to a home that was clean and bright and cheery. The owner led me to her kitchen, which looked to have been freshly painted in white. Sunlight streamed through gauzy curtains that covered a small window.

I sat down at the table, putting my pistol down in front of me. Within minutes she and the other two women appeared, carrying some bread and a generous slice of wurst. I ate greedily, watching as the women exchanged glances.

They excused themselves for a moment. I could hear them whispering in the next room. My fingers moved closer to the gun on the table.

The ladies came back into the room, but the oldest and youngest stayed slightly behind as the mistress of the house took a seat across from me. Her eyes glanced nervously down toward my right hand, which rested close to my gun.

There was great sadness in her voice as she said, "Look, I lost my husband and two sons in a war we should never have fought."

I must have looked at her doubtfully, because for a moment she seemed flustered.

"Does that surprise you?" she asked. "That not all Germans were behind Hitler, or shared his hunger for war and domination? We're human beings too, you know. At least, we can be."

I said nothing. People, I was starting to conclude, would never cease to astonish me. I could testify firsthand to their capacity to do evil. Goodness, on the other hand, was a concept I found much more difficult to accept.

"You're welcome to stay here tonight," she continued. "But we were wondering—would you consider staying on a while longer and helping us? We'll give you a room of your own, and fresh clothes and food. Whatever you need."

"How could I help *you*?" I asked.

There were chores that needed a strong back, they told me. Repairs. Working the field. Cutting down firewood.

Without thinking it over more than a few moments, I agreed. It might be a pleasant change, I figured, and Landsberg would still be there if I decided to return. The three women seemed not to care what my ethnic background was, although they may well have guessed. Thankfully, they did not pry.

After several days I found myself becoming attracted to the daugh-

216

ter. Ilga, I think her name was. She was just a little taller than me, with a pretty face, light brown hair, and a shapely figure that I could not help but notice. Day after day her breasts strained against her tight cotton blouses like twin peaks in the Tatras, or so I fantasized.

Moishe, you have to get some release, or you're going to burst! My uncle's words echoed in my head. I wondered if it was all wishful thinking, or was this girl the enticing little coquette she seemed to be?

I decided I could not stick around long enough to find out. As stimulated as I was by the sight of Ilga, the idea of sleeping with one of *them*—with a German girl—was abhorrent to me. What can I say? I figured I would find someone else eventually. But this was neither the time nor the place.

So after nearly a month I announced that it was time for me to move on. The women were clearly disappointed.

"Good luck to you," the older one called out to me as I walked through their door for the last time.

Ilga was silent. In spite of my ambivalent feelings, I would have given almost anything to know what she was thinking.

"Good luck to you as well," I said in return, and—surprising myself—I realized I meant it.

Then I started back in the direction from which I had come, back toward Landsberg, to face my future, grim and uncertain as it seemed.

I had not walked more than a few blocks when I suddenly stopped on a whim, turned around, and began to head in the opposite direction, past the house I had just left, toward Munich.

It was early. A light cloud cover hinted that the morning might not become unbearably hot. Not that it mattered. In a few hours I would be in the Bavarian capital where, I impulsively decided at that moment, I would catch a train to Salzburg. For I remembered hearing that the DP camps in Austria's American zone were far more livable than those in Germany. I could not imagine ever returning to the filthy Landsberg camp and wondered why it had taken me until now to realize it.

I was wearing striped pants, a lightweight jacket, and a handsome cotton shirt that felt cool against my skin—all expertly tailored to my frame by the women I had just left.

My weight had gone up to 121 pounds or so, the result of not having to stand in line, over the past month, for meager rations. Physically, I felt better than I had at any time since the war began; mentally, though, I still remained largely indifferent to most everyone around me, feeling as if my suffering were somehow unrivaled.

In Munich I found the station and waited patiently for a departing train. Several hours later I sneaked on board an express bound for Salzburg, just across the Bavarian-Austrian border.

217

I had no trouble completing the journey, hiding the entire time from the train's conductors. Compared to my previous feats of subterfuge, this was easy.

From what I had heard, there were three nicely maintained DP camps in the Salzburg region. The largest, reputedly, was Bindermichel. The grandest, according to reports, was some distance away in Badgastein, where the refugees were housed, if you can believe it, in large resort hotels. But the camp I headed for was conveniently located just outside Salzburg. It was a place where several hundred Jewish survivors were being housed in what was formerly a complex of elite SS barracks. It went by the name New Palestine.

As I approached the camp on foot, my lungs filling with clean alpine air, I saw the complex in the distance, shimmering in the morning sun. It looked just as I had imagined it would—a sleek, modern settlement. I picked up my pace, and when I got closer, my heart beat even faster as I thrilled to one small detail that completed the picture:

There, framed against the dramatic backdrop of blue-white mountains, was a flag flying high over the complex of buildings. It was white, with a blue Star of David positioned boldly in its center. It was a *Jewish* flag, the flag of Palestine and the Zionist movement, a flag of promise and deliverance, here, here in what had been the belly of the beast, and it was without a doubt the most beautiful sight that I, in my twenty-one tumultuous, harrowing years, had ever seen.

At Camp New Palestine the roads and barracks were clean, there were modern sinks and flush toilets that worked, and meals did not require a two-hour wait. For me it was almost paradise.

I encountered no problems when I presented myself to the camp administrators. Here, UNRRA and another organization, AJDC—American Joint Distribution Committee—ran the camp. They were aided by a small group of swarthy men who spoke perfect Hebrew but very little Yiddish. It was my first encounter with Jews from Palestine.

The kibbutzim in Camp New Palestine were highly organized. Some were liberally Reform, others devoutly Orthodox. I joined the branch of Hanoah Hatzionim here and was immediately immersed in Hebrew studies that lasted all day, six days a week.

Then, after about three weeks in my new surroundings, I was introduced to something that was, in reflection, probably long overdue.

Measles.

For in spite of having lived on the run for four years and having slept outdoors in the worst kinds of weather, I had escaped illness just as neatly as I had evaded bullets and bayonets.

When the spots broke out, I was immediately transferred to the quarantine unit of a nearby hospital, where I discovered my malady was minor compared to the screaming patients I heard through the walls. Those men, I was told, were suffering from syphilis.

Maybe Uncle Isak was right; without female companionship I'll burst, I reminded myself. *But it's a hell of a better alternative than what these men are going through.*

When I returned to the camp a couple of weeks later, I was selected by the Palestinians to augment my hours of Hebrew with a new curriculum: weapons and combat training. But it quickly became evident to them that I was already well versed in both survival and combat skills. In fact, I found myself teaching *them* a thing or two; Kopec had prepared me well. He had given me an education in survival that no one, not even the rugged Jews from Palestine, could have taught me.

Little by little I began to open up and reveal some of my past exploits to those around me. I have to admit my experiences as a saboteur and unwitting underground fighter in Poland elevated me in the eyes of my fellow survivors. As former prisoners of concentration camps, they looked up to anyone who had had the opportunity to strike back at the Germans.

My background and understanding of weapons and combat also piqued the interest of the Palestinians. They included me in a group selected for illegal migration to their homeland. And they asked me to join their own group, right there in Austria.

"We're fighters too," they told me. "We belong to the Haganah."

The Haganah, a Jewish underground militia, was first formed in Palestine during the 1920s to protect Jewish settlements against Arab attack. It had been reactivated within Europe after the war with the task of organizing clandestine transport to Palestine. They used truck, rail, and specially outfitted cargo vessels for the long and dangerous journey. All such immigration was highly illegal, of course. It was run by an institution known as Mossad Le'Aliyah Beth, whose members were recruited from within the Haganah.

"We can use a guy like you in the Mossad," a man named Shmuel said to me. "You're tough, and you seem to know several eastern European languages. We have a mission, and you can help."

"A mission?" I had hoped never to hear that word again.

"To find Jews who are still in hiding or who haven't been able to cross their border to come to a camp like this one. You don't need the training we offer here; you've had more experience in combat than many of us. We'd like you to travel with us."

I did not know what to say. "Travel where?"

"Hungary, primarily. Damn strange language. Probably Slovakia, as well. You can speak in either tongue?"

"Yes, a little. Enough." I knew I could manage well enough to be understood. But there was one important consideration that I could not overlook.

"What about Palestine? If I work with you here, when do I go to Palestine?"

Shmuel smiled. "I promise that within six months you will personally join a group to the homeland. We'll need you there. But right now we need you here even more."

That was good enough for me. I shrugged and spoke the words that had come out of my mouth many times before: "Why not? I have already lost everything. What more do I have to lose?"

It was mid-September when I began traveling with two, sometimes three, men from the Mossad in search of survivors who could be channeled into Palestine via the ever-changing secret routes. My first trip was to Budapest, with stops in numerous small towns along the way.

This time, I am happy to report, no killing was necessary to cross borders. My small unit had ample money and plenty of cigarettes for bribes, most of it the result of donations from American Jews. And we had visas—which at the time I assumed were legitimate—to aid our passage. I never realized until much later that the Mossad prided itself on the forgery of perfect passports and certificates from any country in the world.

We traveled on passenger trains, and this time I did not have to ride above or below the carriage or hide within it. While my command of the unusual Hungarian dialect was less than perfect, I could still speak and understand it better than my companions. Together we successfully located Jews—many of whom had been hidden by gentile families—who were eager to go to Palestine.

Throughout the autumn months and into winter I made more than half a dozen such trips with the Mossad. Twice we found entire families who had hidden together and survived. I knew I should have rejoiced for them, but I could only think of how my own family had all been killed. That's when the familiar bitterness, like magma, came bubbling up to the surface.

The Jews we uncovered were turned over to other Mossad operatives, usually in Vienna, which had become the major center for Jewish exodus. There the refugees were given a physical exam and an UNRRA identity card.

But the depth and extent of Haganah/Mossad operations went far beyond that. From Vienna, as I understood it, the refugees often traveled by truck across the Brenner Pass, into Italy. There they were transferred to one of several small ports for their Mediterranean crossing. From that point on it was simply a matter of luck whether they got past the British and into Palestine. Some did; many more did not.

My small part in it all was just another job to me, frankly. The means to an end. The bitter winter of 1946–47 seemed even worse than the one before, and by the start of the new year, I counted the days until my six months would be up. Then I would make the trip myself, even with all its uncertainties. I was sure of it.

It was on March 6, 1947—just two days before I was finally scheduled to leave for Palestine—that I was picked up by the U.S. military while on my way to Vienna in a crowded bus. I was taken by truck to military headquarters at Frankfurt.

There, I was interrogated—that can be the only word for it—by a large-boned Dutch woman (an UNRRA official?) who sat behind a massive desk and held a slim file with the name "Goldner" on the extended tab. She already knew my birthplace and family background. I assumed she got that information from my registration at the Landsberg camp.

"Why do you want to go to Palestine?" she demanded.

Clearly it was no coincidence that I had been picked up just as I was getting ready to undertake the illegal journey.

"Why do you want to go to Palestine?" she asked again, sharply this time, speaking German in an attempt to find a common language. I can still hear her exact words that followed: "You just came out of one fire, and now you want to jump right into another one?"

By this time I had reached a boiling point. I was tired from the long journey by road, annoyed at being intercepted, furious at the treatment I was receiving from this . . . this *administrator,* whoever the hell she was. She could not remotely understand the fire I came out of, it seemed to me.

"Where the hell were you when they were killing us by the millions?" I demanded. "I'm not afraid of more fighting; fighting is all I know. At least in Palestine I could fight for a place to belong, not a place to get away *from.* Who are you to tell me I can't go there? Who made *you* the boss?"

The woman did not seem the least bit put off by my response. She pursed her lips together, looked down into her "Goldner" folder, then looked back toward me.

After a moment's silence she said, "You know, you have family in the United States. An uncle. Aunts. Cousins."

A statement, I realized. Not a question. This caught me by surprise.

"I think . . ." I stammered, "I believe my father had . . . has . . . a brother and two sisters. They left for America when I was very young. I don't know them. And I don't know any cousins."

"Well, your uncle in Chicago—Louis Goldner, it says here—he, for one, knows about you."

"How can that be?" I did not have a glimmer of an idea where this place was that she called Chicago.

The woman pushed her nose back in the file. "He has a son. Your first cousin, that would be. Irving Goldner. An officer in the U.S. Army. Looks like he did a search for surviving family. Learned about you through records in Landsberg, then Salzburg. We've been trying to catch up with you for several months, Mr. Goldner. Oh, and it looks like you have cousins in New York as well."

She waited several moments for this new information to sink in. Then she said, "You're a very lucky young man, Mr. Goldner. You have sponsors in the United States."

I had not thought much about America before. I was despondent that after everything I had been through, I still could not shape my own destiny.

"I suppose this means I'm not going to Palestine," I said glumly.

19

America

AFTER A LONG AND difficult crossing, the SS *Marine Flasher* slipped past the Statue of Liberty and docked in New York. The date was March 14, 1947.

I stood at the railing with other refugees as the ship glided into its berth. This was not the Palestine of my recent dreams; I remained bitter at having my wishes ignored. Still and all, I had to admit that this place at least was far from the nightmares of my recent past. I said a silent "thank-you" to Jan Kopec, words I would never get to say to him face to face. He was the reason I had come this far. He was the only reason I was alive at all.

I looked toward shore, the landmass called America, with feelings of both anticipation and trepidation. I had no idea of what to expect from this new country or from my new family, nor could I fathom what recent quirks of fate had even brought me to this point, so far away from the death and decay of Eastern Europe.

Hours later military personnel processed my papers. That's when I discovered they had changed my first name from Moishe to Morris. *Fine. Call me Morris. What's another name?*

I was put up with other young refugees in a building in Brooklyn— an orphanage, perhaps? Something in the back of my mind . . . I do recall that I was given new clothes and three filling meals each day.

Soon I began to explore the streets in my new country. I was overwhelmed by the tall buildings, the lights, the heavy motorcar traffic, the horns, the smells from sidewalk vendors, the store windows with strange and wonderful things for sale. Gone was the devastation and abject poverty of Germany and Eastern Europe; in their place was hope and opportunity, freedom and possibilities. I did not know quite what to make of it.

Just two weeks after I settled in Brooklyn, I was contacted by a man who said he was my cousin. "Can you come for Shabbes dinner?" he asked, speaking Yiddish. Nervously I agreed.

On Friday my cousin came to Brooklyn and escorted me to his home in the Bronx. It was my first time on a subway; its loud screeches took me back, just for a moment, to the artillery barrage in the Blizna Forest.

My cousin, who lived in a comfortable apartment with his wife, made me feel welcome. Although I knew a little English by then, we communicated in Yiddish. They didn't press me for many details of the war, for which I was grateful. They talked instead about family, about America. After dinner they asked me to accompany them to Sabbath services.

It was the first time I had set foot in a synagogue in eight years. And this time—thanks to my extensive Hebrew schooling in Landsberg and Camp New Palestine—I actually understood the liturgy. But I chose not to join in.

After services my cousin introduced me to the rabbi, who warmly clasped my hand. We exchanged a few pleasantries in Yiddish, then fell into a brief silence. At length I spoke up. I could not stop myself from blurting out what had been troubling me. And, I must confess, it troubles me still.

"May I ask you something, Rabbi?"

"Of course. Anything."

"You talk about God. You pray to God. You worship God." The anger had been building up in me for years. "If there really *is* a God, where was He? Where was He when my grandparents were machine-gunned? Where was He when my mother and sister were taken away to die? Where was He when my father was killed at the hands of his so-called friend, when I had to live like a wild animal in the forests, when millions of innocent people were tortured and beaten and killed? How could He let it happen?"

It surely was not the first time the rabbi had been asked this question, yet he looked—how should I put it?—stunned, I would say.

Choking back tears of his own, he put his arm gently around my shoulders and gave me the only answer he could, the only answer he knew to be the truth, and his heart must have ached as he said it, for it was no answer at all.

"I don't know," he replied in a small, trembling voice. "I . . . don't . . . know . . ."

For the next three months I settled into a pleasant routine, visiting my cousin nearly every Friday evening and continuing to explore the strange and colorful streets of Brooklyn. The rest of the time I took classes in English administered by one of the Jewish agencies.

Soon it was summer, and at long last I held a ticket in my hand for the passenger train to Chicago. Such a train it was! I knew I would be living with my relatives in that city—they had contacted me several times by mail—and there I was destined to begin my new life in earnest.

Within days I would arrive in that unfamiliar city, bringing with me all my worldly possessions—namely, the clothes on my back and a few changes, courtesy of UNRRA. I carried them easily in a single paper bag.

And along with my clothes I brought just one other item. The one last thing that belonged to me, that had been by my side through hell and back.

You may have guessed it was the Luger. The captured Luger that some partisan, fighting for a free country, had pried from a dead German soldier's hand during my first real act of sabotage.

It was not that I planned to use the weapon ever again, although the urge to do so would come over me many times during my first few years in America. I don't know; perhaps the gun had become a symbol to me, a token of what I had been forced to become, a metaphor given form and shape for all I had endured. It was an evil thing, I knew that, crafted by people who had succumbed to an insane doctrine of domination and annihilation. But like it or not, the weapon had been a close and necessary part of me, and for some reason I could not throw it away any more than I could discard who I was.

I cannot explain my motive any better than that.

As I boarded the magnificent train, my future seemed filled with both anxiety and promise. Life would not be easy, I was certain of that, but this was America. Here I would be free to make something of myself. Here I could rise above the terrible things I did while I struggled, against overwhelming odds, to make it through the war.

Our time together has made you tough as nails, Kopec told me once.

So it had. But it was not just being *around* him that had made me tough. For once he did not give himself enough credit. It was Kopec himself—his consistent training, drilling, and meticulous rehearsals before each mission—that forged and pounded and shaped me into the survivor I had become.

But that was no longer enough, I realized. I could not continue to justify a life where I simply existed, one day at a time. If the memories

225

of Mama and Papa and Gita and my beloved grandparents were to be preserved—if there was to be any meaning to the reality that I, over all the others, had been spared—then I could not just survive.

Now I must learn to live.

How does one prepare for such a lesson? We're born, we develop a unique personality, we observe our parents and those around us, and before we know it, we're filled with the stuff life is made of: obligations and pleasures and friends and interests and dreams. Can this all be relearned if it has been taken away, if one has been forced, by necessity, to bear malice, to destroy, to shun human contact, to fantasize not about something pleasurable, but—dare we dream?—something that merely brings less pain?

To live again would not be easy. I knew it then, and I can tell you now, it was harder than I ever imagined. Those early years in Chicago were especially difficult.

When I arrived at Union Station, I was met by my aunt and uncle. Louis Goldner was my father's brother, and his resemblance to my father triggered a surge of longing that almost brought me to tears. He, along with my cousins Irving and Esther, all showered me with kindness and understanding. Still, I could not help feeling that I was a burden.

Uncle Louis begged me to get a "good American education," which in his mind included college. I agreed at least to attend night school to earn my high school diploma. But by day I was determined to learn a trade, any trade, that would pay decent enough money to allow me to be self-sufficient. Never again, I vowed, would I beg, borrow, or steal anything from anyone.

One day I learned about an opening for a fabric cutter at a company that manufactured, of all things, baseball jackets.

"I want to learn the trade. I want to be a cutter," I told the owner boldly, in my heavily accented English. I did not know anything about the garment business, but I could learn. I even offered to work for nothing while he taught me the trade. That piqued the interest of the owner, a cherubic fellow named Harry Weinstein. He looked at me suspiciously.

"You'll work for nothing?" he asked. A wry grin spread across his face, and he patted down the narrow thicket of hair that ran in a semicircle behind his head from ear to ear. "Very well then, you'll start by using this."

He handed me a broom.

Every day for the next week, there I was with my broom, with a mop and a bucket, sweeping and scrubbing the factory floors. Enjoying the free labor, Weinstein seemed not the least bit upset that I was not learning the garment trade as he had promised.

Finally I could no longer hide my anger. I charged into the man's office, broom in hand, a five-foot tempest.

"You know, Mr. Harry," I snarled, "I killed people like you for a hell of a lot less. If I had run into you back in Poland, I would have put a bullet in your head without thinking twice."

The man sat frozen to his chair, too startled, I think, to react.

I was not finished with him. "Here you are, a Jewish man, and do you ever ask me where I come from or what I've been through? Do you ever think to ask if I have carfare, or if I am hungry? Do you give a damn what happened to millions of people over there? Do you ever stop to think that it could have happened to *you?*"

Weinstein opened his mouth to speak, but I cut him off with a wave of my hand.

"I offered to work for *bubkes,* for nothing, but that was so I could learn a trade, so I could make something of myself, not just sweep your floors. You took advantage of me, mister. Here's your broom back"— I flung it in a wide arc, and it glanced off the corner of the man's desk— "go sweep the goddamn floors yourself."

Weinstein, I am sure, stared in amazement as I stormed out the door. But to my surprise, he called me the next day. Apologizing profusely, he asked me to return to his factory, promising he would train me at once to be a cutter, just as he had originally promised.

This time he was true to his word.

My first day I was laying out fabric almost as if I was born to it. After a couple weeks I was not only cutting but getting the job done ten times faster than the *alte kuckers*—the old timers—who made up most of Weinstein's work force. I was driven to seek salvation through hard work.

For I discovered that work cleansed me, freed my mind from looking back. I did not need much sleep, which was just as well, because with sleep came the nightmares. They were real, these terrors; they were form and flesh, my immediate past. I found I could usually shake the hellish images during the day, but when they did surface, I revealed very little of them to anyone. After all, who would believe what I had seen, what I had been through? I could barely believe it anymore myself.

So I worked with a speed and skill—immodest as this may sound— that they had never seen before. Before long I had earned quite a reputation for myself, and next thing I knew, I was lured away by Mr. Kalish, who offered me better pay at Debutante Fashions.

It was there an incident happened that opened all the old wounds that were just beginning to heal.

I was hunched over my cutting machine one afternoon when I sensed somebody standing behind me. As I turned and looked up, my eyes met the cold glare of the man who worked a sewing machine at the back table, an older German-born fellow whom everyone called Jimmy. The man was barrel-chested and equally full in the waist, with thick spectacles perched on a ruddy, roundish face. Although Jimmy was well under six feet tall, when I turned to face him, I came up only to his chin. I noticed a nervous tic playing across one side of his face and sensed an attitude of loathing in my coworker's narrowed eyes. I had seen it before, this look, hundreds of times. But not here. Not in America.

Jimmy regarded me with a sneer that even carried over to the inflection of his voice.

"Tell me, you industrious little asswipe, what country are you from?"

I unflinchingly held the man's gaze. "Poland," I said, offering nothing more.

A low growl came from Jimmy's throat; then he snarled, "Obviously Hitler didn't do a good enough job. You got away."

Jimmy, I am sure, never saw my fist that slammed with resounding force into his ample stomach. It caused him to double over in pain just before my second blow sent his glasses flying, along with a couple of teeth. In seconds he was on the ground, blood pouring from his mouth, no doubt trying to comprehend how he could have so underestimated a little guy like me.

At that moment—how can I explain this?—I was no longer in the factory of Debutante Fashions. I was back in Poland, filled to the bursting point with Kopec's cold and calculating bravura, and once more I had the enemy at my feet. Only this time, it seemed, it was not just one man trying to deflect my powerful blows, but every German and Pole and Ukrainian who ever threatened me or my family. I did not have a weapon to use, but my rage was enough, so I kicked and pummeled and beat my enemy into unconsciousness, and even then I did not stop . . .

The other workers ran over to pull me off their pitiful, broken coworker, who lay on his back, bleeding and torn, his breathing erratic and labored. It took several men to forcibly hold me back until my fury subsided.

The defeated man was carried off. Work tenuously resumed.

A short time later Mr. Kalish called me into the large glass-walled office that overlooked the factory floor.

"You're such a quiet, gentle boy," he said softly, sitting informally on the front edge of his beat-up metal desk. "What brought this on?"

I stood there awkwardly, eyes downcast. Finally I responded slowly in measured English, my voice void of any emotion.

"If I had my Luger here at work with me, I would have used it. I would have shot that bastard dead."

Mr. Kalish registered no surprise at my rancor. He simply asked, "What exactly did Jimmy say to you?"

I told him.

Mr. Kalish shook his head from side to side and sighed deeply. "When the man recovers I will fire him, of course," he said. Still, it was little consolation. It seemed to me there would always be more Jimmys.

"I can't begin to imagine what you've been through," Mr. Kalish said to me, his voice filled with compassion.

"That's true, you can't," I responded flatly. "I doubt anyone can."

Shortly after that incident I left the company. Mr. Kalish begged me to reconsider, but I had to move on.

I began cutting for a succession of garment houses—Franklin Dress, I. Doctor. Each job was better than the last; each new employer was anxious to hire me based on my growing reputation. I did it all—cutting, sizing, drafting—often for two different companies in the same eighteen-hour day.

The whole while, I lived frugally and saved my money. Soon I had enough for a down payment on a six-unit apartment building. You really can do that in America, I realized. You can work hard and earn fair pay in return and not ever have to answer to anybody.

After a time I stopped wondering what my life would have been like in Palestine. More fighting, certainly. But the fighting was behind me now, I realized, people like Jimmy notwithstanding.

I still did not go out much. When I did get together with other people, it was at an occasional B'nai B'rith Organization social function. Dancing, socializing—kibbitzing—did not come easily to me. More often than not, my cousin Irving had to cajole me into going.

Which is exactly what he did one balmy spring morning. Throughout that entire day I debated about attending the dance and social after work. At the last minute I decided to go, if for no other reason than to stave off my cousin's inevitable kvetching if he learned that I had stayed home.

What I could not foresee, as I shuffled out of the garment factory that evening, was that I was about to meet the woman who would be my wife and the mother of my three daughters. She was an attractive Russian émigré named Eda. She, too, had come because someone—a girlfriend, in this instance—had coaxed her.

I saw her standing off to one side, this petite young woman of exactly my height, and was struck at once by her beauty. Familiar words popped into my head: *What have I got to lose?*

I walked over and asked her to dance. She looked me over as I approached, which raised my hopes that her attraction to me was just as immediate. Turns out, I was not mistaken.

Well, we danced and danced, this free-spirited girl and I. And today, some fifty-two years later, we are dancing together still.

But back at that social we also talked, conversing easily in Yiddish well into the night. She told me she had come to America from Russia before the war, when she was eight. I think I muttered that I had been in this country only a couple of years, that America was not my first choice, but that somehow fate always seemed to know what was best for me.

"What do you do for a living?" she asked after a time, trying to draw me out a little.

"I am a cutter," I replied proudly. "In the garment trade."

"So, Mr. Cutter, tell me something about yourself," she said, her eyes sparkling with obvious interest. "Tell me something, or tell me everything. You must be keeping a lot inside, having been . . . over there . . . during the war."

I was startled by her directness, for my recent past was something most everyone else had tiptoed around. At the same time I found her refreshing, captivating. I looked into her gentle eyes, and—surprising myself—I smiled warmly. It came from somewhere deep within me: warm, genuine, unguarded.

"How much time do you have?" I asked.

Author's Postscript
Straszęcin, Present Day

BEFORE I COULD BEGIN TO WRITE Morris Goldner's story, I felt compelled to go to Poland. To Straszęcin, where he grew up. To Dębica, Grabiny, Tarnów, and the forests along the Wisłoka. I was drawn there by the power of Goldner's remembrances, by the siren of his words. I went because I wanted to walk in his footsteps, meet anyone who might remember him and his family, see if anything from his time there still survived.

I went with no expectations, only hope that the trip would offer some worthwhile insights into Goldner's past. I had located (through a serendipitous Internet contact) one of Jan Kopec's children, still living in Straszęcin, and we exchanged mail. She was too young to remember Moniek, she wrote, although she was sure her older sisters remembered him. Still, she knew many stories about Moniek being with her father. She said she'd be delighted to meet with me at her home and would bring together her three surviving siblings, who also lived close-by. Bring a translator, she advised; none of us speaks English. It was all I needed to begin making my travel arrangements, though beyond this meeting, I had no idea who or what I might find.

Dębica, I discovered, is a mid-sized, modern city—reasonably attractive, I suppose, though not remarkable. The synagogue Goldner attended is still standing on Krakowska Street, practically in the center of town. When I was there, its gutted interior housed a small department store. Since my visit I've learned that the store has been closed. The mayor of Dębica declared that the synagogue will be preserved as a museum, in memory of the Jews who once made up nearly half of the town's population.

While in Dębica I met the elderly and disabled Home Army veteran called Kryzak in these pages. He knew Jan Kopec personally, having

231

spent some time with him after the war, in that brief period before Kopec's death. He also revealed that he met Moniek several times (although Goldner does not remember him). While he said it was common knowledge that Moniek had been saved by Kopec and kept by his side in the forests, Kryzak knew nothing of what they did together. Kopec, for reasons I understand only too well, did not disclose any of their activities to the Home Army leader.

When I gave Kryzak just a hint of their exploits, he expressed surprise. "Kopec was capable of anything," he said. "But Moniek? He was such a quiet, gentle young boy. A short little guy, soft-spoken and submissive. I can't see him committing acts of sabotage and resistance. Just didn't have it in him."

I smiled to myself, then changed the subject.

"Did Kopec ever mention why he saved the boy in the first place?" I asked, knowing how important the question has been to Goldner. Here was Kryzak's reply:

"Kopec never told me specifically why he saved Moniek, but this may help to explain it: What he saw while he was in Auschwitz . . . it changed him from the man he used to be. He couldn't believe what was happening to people until he saw it with his own eyes. He told me one thing, I remember, that disturbed him greatly. He told me that one day in Auschwitz he was carrying lumber, to be used to build new officers' quarters or something. He passed an area where little children—babies, really, one, two, three years old—were being brutalized by Nazi soldiers. He saw those bastards pick up the shrieking babies by their legs and feet, one after another, and plunge them headfirst into a deep trough of water, holding them there until their wriggling bodies went limp.

"How could something like that not affect someone? How could it not stir even someone as callous as Jan Kopec?"

Following the road to Goldner's (and Kopec's) home village of Straszęcin took no more than a few minutes by car; Straszęcin today is not so much a separate village as it is a suburb of Dębica, separated from it only by the Wisłoka River. There are still farms and fields in the community, though, and even now plowing is often done by horse and plow, because parts for tractors are hard to come by. But Straszęcin no longer resembles the uncluttered farming village of Goldner's day. It even boasts a small strip mall.

All around the area stand many forests, although I suspect time and the progress of civilization have diminished their size and number. In many of these forests memorials and markers have been erected

232

over the site of mass graves, and often one can still see evidence of bunkers dug by the partisans and Jews who were in hiding.

Perhaps I stepped where Goldner and Kopec had once stepped, or slept, or fought; certainly I walked over ground where countless thousands of men, women, and children had died. Only a still silence offered testimony to their fate, and it screamed louder than any voices ever could.

The "palace" that once belonged to Stubenvoll is still standing behind a fence on heavily wooded grounds. It looks more like an ordinary and quite unimpressive two-story house, actually, than anything remotely resembling a palatial estate. When I was there, a small factory occupied the grounds. I was told that Stubenvoll's two elderly daughters sold off the property some time ago and moved to Kraków.

The old schoolhouse that Moniek and Gita attended is gone, replaced by a modern elementary school on the same spot. A block away a sturdy iron bridge has replaced the old wooden structure that crossed the stream that wound through the village.

On the corner by the bridge is a house painted a bold yellow hue; it had been remodeled and reduced in size, I was told, but it was the house where Moishe lived and ran his little store. It was into this house that Jan Kopec moved his family after the liberation and, from what I understand, was where he died.

The Kopec daughter I originally contacted lives just a few blocks away, in a comfortable and modern home. It was here that I met her and her siblings, who ranged in age from mid-fifties to upper sixties. Kopec's wife, Stefania, died several years earlier, so his children could tell me only the little fragments they remembered from their childhood, along with stories their mother had passed down over the years. They were very much interested to hear what became of Goldner; what's more, they seemed disappointed that he didn't come to Poland with me. After all, he saw more of their father than they did. And he was the only person who knew exactly what their father was up to during the eighteen months they were together.

For this reason alone, it was probably for the best that Goldner stayed behind, since I'm reasonably certain the children have no idea of their father's criminal past. Is such secrecy possible, when several elders in the area confided to me that Kopec's nefarious exploits were, indeed, widely known?

"Jan Kopec never worked an honest day in his life," Kryzak told me confidentially. "But why dig up the past? What's done is done. His children live here. We don't speak of it anymore."

A second source echoed the same sentiment. "[Kopec] was chased and wanted by the police long before the war . . . but we don't discuss it because it would make things uncomfortable for his children . . ."

Needless to say, I didn't speak of it either, nor did I refute his children's belief that their father had been a laborer before the war and, after his escape from Auschwitz, a Home Army partisan. I must say, it's my hope they don't learn the truth about him here. If, however, this material should reach them, I believe they can still find a source of pride in their father. After all, Jan Kopec did save one Jewish boy's life and kept him alive. And regardless of his motives, he did strike out against the German oppressors with consummate skill and bravery and undeniable courage.

Surely there has to be a measure of redemption in that.

In the village of Grabiny, just south of Straszęcin, a small concrete-block train station has replaced the old building against which Moniek and his father were shot. Nearby lives the Home Army veteran I called Tadeusz Kozera, a friendly, elderly man with a thick middle and a warm smile. He's the man who confirmed that Pozniak was a Nazi informer whom the partisans repeatedly and unsuccessfully tried to eliminate.

"Is Pozniak's house still standing?" I asked him, assuming Goldner's grenades inflicted only partial damage. He wasn't sure. A few homes in the area remained unchanged since before the war, but he didn't remember if Pozniak's house was one of them. The man has been dead a long time, after all. Natural causes, as far as the old veteran could remember . . .

I thanked him for his time, then headed back into Straszęcin.

About a block north of the bridge, a large wooden storage shed stands along the road to Wola Wielka, on the very spot where the Goldner home had been. Sometime after the war, apparently, the home had been torn down and the wood sold for firewood or building materials.

Directly across the quiet road is a home and farm that looks today exactly as it must have looked when the Goldners lived across the street. Behind the main house stands—barely stands, more precisely—a rickety old barn and an outhouse. There is no plumbing, even though modern homes have sprung up all around.

In that house lives a portly old woman with a craggy lined face and white hair covered by a patterned babushka. Yes, she said, she recalled the Goldner family and the Jewish shopkeeper who insisted they call him Moishe. Like Goldner neither she nor anyone else in the village could remember Moishe's last name.

She related how, several years after the war, one of the first television programs she ever saw showed a picture of three emaciated girls, wearing only thin T-shirts. The announcer said the Nazis did experiments on these girls, injecting them with the blood of rats, among other things, and the girls didn't speak and weren't even in their right minds, and the announcer asked did anyone recognize them?

"They were Moishe's girls," she insisted. "I knew it the moment I saw their picture, no doubt whatsoever. But I never told anyone. If I admitted I knew who they were, I might have had to travel to Warsaw."

Her implication was clear: traveling to Warsaw would not have been convenient. She could not be bothered to come forward to help identify the girls whom she once saw almost daily.

But not everyone felt that same indifference. For back across the road again, just to the side and behind the storage shed that stands on the former Goldner property, is the home of Wladyslaw Reguła. Reguła, the neighbor who'd been a friend to Leap, whose daughter, Anna, had been Morris's first infatuation. Here is the very house in which young Moniek often played, in those sweet, innocent days before the German occupation.

The thatched roof has been replaced with corrugated metal, but in every other way the house looks as I imagine it must have appeared during the war years. Inside I found white plastered walls and sparse furnishings—a simple table and chairs, an old wooden wardrobe, a cot against the wall, an ancient, wood-burning stove. Electricity has been added for light, but in most every other way the house seems unchanged by time.

I was ushered inside by Anna Blezien—*the* Anna—who lives in a modern home just down the road. For many years, she told me, she begged her father to move in with her and her husband, or to at least modernize his own home. Reguła would have none of it.

Before I entered she explained, "My father isn't well, but he speaks of Moniek Goldner often and will be thrilled, as I am, to know he's alive and well."

Moments later I stood face-to-face with Reguła himself—an expressive, animated, ninety-year-old man. If he had been ill, he didn't show it. The early September weather had been cool; he wore warm, shiny pants and a thin cotton sweater that covered a plaid shirt. On his feet heavy work boots came up to midcalf. His face and neck were webbed with lines, yet his eyebrows were bushy and dark. Above a high forehead his considerable hair was only partially white; it lay tousled every which way, looking like a small haystack.

When he spoke of the Goldners, of watching them being taken

away that day in 1941, he spoke with emotion and with tears in his eyes, as if it had all just happened. My translator had a hard time keeping up with him.

He walked around his modest home as he talked, gesturing wildly and passionately, telling stories about tricking Moniek into plowing his field, about hearing of Leap's death, about giving food to Moniek when he was in hiding and having to turn him away when new boarders made such aid unsafe for them all. He said he still had dreams about the Goldners, especially about Moniek, and he'd often wondered whatever became of the boy.

He shed more tears at the news that Goldner was happy and well in America. He said he hoped the boy he so fondly remembered would write to him.

It was with great reluctance that I left Reguła's home a short while later. And it was with even greater sadness that I learned, in a letter from his daughter, Anna, that Wladyslaw Reguła passed away just four months after my visit. At the time of his death, she wrote, he was still hoping to hear from his courageous neighbor, Moniek Goldner . . .

Several days after I returned from Poland, Goldner came to my house with Eda, his wife of more than fifty years. I shared my discoveries and told him about the many people I had met. I spread out dozens of pictures I had taken.

Goldner was genuinely surprised that anyone back in Straszęcin still remembered him. He smiled in recognition of his old synagogue. He grew excited at seeing several still-standing landmarks around his old neighborhood. And he became misty-eyed as more painful memories came flooding back.

I told him again that I found it amazing he was able to rise above his inconceivable experiences. Yet he still maintains there's nothing special about him, that he simply did what he had to do in Poland, did what he was driven to do in America. And while he insists if he had to relive his wartime experiences over again, he'd sooner die, he does wonder, just a little, if the blessing of his family and life in this country has been some sort of divine repayment for his suffering.

"I don't know, maybe someone was watching over me," he says quietly, almost reluctantly, for he still struggles with the concept of God. "What I have seen . . . I just can't understand how a loving God could let such things happen. I try to believe, I really want to believe, but how can I?"

Aside from this one conflict, which he strives to reconcile, Morris is a gentle, active man who has let go of the old bitterness, who has learned how to laugh but still can't stop the flood of tears that come, inevitably, when he opens up about his past.

And with the hundreds of hours of interviews that led to this book, some of Goldner's nightmares have been stirred anew, but he has learned to deal with them too; such is the urgency he feels to share his story.

He still dreams of the last time he saw his mother and sister, of the death of his father and the resignation of Moishe the shopkeeper. He dreams of closed spaces, of wheat fields and church barns; of grenades and *katyusha* shells, of mayhem and killing and random acts of kindness—a bit of bread, a small chunk of sausage, a warm pair of boots. But of all his dreams, he insists, few remain sharper or more pervasive than the recurring images of Jan Kopec that possess him still.

"What happened between us in the forests over those eighteen months—it seems impossible, considering how different we were. Boy, we made some pair, the two of us."

For the first time he's beginning to understand that each gave something of himself to the other. Goldner taught the master criminal, the man to whom bullying and robbing had long been second nature, that it was all right to care for another human being, even a Jew. And Kopec taught the once-sheltered teenager—the naive boy whose only broken commandment before the war might have been the eating of *traif*—to channel all fear, to stand up to any adversary, to grasp for life and live to the fullest in all things. And although Kopec never intended this, his coarse way of showing care for the boy led Goldner to realize one thing more as he matured: that if you look deep enough and hard enough below the surface, you can sometimes—*sometimes*—find something good and decent in even the most hardened scoundrel.

Fate, it would seem, served both master and student well in throwing them together. Both emerged from the war changed men, in no small measure due to their influence on each other.

Had Kopec lived, it's fair to say, there's no telling what ignominious habits he might have changed, given half a chance.

As for Goldner, he's happily retired these days, but occasionally his phone still rings with a request for his skills as a cutter. Every once in a great while, when he accepts a small job, he can be found cutting and resizing patterns somewhere in Chicago, because this is what he does so well, what perhaps he was always destined to do.

But his real passion is his family, for now he finally has the time to devote to his wife, daughters, and eight grandchildren. He was a capable father when his children were young, although his wife, Eda, tells the story of how, when their first daughter was born, it took many months before he'd hold her. The once-fearless Goldner admits it. "These were hands that fought, that I used as weapons. They were powerful hands. How could I hold a little baby in them? How could I? It did not seem right. I was terrified."

With his career behind him, however, he's admittedly even better at being a grandfather. Because the years have softened him, helped him to control his anger, to be at peace with himself. Time has gently shaped his resignation that we cannot always understand why things happen, that sometimes it's better to accept and move on.

Truth be told, Goldner no longer feels a compelling need to search for answers. When he sits in his daughters' homes, and talks with his grandchildren, and delights in their beaming faces, and sees his reflection in their luminous eyes, he knows why he was given the strength, so long ago, to endure.

And that's why, as he sat at my table, eager to hear stories of my own adventures in the village where he grew up, he listened with interest, and he listened with a full heart. But he listened from afar, safe in the country he's come to love and the city he calls home, having no desire ever to revisit the terrible, haunted forests that failed to claim him among the wretched millions.

Acknowledgments

This book could not have been written and published without the help and encouragement of:

Frank Kopec, the proud Pole and advertising media wizard who generously allowed me to borrow his family name. This Kopec is not like the bandit in these pages; Frank, actually, is older.

Rabbi Dov Taylor, for putting me in contact with helpful parties in preparation for my research trip to Poland.

Jaroslaw Szyc of Warsaw, for his indispensable services as guide, translator, and sounding board during my trip to Poland.

Dorothy Kultys, paralegal and Beautiful Person at Lewis, Davidson & Heatherington, for her enthusiastic and unerring translations of my correspondence to and from Poland as well as of long passages from several resource books written in Polish.

Sandi Wisenberg, literary talent and dedicated book doctor, for her sage advice and edit on my first draft, which, thanks to her input, bears little resemblance to this finished work.

My close friends Marge and Keith McClintock, for perceptive editorial comments and overall cheerleading that has meant so much to me.

The Lake Forest Newcomer's Club, which previewed an earlier draft of this manuscript and confirmed this story's potential for a diverse audience.

Sam Gilman, Rock Island legal eagle (and, in a supporting role, uncle) whose observations and line edit blew me away with their depth and perspicuity. I am greatly indebted for his interest and caring.

Andrew Stuart of the Stuart Agency, New York, for recognizing that this work deserved to be published and taking it on in spite of the general big-press malaise toward the "Holocaust genre."

Alan Adelson, director of the Jewish Heritage Project, New York, for stepping up as my mentor, advisor, and co-agent, helping me to craft the final draft and bring this project to fruition.

Raphael Kadushin and the folks at the University of Wisconsin Press, for recognizing the importance of this story and feeling the same urgency to publish it as I felt to write it.

Eda Goldner, for sitting patiently through countless hours of interviews as I prodded her husband's painful memories day after day.

Morris Goldner, for the courage to tell his story, for his faith in me to put it on paper, and for his patience—often tested—over the years it took for him to hold this finished book in his hands.

Finally, my wife Loraine, for her own patience, insights, research assistance, and never-failing confidence in me. It was she who first met Goldner and introduced us. The rest, as they say, is history.

Bibliography

Following is a partial list of references that proved invaluable in helping to provide an accurate historical context to some of the events, people, and places described in the preceding pages.

Auschwitz Nazi Extermination Camps. Warsaw: Interpress Publishers, 1985.

Bartosz, Adam. *Tarnowskie Judaica.* Warsaw: Wydawnictwo Pttk. "Kraj," 1992.

Bauer, Yehuda. *Flight and Rescue.* New York: Random House, 1970.

Botting, Douglas. *The Aftermath: Europe.* Alexandria, Va.: Time-Life Books, 1983.

Chodakiewicz, Marek J., Piotr Gontarczyk, and Leszek Zebrowski, eds. *Tajne oblicze GL-AL: I PPR: Dokumenty* (The secret face of the People's Guard/People's Army). Vols. 1 and 2. Warsaw: Burchard Edition, 1997.

Czech, Danuta. *Auschwitz Chronicle 1939–1945.* New York: Henry Holt, 1990.

Duffy, Christopher. *Red Storm on the Reich: The Soviet March on Germany, 1945.* New York: Atheneum, 1991.

Encyclopedia Judaica. Jerusalem: Kiter Publishing House, 1971.

Encyclopedia of the Holocaust. New York: Macmillan, 1990.

Friedrich, Otto. *The Kingdom of Auschwitz.* New York: Harper Perennial, 1994.

Garas, Jozef. *Oddzialy Gwardii Ludowej i Armii Ludowej, 1942–1945* (Units of the People's Guard and People's Army, 1942–1945). Warsaw: Wojskowy Institut Historicalczny, 1971.

Garlinski, Jozef. *Fighting Auschwitz.* London: Julian Friedmann Publishers, 1975.

Goldberg, Lotka. "I Shall Not Die but Shall Live." In *The Rzeszów Jews Memorial Book.* Tel Aviv: Rzeszower Societies, 1967.

Gutman, Yisrael, and Michael Berenbaum. *Anatomy of the Auschwitz Death Camp.* Bloomington: Indiana University Press, 1994.

Gutman, Yisrael, and Shmuel Krakowski. *Unequal Victims: Jews and Poles in World War II.* New York: Holocaust Library, 1986.

Heymont, Irving. *Among the Survivors of the Holocaust, 1945.* Cincinnati: American Jewish Archives, 1982.

Hilberg, Raul. *The Destruction of the Jews.* New York: Holmes & Meier, 1985.

Kagan, Joram. *Poland's Jewish Heritage.* New York: Hippocrene Books, 1992.

Korbonski, Stefan. *The Polish Underground State 1939–1945.* Boulder, Colo.: East European Quarterly; New York: distributed by Columbia University Press, 1978.

Kornbluth, William. *Sentenced to Remember.* Cranbury, N.J.: Associated University Presses, 1994.

Krakowski, Shmuel. *The War of the Doomed.* New York: Holmes & Meier, 1984.

Lukas, Richard C. *Forgotten Holocaust: The Poles under German Occupation 1939–1944.* Lexington: University Press of Kentucky, 1989.

————, ed. *Out of the Inferno: Poles Remember the Holocaust.* Lexington: University Press of Kentucky, 1989.

McInnis, Edgar. *The War.* Toronto: Oxford University Press, 1946.

Okecki, Stanislaw, ed. *Polish Resistance Movement in Poland and Abroad 1939–1945.* Warsaw: Polish Scientific Publishers, 1987.

Pogonowski, Iwo C. *Jews in Poland: A Documentary History.* New York: Hippocrene Books, 1993.

Sagajllo, Witold. *Man in the Middle.* New York: Hippocrene Books, 1984.

Schwarz, Leo W. *The Redeemers.* New York: Farrar, Strauss & Young, 1953.

Soifer, Ben A. *Between Life and Death.* London: James Publishing, 1995.

Smolen, Kazimierz, ed. *From the History of KL-Auschwitz.* Translated by Krystyna Michalik. New York: Howard Fertig, 1982.

Stone, I. F. *Underground to Palestine.* New York: Pantheon Books, 1978.

Szulc, Tad. *Secret Alliance.* London: Pan Books, 1993.

Thorwald, Jurgen. *Flight in the Winter.* New York: Pantheon Books, 1951.

Wyman, Mark. *DP: Europe's Displaced Persons 1945–1951.* Philadelphia: Balch Institute Press, 1989.